LOUIS BROMFIELD AT MALABAR

LOUIS BROMFIELD
at Malabar

Writings on Farming and Country Life

edited by Charles E. Little

The Johns Hopkins University Press   Baltimore

P 6

The Johns Hopkins University Press
701 West 40th Street, Baltimore, Maryland 21211

The drawings are by the late Kate Lord and are taken from *Malabar Farm* (New York: Harper & Brothers Publishers, 1948).

Frontispiece: The Louis Bromfield Collection, The Ohio State University at Mansfield.

The paper used in this publication meets the minimum requirements of American National Standard for Information Sciences—Permanence of Paper for Printed Library Materials, ANSI Z39.48-1984.

Library of Congress Cataloging-in Publication Data
Bromfield, Louis, 1896–1956.
  Louis Bromfield at Malabar.
  Bibliography: p.
  Contents: The good life on good land/Charles Little—A philosophical excursion—The return of the native—[etc.]
  1. Bromfield, Louis, 1896–1956—Homes and haunts—
Ohio. 2. Farm life—Ohio. 3. Ohio—Social life and
customs. 4. Authors, American—20th century—Biography. I.
Little, Charles E. II. Title.
PS3503.R66Z465   1988   813'.52 [B]   87-37841
ISBN 0-8018-3674-3 (alk. paper)

Contents

Acknowledgments

T he idea for this book emerged from a conference held at Malabar Farm in 1982 under the auspices of the American Land Forum, which I then headed. The conference was on "communicating the land," which Louis Bromfield most assuredly did during his lifetime and which Malabar continues to do as a facility now open to the public, attracting many, many visitors throughout the year.*

And so, the first acknowledgment must be to Malabar, and to all the people who now care for this wonderful place, keeping the memory of Louis Bromfield's works and days alive. I am most especially grateful to Carmen Hall, tour coordinator at Malabar, who helped set up the conference, and who has provided me with many significant details on Bromfield's life for this anthology.

I am, in addition, indebted to Linda R. Safran of Harper and Row, Bromfield's publisher, for facilitating the permissions necessary to reprint these essays, and to the Bromfield estate for so graciously allowing publication of this book.

George F. Thompson, of the Johns Hopkins University Press, became virtually a co-editor of this work. It was he who first urged me to go ahead with the anthology when I mentioned the possibility to him casually in a phone call. He, along with the Press's director, Jack Goellner, Gregory Conniff, and Wendell Berry, helped shape the selections and thereby the book, and he kept the project on track through manifold exchanges of correspondence between me, Bromfield's publisher, and his own colleagues at Johns Hopkins. Anne M. Whitmore deftly edited the text and organized and integrated the book's many elements.

*The mailing address for Malabar Farm State Park is Route 1, Box 469, Lucas, Ohio 44843.

Finally, the greatest debt is owed to Louis Bromfield himself. He was a man of large spirit and great gifts. My study of his work at Malabar has enriched my own life and writings immeasurably. I would give anything to have known him personally. Putting this book together is, I suppose, the next best thing.

Introduction: The Good Life on Good Land

I f you will take a look at the 1928 year-end issue of *Vanity Fair* magazine, in a section entitled "Nominated for the Hall of Fame" you will find the picture of a handsome young man, Louis Bromfield. He is described as "the most prominent of our younger novelists" and winner of the Pulitzer Prize. He is thirty-one years old. Pictured with him are Thomas Mann, Pablo Picasso, Walter Gropius, Serge Diaghileff, S. M. Eisenstein, Jed Harris, Max Reinhardt, Countess de Chambrum, and Ernest Hemingway. Today, the buildings of Gropius, the incredible literary influence of Hemingway, the ballets of Diaghileff, the paintings of Picasso are still with us. Where is Louis Bromfield?

This anthology is meant to provide the answer to that question; for, in the end, his novels turned out to be post-Victorian rather than prelusively modern. Rather than in fiction, Bromfield's influence was best expressed in the hill country of Ohio, at a place called Malabar Farm. The establishment, in 1939, of what was to become the most famous experimental farm in the United States, was Bromfield's most creative act—more creative than all his novels, plays, and films put together. And his writing about Malabar—in five books about his life on the place—was the best writing of his career: more deeply felt, a whole order of magnitude better than any of his earlier books of fiction, and the most lasting of his literary achievements. Bromfield's effort to show how traditional rural values could be reconciled with the modern, industrialized agriculture he saw emerging during and after World War II offers lessons as valid today as they were then. As the proprietor and chronicler of Malabar, Bromfield was far ahead of his time. In fact, sometimes Bromfield-at-Malabar seems ahead even of ours.

America is now in the midst of an historical change in the structure of agriculture and in the patterns of rural settlement.

For most of the 1980s, farming has been in financial crisis, with mounting farm bankruptcies despite seemingly boundless levels of government subsidy. Soil erosion rivals that of the 1930s, and the misuse of agricultural chemicals has created groundwater pollution levels in the countryside that exceed those in many a city and suburb.

At the same time, and not entirely unrelatedly, more and more people are moving away from cities, hoping to find greater meaning in life a bit closer to the land. The number and skyrocketing circulation of "country" magazines is a publishing phenomenon. Recently, the U.S. Department of Agriculture set up an Office of Small-Scale Agriculture to address the needs of part-time farmers, the only sector of U.S. agriculture that is, in fact, growing; indeed it is growing rapidly. There are over six hundred thousand such farms today.

Remarkably, Bromfield's farm books, published in the decade 1945–55, speak directly to our contemporary rural problems, needs, and aspirations. These books are not quaint artifacts, as perhaps his novels have become, but are wholly relevant to the issues of farming and country life as we find them today. With an extraordinary display of prescience, and with more intellectual depth and balance than anyone since, Bromfield discussed the "family farm," self-sufficiency, soil stewardship, water resource management, advances in tillage technique, sustainable agriculture, rural landscape aesthetics, the overuse of chemicals, the "direct" marketing of produce, and a number of other topics that are of quite immediate concern.

And he did it with *style*. He used his literary gifts to the fullest in the effort. His writings on Malabar are as inspiring a testament to the inherent values of farming and rural life as any in American literature. The whole of it is recorded in *Pleasant Valley* (1945), *Malabar Farm* (1948), *Out of the Earth* (1950), and *From My Experience* (1955). (The fifth book, *Animals and Other People,* also published in 1955, is a collection of animal stories that appeared in earlier works.) Some of these books are hard to find. All are out of print.

This anthology, accordingly, draws into a single volume the most currently relevant, the most interesting, and the most representative chapters of the farm books. It is a task that

Bromfield himself might have done at some point had he not died so prematurely, in 1956 at the age of fifty-nine.

Malabar Farm is located just ten miles southeast of the small city of Mansfield, Ohio. Ohio is, you might say, the all-purpose American state. It combines the industrial Northeast with a bit of the hillbilly South and, beginning somewhere around Mansfield, is where the greatest patch of farmland in the whole world begins. Stretching from central Ohio westward to the middle of Colorado, where the Rocky Mountains rise from the Great Plains, is a one-million-square-mile region of land—the great agricultural epicenter of the nation.

It was here, in that geographical muddle of North and South, industrial city and agrarian heartland, that Louis Bromfield was born—in Mansfield, Ohio—in 1896; and it is here that he was brought up. That biographical fact is a controlling one for understanding Bromfield and his vision, in both literature and fact, at Malabar. For the rest of his life he tried to identify and sort out the conflicting values implied by the geography of his childhood.

Near the city of Mansfield, located in the rolling, morainal landscape of that part of Ohio, was a multigeneration family farm that had been left to Bromfield's maternal grandfather, Robert Coulter, who was the founder of the Ohio Grange and, Bromfield says, "one of the best farmers in the state." Bromfield remembered the Coulter farm fondly as a young child, yet during a good part of his growing up Grandfather Coulter had lived in his son-in-law's house in town, a farmer no longer. He continued to hang on to the place, renting it as he could. Ostensibly, Grandfather Coulter lived with the Charles Bromfield family because of his advancing years and an injury sustained in a fall from a haymow. But his grandson Louis knew that there were reasons for his abandoning the family farm that went well beyond these.

One of the reasons was Louis Bromfield's mother. Having grown up on the farm, she knew its hardships and how people could be tied to land, with no chance to make their mark in life. This was not to be for her Louis. From time to time her husband, Charley Bromfield—a popular city official, sometime banker, and dabbler in real estate—suggested they move out to the old Coulter place, but Annette would have none of it. Even so, Charley would take Louis out into the countryside òn political business and to look over abandoned farms.

In 1914, the year Louis graduated from high school, the Bromfields suffered severe financial reverses, and Charley convinced Annette to sell the house in Mansfield and move back to the farm. Accordingly, it was decided, against Annette's better judgment, that Louis should attend Cornell, where the great Liberty Hyde Bailey was dean of the college of agriculture.

But Bromfield hadn't even finished his first year when he got an emergency message to return home. Grandfather Coulter had died. Louis was needed to help out on the farm. His presence there did not really help matters, though. Charley was a good man but no farmer, and Louis was too young to take over completely. Moreover, his mother had ambitions for her son. For these reasons and more, the farm had to be sold. It was a bitter loss, nevertheless, for a pattern had been broken—a family-farm heritage as well as an agrarian way of life that had steadily given way to the industrialization of Ohio.

If it is true that the ideals of one generation are based on the broken dreams of those immediately preceding it, then it fell to Louis Bromfield to make good on the lost Coulter farm, and by extension on the lost promise of Ohio. Whether he knew it or not at the time, this was his true vocation.

The story of how Ohio fell from agrarian grace is recounted in Bromfield's fictionalized family biography, *The Farm,* published in 1933. In the great tug of war between the Hamiltonians and the Jeffersonians over America's economy as well as its soul, Ohio, Bromfield asserted, went to "the money men," whose avarice destroyed the agrarian fortunes of his own family, of Mansfield and the state of Ohio, and ultimately corrupted the nation itself. To Bromfield, Jefferson's great American Dream —a life of plenty, of dignity, education, and culture produced by an agriculturally-based rural society in which class lines were erased and from which a natural aristocracy of the land would arise—seemed almost possible in Ohio. But in the end the dream was smashed by materialistic Yankee industrialists who brought their mills and their stinks and clatters and bangs and moral depravity to the Middle West. In "the Flats," about which Bromfield wrote often in his novels, the laborers imported from central and southern Europe lived in near-hovels huddled at the factory gates, their only lot despair. For Bromfield, their exploitation was emblematic of what had gone wrong with the idea of an egalitarian, land-based society, and it stood in stark contrast to the possibilities presented by the Middle West for developing a way of life to which America could aspire. The broken promise of the Enlightenment, as enunciated by Jefferson, was Bromfield's preoccupation all his life.

In the final chapter of *The Farm,* Bromfield writes:

> For a long time the mills and factories had been spreading, to the north and east, over the fields and along the altered channels of Toby's Run. . . . The Farm was sold to a man who bought it as a speculation because now it was within the sound of the mills. The Town would come nearer and nearer until presently the great barn and perhaps the rambling house itself would be pulled down. Streets would cut through it and hard ribbons of cement sidewalks laid down. The long double avenue of ancient locusts would disappear, and presently the whole Farm would cease to be.

He is, of course, describing the loss of his own birthright. But the account could have been composed yesterday. When a farm is lost, something awful—and permanent—has happened.

After the sale of the Coulter farm, there was no more thought of returning to Cornell. There was a brief stint at Columbia (to study journalism), but Bromfield quit in his first year to enlist in the United States Army Ambulance Service. He served in France from 1917 to 1919. He then returned to New York, took on various journalistic assignments, got married, and in 1924 at the age of twenty-seven published *The Green Bay Tree,* a sweeping Victorian novel drawn from his family experiences in Mansfield and reflecting the contest between town and country, the materialistic and the idealistic. It was an immediate critical and commercial success, and Bromfield began his long career as a full-time novelist and screenwriter. In 1925 he moved to Senlis, France, forty miles north of Paris, and within a few years had taken a fifty-year lease on a *presbytère* where he thought he might live for the rest of his life.

Although Bromfield was not a modern writer of the "Lost Generation" school like his fellow expatriates Hemingway and

Fitzgerald, he became part of the Paris literary scene, entertaining and being entertained in the salons, including that of Gertrude Stein and Alice B. Toklas. Gertrude Stein especially liked to visit the Bromfields at Senlis, where Louis tended a three-acre plot of flowers and vegetables. She much admired his knowledge of gardening. Though the Paris years were filled with fame, fortune, and fun, Bromfield felt a nagging sense of dissatisfaction that grew with each best seller. Increasingly, the literary life seemed somehow unreal; and, even though he could write passionately about the issues of the Farm and the Town in most of his novels, his own life seemed spiritually uncentered and adrift.

After publication of *The Farm,* in fact, Bromfield began talking about buying a farm back in the United States. Then, in 1933, he visited India, whose emergence as a modern society was just beginning. Bromfield and other idealists were, at the time, hopeful that India could modernize without adopting the kind of destructive industrialism that had come to dominate the landscape of the Middle West—that, at least in India, a version of Jeffersonian rural society might have a chance to emerge. He even toyed with the idea of buying land on the beautiful Malabar coast of the country and made a second visit in 1935.

But when he returned to France later that year, the relentless march of fascism began to occupy his time and thoughts. After the Fascist victory in the Spanish Civil War, Bromfield became concerned for his family's safety and sailed to America to establish a home in Ohio for his wife and three daughters. He intended, for the time being, to live alone in Senlis and from that vantage point continue to raise funds for the Abraham Lincoln Brigade, to write dispatches and pamphlets against Chamberlain's appeasement policy, and to make speeches to alert America and the rest of the world to the threat of fascism, maintaining that fascism, and not bolshevism, posed the most immediate danger to freedom.

And then, in 1939, it became clear that Bromfield would have to leave Senlis, perhaps permanently. As the German army prepared to invade France, he returned to his beloved Ohio countryside. Of his return Bromfield wrote (in the first chapter of *Pleasant Valley,* and of this anthology), "As the car came down out of the hills and turned off the Pinhook Road the whole of the valley, covered in snow, lay spread out before us with the ice-blue creek wandering through it between the two high sandstone ridges where the trees, black and bare, rose against the winter sky. And suddenly I knew where I was. I had come home!"

Louis Bromfield had just turned forty-two. He had come home again and he was home to stay. Though he wrote many novels and screen plays after that, his career as a writer of fiction was, for all intents and purposes, behind him and his career as an apologist for the good life on good land had begun.

Bromfield was, among other things, rich. So he bought three farms, not just one, and, with later additions, ultimately acquired a thousand acres near the rural hamlet of Lucas, in Pleasant Valley. He called this aggregation Malabar Farm and hired a young, well-trained farm manager named Max Drake to work with him on "the Plan" for the farm. Max Drake was the hard-headed one, Louis Bromfield the dreamer—he called himself a bit "teched," by which he meant that he had a certain mystical understanding of farming that defied both rational analysis and farm economics.

What Bromfield wanted was a model, self-sufficient, diversified farm, somewhat like the farm he might have inherited himself had he, Ohio, and the world been a little bit different in 1914. But he wasn't interested in turning back the clock. He wanted to explore the techniques of the "New Agriculture" developed since Grandfather Coulter's day by the exponents of soil conservation, by the inventors of new farm machinery such as the deep cultivators that could penetrate the hardpan built up over the years, by the scientists who were beginning to understand the value of trace elements in the soils, and by the geneticists who were bringing new hybrids into agriculture. The idea was decidedly *not* to have a farm whose economic existence could be achieved only by continued subsidy. Rather, he wished to conduct an experiment in agriculture that could make its own way economically so that what it demonstrated was that, with scientific agriculture, a Jeffersonian way of life could yet be achieved.

The plan that Max Drake and Bromfield worked out was,

pre-eminently, to restore the soil, much of which had disappeared, as Bromfield put it in *Pleasant Valley*, "down Switzer's Run into the Clear Fork and thence into the Muskingum, the Ohio, and the Mississippi, where so many billions of tons of our good American soil have gone since first we cut off the forests and plowed up the grassbound prairies." Another element of the plan was for the farm to be self-sufficient, in the manner of Ohio farms of the mid-nineteenth century, as opposed to those of the mid-twentieth, many of which had succumbed during the miseries of the depression. Bromfield believed that, if you could grow your own food and not get heavily into debt, you could survive the kind of economic and civil disasters that have plagued this century, disasters which Bromfield knew at first hand not only in the United States but in Europe and Asia as well. On this point, Bromfield and Drake had a decided difference of opinion. Max Drake, who was better trained in the economics of modern agriculture, knew that a nineteenth-century diversified farm was fun to dream about but wouldn't make it. Also, Drake was not averse to the use of credit as a way to raise the substantial capital that even then was required for entry into farming. The credit point was moot, however, since Bromfield had the money anyway. As for diversification, Max and Bromfield finally agreed that Max would be in charge of the farm and Bromfield ("the Boss," as they all called him) would be in charge of self-sufficiency. "I meant to have as nearly everything as possible," Bromfield wrote. "Not merely chickens and eggs and butter and milk and vegetables and fruit and the things which many foolish farmers buy today; I meant to have guinea fowl and ducks and geese and turkeys which could live off the abundance of the farm without care in a half-wild state as such birds live in the *basse-cour* of a prosperous French farm. I meant to have grapes in abundance and plums and peaches, currants, gooseberries, asparagus. . . . "

The most inventive aspect of "the Plan" was the corporate structure it called for. Bromfield was concerned about the demise of family-sized farms and the way the high cost of farm machinery made it almost impossible for young people to become established without inheriting land or having the money in the first place to buy an operation big enough to make a whole living. The idea of Malabar was not to have a small, not-very-viable farm, but rather to have a big farm—with the crucial difference that, unlike other big-farm operations, it would not displace the small-farm people in the process. Hence, Malabar was modeled after a Soviet collective farm, in which Bromfield was "the state," supplying the capital and taking a modest profit if there were one. The families that came to work on the farm would have "a house, rent-free, with light and heat, bathrooms and plumbing, all [their] living save only coffee, spices, and sugar, as well as a salary above the average"—plus a share in any profits above Bromfield's skim of five percent.

It was a wonderful plan and was put into effect. Bromfield built the "Big House," and it became, like the *presbytère* at Senlis, filled with celebrities from abroad, at home, and from Hollywood. Joan Fontaine was a visitor. Lauren Bacall and Humphrey Bogart were married there and even spent their honeymoon at Malabar.

But the best visitors in Bromfield's view were the "real dirt farmers," which is how he liked to classify himself. On one farm field day, eight thousand farmers came to Malabar. Still, Louis Bromfield was a "great man," not a "little man," as the language of the depression had it, and inevitably he became a major figure in the politics of agriculture, and in politics generally, tending increasingly toward conservative views. He was a prime mover in an organization known as Friends of the Land, now defunct, and a mainstay of its journal, *The Land*. In this work, Bromfield even hobnobbed with Henry Wallace of whom he mightily disapproved. Dwight Eisenhower was on the board of Friends of the Land at the time that he was president of Columbia University.

Finally, Bromfield stopped writing novels altogether, thinking the work to be shallow and inconsequential compared to his writings about Malabar, agriculture, and the possibilities for improvement in the modern world. He had become a propagandist for optimism rather than a novelist concerned with the realities of despair. He writes as follows in the concluding chapter of *Pleasant Valley:*

> I believe that one day our soil and our forests from one end of
> the country to the other will be well managed and our supplies
> of water will be abundant and clean. I believe that there will be

abundance for all as God and Nature intended, an abundance properly distributed when man has the wisdom to understand and solve such things. I believe there will be no more floods to destroy the things man has worked to create and even man himself, and that the abomination of great industrial cities will become a thing of the past, the men and women, and above all else, the children, will live in smaller communities in which there can be health and decency and human dignity, and then when that time comes, the people then living will look back upon us and the stupidity of our times as we look back with unbelief at the squalor and oppression and misery of the Middle Ages.

Later, Bromfield was to moderate his views somewhat, to adjust to the realities of modern agricultural economics. But for Louis Bromfield, the economic side of agriculture was not a matter of bigger and better tractors, as it tends to be today, but of the careful application of scientific agriculture. The alternative was what Liberty Hyde Bailey called "moon farming," using phases of the moon, rather than scientific technique, as a guide to cultivation. Bromfield wanted scientific agriculture to be consonant with, and to support, the Jeffersonian ideal of rural life—for Jefferson himself was an exponent of science—not a scientific agriculture dependent on expensive machinery, irrigation techniques, chemicals, and other "inputs" as propounded by agribusiness and its minions in the U.S. Department of Agriculture.

Modern advances in scientific agriculture might be a way to democratize farming rather than make it prohibitive to all save those who could afford high capital costs. "There has always been one iron-clad restriction at Malabar," Bromfield wrote in *From My Experience:* "Nothing should ever be done there which *any* farmer could not afford to do." He was fully aware of the pitfalls of simply being the gentleman farmer, practicing scientific agriculture without reference to the social and historical implications that such a status would confer. He continually adjusted his program at Malabar in the interest of making his findings as completely applicable to small and medium-sized farmers as he could.

As he wrote in *Malabar Farm:*

We were fourteen in all in the Big House [which he built new but which looked like an old "Western Reserve" house that had been added onto by generations of family owners]—from Butch who is seven to Ma who is 83. It reminded me of the meals at my grandfather's farm long ago when the farmers somehow lived better than most of them do today. I believed it could be done and it has been done, but best of all every other family on the place was having the same kind of meal. Today the acres at Malabar support more people than ever before in their history. And the families live better, having more comforts and a higher standard of living than any living on the same land in the past. We have dispossessed nobody. On the contrary, we have been able to make much of the land, poor and run down when we took it over, do a better job than when it was virgin soil, freshly cleared of forest.

The crucial issue on those beat-up Ohio farms was, of course, the soil. And it was here that Bromfield spent most of his effort as a farmer and as a conservationist. Although he was less than enthusiastic about many of the New Deal programs of the 1930s, he was a booster of the new soil conservation programs under the leadership of Hugh Bennett, the father of soil conservation, who was later to become a friend.

As head of President Franklin Delano Roosevelt's new Soil Conservation Service, Bennett preached a program of crop rotation, strip planting, contour plowing, and swales permanently planted to grass to lead off potentially erosive water. Then, as now, the question was whether farmers should be *required* to introduce conservation practices on their land. According to historian Arthur Schlesinger (*The Coming of the New Deal*), F.D.R.'s views tended toward requiring them. "The nub of the whole question is this," said the President. "If a farmer in upstate New York or Georgia or Nebraska or Oregon, through bad use of his land, allows his land to erode, does he have the inalienable right as owner to do this, or has the community, i.e., some form of governmental agency, the right to stop him?"

Bromfield did not believe much in conservation by coercion, or even by direct or indirect subsidy as it is carried out today. In fact, he thought that subsidies were part of the problem rather than the solution. "A subsidized agriculture," he wrote in *Malabar Farm*, "is necessarily a static agriculture in which . . .

subsidies serve mainly to protect and maintain the poor and inefficient farmer or absentee landlord who is always looking toward high prices rather than production per acre to give him economic solidity and prosperity." But Bromfield subscribed entirely to Hugh Bennett's religion of soil conservation and put it into practice on the "run out" farms he had bought in Ohio. "All our contour plowing, cover crops, and strip cropping have paid us great dividends," he wrote. "Throughout the drought [a post-dustbowl dry spell in the Midwest], when farms all over Ohio were hauling water, our springs kept their flow, because the methods to stop erosion and the run off of surface water had stored up great quantities of water underground."

And so, Malabar became a show-place of the practical results of conservation. "Wherever there was desolation and sterility," Bromfield wrote in *From My Experience*, "it had been created by man, by ignorance, by greed and by a strange belief inherent in early generations of American farmers that their land owed them a living."

Louis Bromfield set out to show—to the extent of twenty thousand visitors to Malabar a year, as well as with his best-selling books—that man belongs to the land as much as the other way around and that, when this fact is understood, a life of security, dignity, and happiness will ensue. Toward the end of his life he wrote in *From My Experience*, "And so, for fifteen years I have worked and suffered and sometimes spent money which I should not have spent, not merely upon restoring land and achieving rich crops, but in the creation of something more than that . . . a whole farm, a whole landscape, in which I could live in peace and with pride and which I could share with others to whom it would bring pleasure."

LOUIS BROMFIELD AT MALABAR

A Philosophical Excursion

In the immediate postwar years, Malabar Farm was not only the best-known experimental farm in the United States but also an establishment that embodied America's deeply held belief in the virtues and values of life on the land. Each generation of Americans discovers this belief in its own terms, from Jefferson's time to ours. But, as Louis Bromfield points out in perhaps the best one-paragraph apologia for farming extant in the literature, "the essense of the farm and the open country remains the same."

This passage, chosen to serve as prologue for this anthology, is taken from Bromfield's most technical farm book, Out of the Earth, *but it is probably his best short statement of his overall philosophy. As a kind of manifesto for farming and country life, it may seem to many readers especially relevant today. The theme of working with nature to create not only a whole farm but a whole life recurs throughout Bromfield's works, both fiction and nonfiction, and was the idea that Malabar Farm was created to demonstrate.*

A t Malabar when the shadows grow longer across the valley and each day the Big House falls earlier beneath the deep shadow of the low sandstone cliffs, we know that winter is closing in. On a still day when we hear the whistles of the big diesels on the Pennsylvania Railroad six miles away we know that we shall have fine clear weather, and when the sound comes from the opposite direction from the Baltimore and Ohio, we know that there will be clouds and rain. We know the time by the flight overhead of the big planes going north and south, and some of the pilots know us so well that on summer nights they blink their lights in greeting as they pass through the clear, still sky overhead.

In the barns and the fields, Al and Simon know their cows—a hundred and twenty of them—by name, and they know their dispositions and what they like or do not like, from Jean, the bossy old Guernsey who must be started homeward first on her way from pasture before the others will go properly, to Inez, the Holstein, smart and temperamental, who once struck up a feud with Mummy, the feed-room cat, and was observed on two occasions shaking Mummy as a dog might shake her, when the unfortunate cat came within reach.

As Philip, who lived with us until he grew up and went away on his own, once said, "The trouble with Malabar is that it's always characters—characters, never people . . . even down to the ducks." That's true of most farm people and especially true of farm people in hill country where over each rise in the land, just beyond each patch of woods, there lies a new world. In the old days before automobiles and telephones, "character" developed in old age into eccentricity. Today the change is not so great, but the independence, the strength of opinion and willingness to fight for an opinion still remain. These are not regimented people herding at night into subways to return to a cave somewhere high up in a skyscraper, living as man was never meant to live.

For the young people a farm is a kind of paradise. One never hears the whine of the city child, "Mama, what shall I do now?" On a farm no day is ever long enough for the young person to crowd into its meager twenty-four hours all there is to be done. That, too, is true of the good farmer himself. No day is long enough. There is fishing and swimming, explorations of the woods and the caves, trapping, messing about the big tractors, playing in the great mows, a hundred exciting things to do which each day are new and each day adventurous.

But most of all there is the earth and the animals through which one comes very close to eternity and to the secrets of the universe. Out of Gus, the mallard duck, who comes up from the pond every evening to eat with the dogs, out of Stinker, the bull, with his wise eyes and placid disposition, out of all the dogs which run ahead leaping and barking and luring the small boys farther and farther into the fields, a child learns much, and most of all that warmth and love of Nature, which is perhaps the greatest of all resources, not only because its variety and beauty are inexhaustible but because slowly it creates a sense of balance and of values, of philosophy and even of wise resignation to man's own significance which bring the great rewards of wisdom and understanding and tolerance. It is not by senseless accident that the vast majority of the great men and women of the nation and those who have built it have come from farms or hamlets.

There is in all the world no finer figure than a sturdy farmer standing, his feet well planted in the earth, looking over his rich fields and his beautiful shiny cattle. He has a security and an independence unknown to any other member of society, yet, unlike the trapper or the hunter, he is very much a part of society, perhaps its most important member. The sharp eyes with the crow's-feet circling them like small halos, the sunburned neck, the big strong hands, all tell their story of values and of living wholly in an industrial civilization where time clocks and machines rule man instead of man ruling them.

Nothing is more beautiful than the big farm kitchen. It has changed with the times. The refrigerator, the electric stove, the quick-freeze and the cold room have supplanted the cellar, the root storage and the great black old range with its tank of boiling water on the side. The woodpile is gone from outside the door and the horses no longer steam as they stand patiently while the farmer comes in for a cup of coffee and a cinnamon bun. We tell the time nowadays not by the whistle of the old steam locomotives but by the passage overhead of the big flying flagship. But the good smell is still there in the kitchen and the farmer's wife is the same at heart, although in these times she is not bent with rheumatism at forty from carrying water and wood and bending over a washboard. At forty she is likely to be spry and young and busy with her clubs and neighborhood activities—as young-looking as her eighteen-year-old daughter who is a leader in the 4-H Club. And her husband does not rise at daylight and come in weary and bent long after dark. He keeps city hours, but during the day his work is half fun, because the drudgery has gone out of it. He is out of doors with the smell of fresh-turned earth rising to him from the furrow, the sight of a darting cock pheasant rising before his eyes in a kind of brilliant hymn to morning. He, too, is young and sturdy at middle age and able to go places with his boys, to fish and hunt with them and attend their meetings.

A lot of things have changed on the farm of today, but the essence of the farm and the open country remains the same. The freedom is unchanged and the sense of security and independence and the good rich food and the beauty that lies for the seeing eye on every side and, above all, that satisfaction, as great as that of Leonardo or Shakespeare or any other creative artist, in having made something great and beautiful out of nothing. The farmer may leave his stamp upon the whole of the landscape seen from his window, and it can be as great and beautiful a creation as Michelangelo's David, for the farmer who takes over a desolate farm, ruined by some evil and ignorant predecessor, and turns it into a paradise of beauty and abundance is one of the greatest of artists.

Of course, I am talking about the good farmer, the real farmer, and not that category of men who remain on the land because circumstance dropped them there and who go on, hating their land, hating their work and their animals because they have never discovered that they do not belong there, that they have no right to carry in trust the greatest of all gifts Nature can bring to man—a piece of good land, with the independence, the security, the excitement and even the splendor that go with it. The good farmer, working with Nature rather than fighting or trying to outwit her, may have what he wants of those treasures which are the only real ones and the ones by which man lives—his family, his power to create and construct the understanding of his relationship to the universe, and the deep, religious, humble sense of his own insignificance in God's creation.

The good farmer of today can have all the good things that his father knew and many that his father never knew, for in the modern world he lives with all the comforts of a luxurious city house plus countless beauties and rewards forever unknown to the city dweller. More than any other member of our society— indeed, perhaps alone in our society—the farmer has learned how to use machinery to serve him rather than his serving machinery. That is a very great secret indeed and one which the other members of our society need desperately to learn.

The Return of the Native

Like Clym in Thomas Hardy's classic, Louis Bromfield was a native returned from the Continent to his place in the country. For Bromfield the return was a wonderful and renewing one. It was the kind of return that more and more Americans would like to make these days—if not from the Continent, then from an urban milieu that lacks, finally, the satisfactions that a true "place in the country" can provide. Bromfield had great affection for France and for his life there, which he describes in this essay. He left reluctantly. But he did not return to his native Ohio to sink into some sort of depressed literary semiretirement. That was not the idea at all. Instead, he would roll up his sleeves and create an even more meaningful life.

The year is 1939, and the now-famous author, his wife, Mary, and his business manager–secretary, George Hawkins, are scouting out the farms of Pleasant Valley that are to be joined to make Malabar. Louis Bromfield has just turned forty-two.

A s the car came down out of the hills and turned off the Pinhook Road the whole of the valley, covered in snow, lay spread out before us with the ice-blue creek wandering through it between the two high sandstone ridges where the trees, black and bare, rose against the winter sky. And suddenly I knew where I was. I had come home!

All that afternoon we had been wandering through the southern part of the county trying to find the Pleasant Valley Road. It was not as if I had never been there before. Once I had known it very well, as only a small boy can know a valley where the fishing and swimming is good, the woods are thick and cool and damp, and filled with Indian caves. I had known every turn of the creek, every fishing hole, every farm, every millrace, every cave. But that had been a long time ago—more than thirty years—and now finding my way back through the hills was like trying to find one's way back through the maze of a vaguely remembered dream. There were places I remembered when I came upon them, places like the village of Lucas, and the bridge over the Rocky Fork and the little crossroads oddly called Pinhook and another called Steam Corners, no one has ever been able to say why. But like scenes and places in a dream these were isolated landmarks, disconnected, with the roads that lay between only half-forgotten mysteries. In those hills, where the winding roads trail in and out among the woods and valleys, I can lose myself even today after I have come to know the country all over again as a grown man. On that first day I was utterly lost.

I might have asked my way. In the village there was the little bank of which one day I was to become a director, and the village post office where one day I was to do what I could, as an amateur politician, to get Hoyt Leiter appointed postmaster. As I write this I am struck again by the curious dreamlike quality of the whole adventure in which the elements of time and even of space seemed confused and even suspended. It was as if the valley had been destined always to be a fiercely dominant part of my existence, especially on its spiritual and emotional side. It has always existed for me in two manifestations, partly in a dreamlike fashion, partly on a plane of hard reality and struggle. Perhaps these two manifestations represent the sum total of a satisfactory life. I do not know. I think that some day when I am an old man, it, like many other mysteries, will become clear, and that clarity, as one of the recompenses of old age, will become a part of the pattern of a satisfactory life.

I could have stopped and asked my way at the bank or the post office, or I could have stopped the car and asked one of the three or four people who passed us trudging along on foot in the snow. Once we passed a boy in a Mackinaw and ear-muffs riding on a big blue-roan Percheron mare. He raised his hand in greeting. As I passed each one I thought, "That might be a Teeter or a Berry or a Shrack or a Darling or a Tucker or a Culler."

Those were all names which had belonged among these hills since Indian times. The young ones I couldn't know because all of them had been born during the thirty years I had been away. But I peered into the faces of the old ones trying to find there something that I remembered from the days when, as a small boy, I had driven over the whole of the county in a buggy behind a team of horses, electioneering for my father or for some other good Democrat.

Then, as a small boy, I had known all the Teeters, the Cullers, the Berrys and all the others for sometimes we had had midday dinner with them. Sometimes we had tied the horses to the hitching rail and got out and gone into the fields to help ring hogs or husk corn. Sometimes, if the roads were deep with mud or an early blizzard came on, we unharnessed the steaming horses and put them in a stall deep with straw and ourselves spent the night in a big bed with a feather quilt over us. I think my father was welcome in the house of any farmer or villager of the county, Republican or Democrat. They all knew him as "Charley" Bromfield. He was a kindly man, who was a bad politician because he didn't pretend to like people; he really liked them. I think he liked politics, in which he never had much success and in which he lost a great deal of money, principally because it brought him into close contact with nearly all kinds of people. He was one of the fortunate people who like the human race despite all its follies and failings.

And so the faces of the people I saw in the village streets and on the country roads were very important to me on that first day. I was coming home to a country which I had never really left, for in all those years away from the valley it had kept returning to me. It was the only place in the world for which I had ever been homesick. More than half of the time I had spent away from Pleasant Valley was passed in France, a country where I had never been a stranger, even on the first night when I stepped ashore at Brest at the age of eighteen and tasted my first French cheese and French wine in the smoky, smelly little bars and cafés of the waterfront. Often in distant parts of the world, among strange peoples, I had wakened to find that I had been dreaming of Pleasant Valley.

There have been moments in my experience when I have been sharply aware of the "strange intimations" of which Dr. Alexis Carrel writes—intimations which have scarcely been touched upon in the realms of science—"strange intimations" of worlds which I had known before, of places which in spirit I had touched and heard and smelled. France was one of the places I had always known. From the time I was old enough to read, France had a reality for me, the one place in all the world I felt a fierce compulsion to see. Its history fascinated me, its pictures, its landscapes, its books, its theaters. It was, during all my childhood and early youth, the very apotheosis of all that was romantic and beautiful. And finally when, the morning before we were allowed ashore, the gray landscape of Brittany appeared on the horizon, there was nothing strange about it. I had seen those shores before, when I do not know. And afterward during all the years I lived there, during the war when I served with the French army and in the strange, melodramatic truce between wars, it was always the same. Nothing ever surprised or astonished me; no landscape, no forest, no château, no Paris street, no provincial town ever seemed strange. I had seen it all before. It was always a country and its people a people whom I knew well and intimately.

I have had a similar feeling about the austere, baroque, shabby-elegant quality of Spain and about the subcontinent of India. Germany, under any regime, has always been abhorrent, a place where I was always depressed and unhappy and a hopeless foreigner, even in a city like Munich which many people accept as beautiful and warm and *gemütlich*—a feeling which was not improved by spending my last visit there in the Vierjahreszeiten Hotel with Dr. Goebbels. And although, save for a little very remote Swedish blood, I have no blood that did not come from the British Isles, England was always a strange, although very pleasant country, more exotic to me than Spain or India. I do not begin to understand these things, these "strange intimations."

The point I wish to make is this—that during all those thirty years, sometimes in the discomfort of war, sometimes during feelings of depression engendered by Germany, but just as often during the warm, conscious pleasure and satisfaction of France or India or the Spanish Pyrenees, I dreamed constantly of my home country, of my grandfather's farm, of Pleasant Valley. Waking slowly from a nap on a warm summer afternoon or dozing before an open fire in the ancient *presbytère* at Senlis, I would find myself returning to the county, going back again to the mint-scented pastures of Pleasant Valley or the orchards of my grandfather's farm. It was as if all the while my spirit were tugging to return there, as if I was under a compulsion. And those dreams were associated with a sensation of warmth and security and satisfaction that was almost physical.

It may have been because in all my waking hours, during most of those years, I was aware of insecurity and peril, conscious always that in the world outside my own country, a doom lay ahead. During the last few years before the end of Europe, the feeling of frontiers, hostility and peril became increasingly acute, and distant Pleasant Valley, fertile and remote and secure, seemed more and more a haven, hidden away among the lovely hills of Ohio. I think no intelligent American, no foreign correspondent, living abroad during those years between the wars, wholly escaped the European sickness, a malady compounded of anxiety and dread, difficult to define, tinctured by the knowledge that some horrifying experience lay inevitably ahead for all the human race. Toward the end the malady became an almost tangible thing, which you could touch and feel. Many doctors had a hand in the attempt to check it, most of them quacks like the Lavals and the Daladiers, some untrustworthy like Sir John Simon, later honored by a title for his follies and deceptions, some merely old-fashioned practitioners with quaint nostrums patched and brewed together like Neville Chamberlain. One saw the marks of the malady on every face, from the hysterical ones whose follies became even more exaggerated, to the dull or unscrupulous ones who became each an individual thinking only of himself, and rarely of his country.

Toward the end I found myself spending more and more of my sleeping hours in the country where I was born and always what I dreamed of was Ohio and my own county.

And at last when Mr. Chamberlain debased the dignity of the British Empire, took his umbrella and overshoes and went to Munich to meet a second-rate adventurer, I, like any other moderately informed and intelligent person in Europe, knew that the dreadful thing was at hand, and that nothing now could stop it. I sent my wife and children home to America on a ship crowded with schoolteachers and businessmen and tourists whose pleasure trips or business had been cut short by orders from the State Department for all Americans traveling in Europe to come home.

My wife said, "Where shall we go?" and I replied, "To Ohio. That is where we were going anyway sometime."

I myself stayed on, partly out of a novelist's morbid interest in the spectacle, however depressing, and partly because, loving France, I wanted to be of help if there was anything that I could do. I stayed for weeks, more and more depressed, and it was Louis Gillet who persuaded me at last that I could do more for France at home in my own country than I could ever do by remaining in France.

I remember that we talked it all out beneath the great trees and among the magnificence of the ruins of the Abbaye de Chaalis where Louis Gillet held the sinecure of curator. The leaves were falling from the trees in the long gentle autumn of the Ile de France. His four boys were all mobilized. His widowed younger daughter was there on a visit from her quiet farm in Périgord. A second daughter, wife of the head of the Institute de France in Athens, and her two small children, had not returned to Athens at the end of the summer because of the malady, of that doubt and dread which crippled the will and the plans of everyone in Europe, in homes in Poland, in Norway, in Italy, in England.

And as we walked about the great park among the lagoons and the seventeenth century gardens, surrounded by the evidence of all the glorious history of France, Louis Gillet talked, brilliantly, humanly, as he could talk when he was deeply moved.

At last he said, "You must return home. There is nothing you can do here that a Frenchman could not do. You can go home and tell your people what is happening here, what is bound to come. Tell them they will not be able to escape it—to be prepared and ready. We in France and in England too have already lost half the battle by complacency and bitterness and intrigue. The Hun is preparing to march again down across the face of civilized Europe. Go home and tell your people. You can help France most by doing just that."

That night after dinner all of us went out into the moonlit forest of Ermenonville to listen to the stags call. It was the mating season and the stags made a wonderful roaring noise to attract the does. Sometimes in a patch of moonlight you could, if you were down wind and sat quite still, catch a glimpse of a big stag calling, his head raised, his muzzle thrust straight out, sick with love. And if you were very lucky you could witness the magnificent spectacle of two stags fighting over a doe. The deer were the descendants of those deer which François Premier and Henri Quatre had hunted in these same forests. It was the fashion in the autumn on moonlit nights to go out from the provincial towns in the Oise to listen to their calling—*entendre bramer les cerfs.*

It had been the fashion perhaps as far back as the days when our town of Senlis was a Roman city.

Sitting there in the warm sand and lanes of the forest on a moonlit night, surrounded by a family which represented all that was finest in France and therefore in our Western civilization, I experienced a faint sickness in the pit of my stomach. In a day or two I would be leaving all this—the forest, the old town of Senlis, the good people who lived there. I would be saying farewell to France which I had loved and known even before I had ever seen it. And if one day I returned it would never be the same. It would live, because an idea, a civilization never wholly dies but goes on living in some altered form as a contribution to all that follows, but it would be changed, dimmed and dissipated by the violence of war and decadence. I would never again find the France I was leaving.

I was aware too, quite suddenly, of what it was that attracted me to Europe and most of all to France; it was the sense of continuity and the permanence of small but eternal things, of the incredible resistance and resiliency of the small people. I had found there a continuity which had always been oddly lacking in American life save in remote corners of the country like parts of New England and the South which were afflicted by decadence, where permanence and continuity of life existed through inertia and defeat. In the true sense, they were the least American of any of the parts of America. They had stood still while the endless pattern of change repeated itself elsewhere in factories, in automobiles, in radio, in the restlessness of the rich and the nomadic quality of the poor.

The permanence, the continuity of France was not born of weariness and economic defeat, but was a living thing, anchored to the soil, to the very earth itself. Any French peasant, any French workingman with his little plot of ground and his modest home and wages, which by American standards were small, had more permanence, more solidity, more security, than the American workingman or white-collar worker who received, according to French standards, fabulous wages, who rented the home he lived in and was perpetually in debt for his car, his radio, his washing machine.

Sitting there it occurred to me that the high standard of living in America was an illusion, based upon credit and the installment plan, which threw a man and his family into the street and on public relief the moment his factory closed and he lost his job. It seemed to me that real continuity, real love of one's country, real permanence had to do not with mechanical inventions and high wages but with the earth and man's love of the soil upon which he lived.

I knew that the hardest thing for me to bear in leaving France and Europe was not the loss of the intellectual life I had known there, nor the curious special freedom which a foreigner knows in a country he loves, nor the good food, nor even the friends I would be leaving behind. The thing I should miss most, the thing to which I was most attached were the old house and the few acres of land spread along the banks of a little river called the Nonette—land, earth in which I had worked for fifteen years, planting and cultivating until the tiny landscape itself had changed. If I never saw it again a part of my heart would always be there in the earth, the old walls, the trees and vines I had planted, in the friendships that piece of earth had brought me with horticulturists, farmers, peasants, market gardeners and the workingmen whose communal gardens adjoined my own.

They had liked and respected me, not because I was by their standards fabulously rich or because on Sundays Rolls-Royces and automobiles labeled *Corps Diplomatique* stood before my door. They liked and respected me because I grew as good or better cabbages with my own hands than they were able to grow. And it occurred to me that the honors I valued most out of all those I had received was the diploma given me by the Workingmen-Gardeners' Association of France for my skill as a gardener and the medal given me by the Ministry of Agriculture for introducing American vegetables into popular cultivation in the market garden area surrounding the city of Paris.

All of these things had to do with a permanence, a continuity which one seldom found in America. When I returned home, I knew that permanence, continuity, alone was what I wanted, not the glittering life of New York and Washington, not the intellectual life of universities. What I wanted was a piece of land which I could love passionately, which I could spend the rest of my life in cultivating, cherishing and improving, which I might leave together, perhaps, with my own feeling for it, to my children who might in time leave it to their children, a piece of land upon which I might leave the mark of my character, my ingenuity, my intelligence, my sense of beauty—perhaps the only real immortality man can have, so the people would say long after I was dead as they would say in Senlis long after I was gone, "Yes, the American did that. He planted that tree and built that bridge. He made the garden below the river in the old orchard." I cannot see that man could wish a better afterlife than the peace of oblivion and the immortality that rests in houses and trees and vines and old walls.

But on the floor of the forest the November fog had begun to settle down and the first chill of winter had begun to slip in about us. The stags, satisfied, had quit calling. Quietly we walked back to the Abbaye under a waning moon, past the canals built six hundred years before by the monks of Chaalis who were also the first millers of that rich wheat country.

Inside the pleasant house under the pompous bourgeois portrait of the Gillet ancestor who had been a marshal under Louis Philippe, we had a glass of good *vin rosé* and I drove home at last through the forest back to Senlis. It was the last time I ever saw Louis Gillet, with his long, sallow, bearded face and blue eyes. Afterward, week after week, I had letters from him when he was a *réfugié,* proscribed by the Germans, living in Montpellier with one son gravely wounded, another a prisoner in Germany and a third with the Free French in Syria. He kept on fighting with his pen and voice against the Nazis, against German *kultur,* against the defeatism and treason of Vichy. And then we entered the war and the Germans occupied all of France, a steel curtain came down, and I heard from him no more.

By some curious chance on the day I began to write this book, I had word through the French Underground that Louis

Gillet was dead, away from the Abbaye which he loved, a *réfugié* in Montpellier. I do not know whether the Germans imprisoned him, or how he died, but I do know now, six years after we walked beneath the trees in the Abbaye gardens, that all the advice he gave me was wise advice, that all the things he feared and predicted have come true. I know that he was a wise and good man. My only regret is that he never came to see me in Pleasant Valley, to see the land to which I had returned because we both believed it was my destiny and a good destiny. I would have liked him to know, to understand through his own senses, the rightness of all he said that November evening in the forest of Ermenonville before—what must have been for him—the end of the world.

All along, all through the years of homesickness and even after I had come back to America, I had never said to anyone that the county in which I was born was one of the beautiful spots of the earth. I had kept the belief to myself, a little out of shyness, a little because there were times when I, myself, had doubts, knowing that all too often when later in life you revisit scenes you have known and loved as a child, something strange has happened to them. Somehow, mysteriously as you grew into manhood and swallowed the whole of the world, they have become shrunken and different. The houses that you remembered as big and beautiful have dwindled and become commonplace, the stream on which you once played pirates is no longer a lovely gleaming river but has turned into a small and muddy brook.

On that winter afternoon while I searched for Pleasant Valley among the hills and winding roads, I was a little afraid that when I came suddenly upon it, I would find that it had changed, that all the while I had been dreaming of something that no longer had any existence in reality.

With me in the car were Mary, my wife, and George, who had been my friend and managed my affairs for a great many years. You will hear of them again in the course of this story, so it is just as well to explain them now. Mary was born on Murray Hill in New York City, a New Yorker of New Yorkers, and George was born on Long Island. Neither had ever known Ohio —my Ohio—save for the flat uninteresting country south of the lakes where Mary had taken the children on her flight from the doomed maneuvers of Chamberlain and Hitler.

All that afternoon as the car drove southward out of the flat lake country into the rolling hills of Wayne and Ashland County they kept saying, "This is beautiful country, why didn't you tell us about it?"

I had never really talked about it but once. Years earlier during a fit of homesickness in Switzerland, I had written a whole book about it called *The Farm*. I knew now that until the car turned into the wooded hill country, they hadn't really believed what I had written then. They had thought the county and the people I described were imagined as in a book of fiction. Their exclamations encouraged me; perhaps, after all, the valley would be exactly as I had remembered it.

And then we turned the corner from the Pinhook Road and I knew that I was right. Nothing had changed. It lay there in the deep snow, wide and pleasant between the two high sandstone ridges covered by forest. Halfway up the slopes on each side, in the shelter of the high ridges, stood the familiar houses and the great barns, unchanged after thirty years—houses with the old names of the Pennsylvania Dutch and old English stock which had settled the country long ago—the Shrack Place, the Mengert Place, the Berry Place, the big white houses and barns of the Darling settlement set in the wide flat rich end of the valley where Switzer's Run joined the Clear Fork.

And then far away, a mile or more on the opposite side of the valley I saw a small house with an enormous cupolaed barn. The buildings sat on a kind of shelf halfway up the long sloping hill that turned its back on the north winds. It was already twilight and the lower valley was the ice-blue color of a shadowed winter landscape at dusk and the black, bare trees on the ridge tops were tinted with the last pink light of the winter sunset. There were already lozenges of light in the windows of the distant house. Like Brigham Young on the sight of the vast valley of Great Salt Lake, I thought, "This is the place."

I heard my wife saying, "What a lovely, friendly valley!"

On that late winter afternoon, one had a curious sense of being sheltered from the winter winds, from the snow, from the buffetings and storms of the outside world. My wife and George saw a snow-covered valley. They could not see what I was seeing for the valley had no place in their memories. What I saw was a spring stream in summer, flowing through pastures of bluegrass and white clover and bordered by willows. Here and there in the meanderings of the stream there were deep holes where in the clear water you could see the shiners and bluegills, the sunfish and the big red-horse suckers and now and then a fine smallmouthed bass. On a hot day you could strip off your clothes and slip into one of these deep holes and lie there in the cool water among the bluegills and crawfish, letting the cool water pour over you while the minnows nibbled at your toes. And when you climbed out to dry in the hot sun and dress yourself, you trampled on mint and its cool fragrance scented all the warm air about you.

I saw, too, fields with fat cattle and wild marshy land where the cattails grew ten feet high and the muskrats built their shaggy round houses in the autumn, marshes which in April were bordered and splashed with the gold of one of the loveliest of all wild flowers, the marsh marigold. A little later in summer from among the rich tropical green of its spade-shaped foliage the arrowroot threw up long spikes of azure blue. And I saw the old mills, high, unpainted, silvergray with the weathering of a hundred years, the big lofts smelling of wheat and corn and outside the churning millrace where fat, big carp and suckers lay in the deep water to feed on the spilled grain and mash.

And I saw not the winter-naked woods, all snow and ledges of pink sandstone rock, but whole fields of dogtooth violets and trillium and Canadian lilies and Dutchman's-breeches and bloodroot. And in summer the same woods were waist high in ferns and snakeroot and wild grapes hung down from among the branches so that the whole woods seemed a tropical place like Brazil and Sumatra. As a boy in these woods I had pretended that they were tropical forests and that I was lost in them, as very often I was. And now I knew I was right. I had been far in the years between. I had seen tropical forests in Malabar and Macassar which held the same feeling of dampness, of fertility where, as in these Ohio woods, the leaves and tendrils and fresh green shoots were so thick that the whole air seemed green as if one were under water.

And I saw the woods in late February and March when there were no leaves on the naked trees and here and there in

damp hollows the first lush green of the skunk cabbage was thrusting through the dead leaves and marsh grass of the year before. For me there is always something exciting and especially beautiful about the skunk cabbage. Boldly it thrusts its tropical green leaves into the frosty air of dying winter, the first of all plants to herald the awakening and rebirth of life with each spring.

That time of bareness when the skunk cabbage first appeared was the time of making maple syrup and I saw the sugar camp with its roaring fires and the woods streaked with the last melting snow and the fat horses steaming as they drew the sled which carried the great hogshead of fresh sap taken from the budding trees. And the long nights when the run was good and I was allowed to sit up all night with my grandfather and boil syrup while the fire made shadows on the oaken walls of the sugar camp and the wind howled outside.

I was seeing all this which the two others could not see. My heart was crying out, "Wait until spring comes! If you think it is nice now, you will see something you cannot even imagine when this country awakens."

We crossed the valley and the little river half frozen over, with the swift-running clear spring water fringed with ice and rime, and up the hill on the opposite side of the wide sheltered ledge where the small house sat with its little windows blocked with light.

We followed the Hastings Road, a narrow, insignificant township road which led back and forth through woods and up and down low hills to the casual crossroad settlement called Hastings; and halfway up the hill we turned across a ravine with a small spring stream flowing down it, showing blue where the living water, green with cress, ran clear of ice between the dead leaves of last year's sweet flag.

At the house no one answered the knock. I knew it was chore time and so I went to the big barn to find the owners.

It was a big, red barn built in the days when farmers were rich and took a pride in their barns. Ohio is filled with them, barns which are an expression of everything that is good in farming, barns in which their owners took great pride. Nowadays one sees often enough great new barns on dairy farms owned by great corporations, or stock farms owned by millionaires; but these new barns have no character. They express nothing but utility and mechanized equipment, with no soul, no beauty, no individuality. Already they appear on any country landscape commonplace and standardized without beauty or individuality—in fifty years they will simply be eyesores.

The old barns built in the time of the great tradition of American agriculture, when the new land was still rich and unravaged by greed and bad farming, had each one its own character, its special beauty born of the same order in spirit and devotion which built the great cathedrals of Chartres or Rheims or Salzburg. They were built out of love and pride in the earth, each with a little element of triumphal boastfulness—as if each barn was saying to all the rich neighboring countryside, "Look at me! What a fine splendid thing I am, built by a loving master, sheltering fat cattle and big-uddered cows and great bins of grain! Look at me! A temple raised to plenty and to the beauty of the earth! A temple of abundance and good living!"

And they were not built *en série*, like barracks. Each rich farmer had his own ideas, bizarre sometimes, fanciful with fretwork and cupolas and big handsome paintings of a Belgian stallion or a shorthorn bull, the main cupola bearing a pair of trotting horses bright with gilt as a weather vane. They were barns with great, cavernous mows filled with clover hay, two stories or three in height with the cattle and horses below bedded in winter in clean straw, halfway to their fat bellies. Perhaps there was waste space or they were inconveniently planned for doing the chores, but there was a splendor and nobility about them which no modern hip-roofed, standardized, monstrosity can approach. Ohio is filled with them—Gothic barns, Pennsylvania Dutch barns with stone pillars, New England barns attached to the house itself, the stone-ended barns of Virginia and even baroque barns. There is in Ohio no regional pattern of architecture as there is in New England or the Pennsylvania Dutch country. Ohio was settled by people from all the coastal states each bringing his own tradition with him, and so there is immense variety.

In my boyhood nearly all these barns had a rich, well-painted appearance. Those owned by farmers with an ancient Moravian background outdid the barns which only had a single stallion or bull painted on them; they had painted on the big sliding barn door a whole farm landscape for which the farm itself had served as a model and in it appeared bulls and cows, calves and stallions, hens and ducks and guinea fowl, horses and sheep and hogs. They were hex-paintings and their roots lay, not in Ohio or even in the coastal states, but far back in the darkness of medieval Germany, in a world of Bald Mountains and *Walpurgisnächte.* They were painted there on the big barn doors as a safeguard against the spells of witches, against vampires and incubi for it was believed and it is still believed among the old people that the spell cast by any malicious neighboring witch on the cattle in one of these great barns would fall not on the cattle themselves but upon the representations painted on the barn door. Always they were painted artlessly by someone on the farm and some of them had a fine primitive quality of directness and simplicity of conception.

Usually over the doors of these painted barns there hung a worn horseshoe, for it was believed that witches had an overweening passion for mathematics coupled with a devouring curiosity. If a witch sought during the night to sweep through the barn door on her broomstick and found herself confronted by a used horseshoe, she was forced to turn about and have no peace until she had retraced and counted all the hoofprints made by the shoe. The more worn the shoe the better, for it would take her all the longer to satisfy her compulsion, and she would not have completed her impossible task before morning arrived and she had to return whence she came. If the shoe had been worn long enough, the prints it had made would be so numerous that she could never count them all in a single night. As each night she had to begin afresh, she would never be able, even in the long nights of winter, to get through the door to do evil to the cattle.

As a boy I had seen in the early mornings little heaps of corn or corn meal outside each door of a barn owned by some old man whose Moravian blood took him far back into the mists and shadows of Germany. They were placed before the doors for the same reason as the omnipresent horseshoe. A witch confronted by a heap of corn could not go on with her evil purpose until she had satisfied her curiosity by counting every gain. If the corn were ground into meal, so much the better for the task became a thousand times more difficult.

All these memories came flooding back during the short walk from the house to the great barn. Then I pushed open the door and walked into the smell of cattle and horses and hay and silage and I knew that I had come home and that never again would I be long separated from that smell because it meant security and stability and because in the end, after years of excitement and wandering and adventure, it had reclaimed me. It was in the blood and could not be denied. But all of that story I told long ago in *The Farm*.

The Plan

The three farms Louis Bromfield bought in Pleasant Valley in 1939 had once been in a single ownership. They had been broken into the Ferguson Place, the Anson Place, and the Fleming Place—as Bromfield called them. A fourth farm, the Bailey Place, was added later. He eventually farmed a thousand acres. None of the places Bromfield bought were successful operations; they were small and the land had been abused. What he wanted to do was no less than to restore the land to its original productivity, even surpass it, and to make a farm that would support his and other families by itself in a way that could be emulated by any farmer— not just a Hollywood-rich novelist. In this way would he reclaim what he felt to be his family's destiny as members of an agrarian "natural aristocracy," described in his 1933 autobiographical novel, The Farm.

This was no small challenge. In meeting it, the ebullient Louis Bromfield took Daniel Burnham's advice—"make no small plans." Over endless cups of coffee, Bromfield and his first farm manager, the redoubtable Max Drake, figured out a most remarkable scheme, borrowing freely and variously from feudal England, rural France, southern India, Soviet Russia, Thomas Jefferson's Monticello, and, of course, the technical and economic imperatives of modern American agriculture. Max Drake now lives in retirement in Michigan, still fit, humorous, and opinionated, pretty much as Bromfield describes him here. Max (which is what everyone calls him) describes Bromfield as a hardhead, but an interesting and affable fellow nevertheless. Together, they made "the Plan."

I t wasn't a job I could do alone. I had been away from America too long, far too long out of touch with the machinery of agricultural administration, of American agricultural experiment and progress. In some ways I was far more familiar with what was going on in France, in Sweden, in Syria or even India. I was born in a small town where one only had to walk a few minutes in any direction to be in the open country. I had spent half my childhood and boyhood on my grandfather's farm —*The Farm* of which I had once written all the history in the most intimate possible detail. At sixteen I had gone off to Cornell Agricultural College meaning to be a farmer. I might have gone on with that career but for two circumstances, both extremely powerful. One was a potent urge to become a writer; the other was my mother, who was determined that I should not, as she phrased it, "waste my life on a farm."

She was herself the daughter of a skilled farmer, the first Master of the Grange in the state, but in her heart she always carried a bitter resentment of the fact that a piece of land anchored one forever to one spot. She had in herself the seeds of the restlessness which made it necessary for me to see the whole world before I settled down. She always counseled me to be a writer first and then at my leisure become a "farmer." I knew that "a gentleman farmer" was what she meant even then—a man who had a big income from investments, established a "model dairy" or had saddle horses in mahogany stalls. I never had that in mind, even then. It is still less in mind today.

During the first year at agricultural college my grandfather died at a great age and my mother insisted that I come home and operate his farm myself for a year in order to make a decision. Because she was a "powerful influence" I yielded and ran my grandfather's farm, not too badly, for a whole year and learned what she meant by "anchored to a piece of land." There were twelve cows to be milked twice a day, hogs, horses, chickens to be fed, hay to be made, not when one chose but when the hay was ready and the weather right. At the end of the year I knew that it was no good, that I could never settle down until the restlessness was satisfied. At the end of that year, I did not return to the college of agriculture; I went instead to the Columbia School of Journalism. But even that did not last for long. Before the first year was finished I went off to the war. I never gave either university much of a chance to teach me anything, but I never learned anything at all at either one.

I became a writer and I made lots of money and my books were translated into every language in Europe and even into Chinese and Bengali. I don't think my mother could have asked for more, but for all that, the old itch for the land never died. In all my life I lived only three years in a city and they were the three most unhappy years of my life, two of them in New York and one in Paris. They were unhappy because I was bored, despite all the distinguished and celebrated people I knew, and all the supposedly exciting events in which I participated. Always there were two or three hours a day when I did not know what to do with myself. If I had had a weak head or any taste for drink I could have slipped down the path so many writers have gone out of boredom. I just wasn't born for city life. On a farm, if you are born for it, no day is ever long enough to accomplish all there is to be done. No city can offer any excitement comparable to what happens when there is a new pure bred calf or the whole landscape comes alive with the change of season. No excitement can equal the slow satisfaction of witnessing a tired, worn field come back to life and fertility.

And so during all the years away from my country I came to know farmers and agricultural stations in every part of the world, and I learned much, many things that we have not yet learned in agriculture even here in America. And always I had, save for three years, a piece of the earth in which I could work, watching and learning things about earth, water, air, plants and animals.

The first step was obviously to find myself a partner in the undertaking, a younger man who knew all the developments of recent years, who was a farmer and was in touch with the agencies of government, of the extension school, of the agricultural colleges which made easily accessible to the farmer all the knowledge concerning agriculture which they had been piling up for a long time. There were a hundred applicants for the job of taking over and restoring John Ferguson's section of hill and valley land. They were of all kinds, young and old and middle-aged, some the products of agricultural colleges, some rabid theorists, some just plain old-fashioned dirt farmers. They came from all over the country. The selection was a long process and I learned much from talking to all those men. But none of them seemed right; either they knew too little of recent developments in agriculture or they knew too much and had too little contact with the earth itself. Or they were too old and "sot" in their ways, or they were too young and too eager, too innocent of the hard work that is inevitably a part of farming.

A good farmer in our times has to know more about more things than a man in any other profession. He has to be a biologist, a veterinary, a mechanic, a botanist, a horticulturist, and many other things, and he has to have an open mind, eager and ready to absorb new knowledge and new ideas and new ideals.

A good farmer is always one of the most intelligent and best educated men in our society. We have been inclined in our wild industrial development, to forget that agriculture is the base of our whole economy and that in the economic structure of the nation it is always the cornerstone. It has always been so throughout history and it will continue to be so until there are no more men on this earth. We are apt to forget that the man who owns land and cherishes it and works it well is the source of our stability as a nation, not only in the economic but the social sense as well. Few great leaders ever came out of city slums or even suburbs. In France, in England, in America, wherever you choose to turn, most of the men who have molded the destinies of the nation have come off the land or from small towns. The great majority of leaders, even in the world of industry and finance, have come from there. As a nation we do not value our farmers enough; indeed I believe that good farmers do not value themselves highly enough. I have known all kinds of people, many of them celebrated in many countries, but for companionship, good conversation, intelligence and the power of stimulating one's mind there are none I would place above the good farmer.

But there are two other qualities, beyond the realm of the inquiring mind or the weight of education, without which no man could be a good farmer. These, I believe, are born in him. They are a passionate feeling for the soil he owns and an understanding and sympathy for his animals. I do not believe that these traits can be acquired; they are almost mystical qualities, belonging really only to people who are a little "teched" and very close to Nature itself.

Often enough, people discover late in life that they have these qualities, without ever having known it. They did not acquire them suddenly; they were always there. It is only through the accident of a fishing trip or the purchase of a farm, they discovered them. I have any number of friends who spent all their lives as bankers and industrialists or workingmen or insurance salesmen, only to discover at middle age that in reality they were farmers all the time, without knowing it. I know of no human experience more remarkable than that of men whose whole existences are changed and enriched by the discovery late in life that they have a close bond with the earth and all living things, and that they have lost vast and intangible riches by not making the discovery when they were younger.

Conversely, there are many men on farms in America who have neither that love of soil nor of animals. They are the bad farmers who have done us such great damage as a nation. They do not belong on farms. They are there, most of them, because they were born there and have not the energy to quit and go to the cities and factories where they properly belong. There are too many of them in America, and they have cost us dear.

For the good farmer, his animals are not simply commodities without personality destined only to be made into pork chops or beef steaks or to produce milk all their lives. To a good farmer, each animal has its own personality. A good farmer cannot himself sleep if his animals are not well fed and watered and bedded down on a cold winter night. Watch any good farmer showing his sheep or cattle or hogs at a county fair or an international stock show and you will understand how much he respects the animals that are linked into that chain of life which explains and justifies the whole of his activity. Or watch any 4-H Club boy or girl with tears in his eyes when the moment comes for him to part with the fat steer he has raised and brought to a cattle show. He has slept in the straw in the stall beside his steer for days. The steer is a part of the richness of his own existence. He will go cold himself or go without food and water before the steer shall be deprived of these things.

Looking for all these qualities among a hundred or more

strangers was not an easy job, but I found them at last in a young fellow called Max Drake. He was thirty-two years old, with a wife and son. He was himself the son of a good farmer. He had a brilliant record in the state agricultural college. He had worked with 4-H Clubs and been a substitute county agent. He was interested in anchoring the soil and salvaging what remained of our good land. And he was interested also in the whole intangible side of a farmer's life which had to do with farm institutes and square-dancing and fun.

We made a deal and Max and his wife and son came to live in the miller's house where "Ceely" Rose had done away with her parents and two brothers. Fortunately they were not superstitious people. They liked the little house with its big spring and its huge elm tree and the wide view up and down the valley across the bottom pasture where the dairy cows fed. It was still winter when they came there.

As winter broke into spring we sat night after night beside the big stove in the miller's house or in the big ugly house on the Fleming Place where I came with my family to live until the changes had been made in the old house above us on the side of the hill. I think that for both of us, there had never been or ever will be a more stimulating experience than the working out of the Plan. We had between us six hundred and forty acres of woods and pasture and farmland and springs and streams, a small kingdom which we sought between us to bring back to life. It was a little like planning the re-creation of a world of our own, secure and complete and apart.

The Plan grew, slowly at first and then more and more quickly, out of the lives, the education, the experience of both of us. Both of us knew pretty definitely what we wanted to do. There were disagreements and compromises but in the end the Plan emerged. It was something like this:

There was first of all the soil itself which was the foundation of our own well-being and security as it was of that of the whole nation. Much of it was already gone, washed off our hills, down Switzer's Run, into the Clear Fork and thence into the Muskingum, the Ohio and the Mississippi, where so many billions of tons of our good American soil have gone since first we cut off the forests and plowed up the grassbound prairies. We had first of all to stop that destruction and heal the gullies which made ugly scars in every sloping field. And we had to bring back to the soil the fertility which, save on the Anson Place, had been dissipated by ignorant and greedy farming.

We had to remodel the big old barns built in a more leisurely time when labor was cheap and the rich soil had not yet been raped of its fertility. Those barns were planned too before the days of machinery and to operate them it took too many man-hours, more hours than any farm could afford and succeed in a time when labor costs had doubled and tripled.

And there was the question of livestock which was vital in the production of manure to bring back the fertility of the wasted fields. We decided that whatever we sold off the farm would have to be able to walk off, a sound principle of any farm, rich or wasted. No straw, no hay, and a minimum of grains would be sold off the place. It would be fed and the animals who ate it marketed, leaving behind them the tons of manure which spells wealth to a farmer anywhere in the world.

And there was to be a whole program of green manures, the clovers and other legumes, rye and rye grass to be plowed under to restore both nitrogen and humus to the tired, worn-out soil. And there was the question of lime and phosphorus and potassium and other minerals and trace minerals which had been leached out by erosion and removed by greedy "mining" of the land—all these minerals without which plant life remained sickly and feeble and animals which fed upon it small-boned and anemic.

We knew, too, that poor worn-out land made not only poor crops and scrubby cattle; it made poor, underdeveloped, undernourished people as well. That was one of the great problems of American agriculture—the decline of human stock through the decline in fertility and mineral content of the soil itself. "Poor land makes poor people" is a saying every American should have printed and hung over his bed.

And there was the question of the timbered land which had gone the way of most farm woodlots in America. Long ago most of the bigger trees, save only the sugar maples, had been stripped from most of the land for quick cash profits. Into what was left of the woods sheep and cattle had been turned to feed for many years. The pasture was poor and scrubby and the cattle and sheep got little or no nourishment from it, and in their hunger they had eaten off the young seedlings year after year until there was no new crop of trees coming on to supply the farmer and the nation with timber. The men who had farmed these three farms were getting neither pasture nor timber from the woodlots and as most of the woods were on steep ground unfit for farming, the soil was washed badly in spots and gullies occurred even on the wooded land. To check all that, we planned to shut out all cattle from the woodlots and give the forest a chance to seed itself and become productive once more.

There would be other benefits as well. A forest floor green once more with seedlings does not permit the water to rush across it, cutting gullies, carrying away topsoil and encouraging the rainfall to escape into the Mississippi and the Gulf of Mexico instead of staying in Ohio where we needed it desperately for crops and springs and industrial and urban use.

There was too the question of restoring the native pastures of bluegrass and white clover, perhaps the finest pasture for livestock in the world. Our bottom pastures which lay along the little creek were alluvial and deep-soiled and most of the land had never been cultivated since the trees had first been cut away; but in the course of years both lime and phosphorus as well as other minerals and trace minerals had been leached away even there or consumed and carried off in the bodies of the animals which fed off it. On the hill pastures the topsoil was often gone along with the minerals and where there should have been bluegrass and white clover, there was only poverty grass and the tough wire grass that moves in on poor land. In many of the pastures the animal droppings of years provided nitrogen, but nitrogen alone is not enough to produce good grass. All the pasture land would need both lime and phosphorus, not only in order to grow better grass, but to feed these minerals into the bones and sinew of cattle, horses and sheep, and the growing children on the farm.

As the new pioneers bent upon restoring the land, we had to put back by every manner of ingenious means the very elements the first pioneers had removed recklessly or permitted to disappear through erosion and neglect. The problem was, on the surface, a simple one but both Max and I knew that it was not so simple as it appeared to be. Working *with* Nature, we would be recompensed by her sympathy, but beyond a certain point Nature could not be pushed. To build the precious topsoil which had been treated so carelessly by our predecessors, it had needed millions of years in the natural process of the disintegration of rock and clay and rotting vegetation. With the aid of the knowledge and experience of agricultural civilization, we knew that we could restore the soil infinitely more quickly but only if we worked *with* Nature rather than *against* her as our predecessors had done.

One thing was in our favor. All our land was glacial moraine, of the soil type known as "Wooster"—great hills of gravel, sand and clay, scraped from the surface of the land north of us for a distance of fifteen hundred miles north to the borders of Hudson's Bay. Some of it, alluvial in character, had been washed from beneath the vast glacier as it began to disintegrate with a softening of climate that had happened a million years before John Ferguson came into the valley. Mixed in these hills, all the way down, were gravel, lime, phosphorus, potassium, fluorine, iodine and countless other elements. It was good stuff to work with, to build upon. In creating new topsoil, the process required most of all masses of decaying organic matter to hold the moisture, the volatile nitrogen and anchor the minerals we planned to use in the replenishing process.

In our case when the topsoil had disappeared we did not come upon rock, or hardpan, or blue clay as happened in the case of so many thousand worn-out farms in America. When that happened, a farm was really dead and gone, a total agricultural loss, fit only for reforestation or to be abandoned as man-made desert. But Max and I knew that millions of acres of good American land, based upon hardpan or shale, had been reduced to desert conditions. It could never be restored quickly by any process now known to man. We were lucky—where the dark topsoil was lost we came down to glacial drift, made up of many kinds of soil stirred together by the great glacier. We had something to build upon.

But the plans we had in mind were not concerned alone with the soil. They had social and economic aspects as well, for we both knew that agriculture in America was sick, with a wasting illness which no amount of subsidies or superficial measures *imposed* by a highly centralized government could cure. We knew too that when agriculture is sick, the illness in time pervades the whole of the economic structure of the nation. That much was history, unarguable, confirmed by the story of more than one dead or decaying nation since the beginning of time.

Some of the reasons, like the wasting of the soil, lay with the farmer himself, born of ignorance or greed or carelessness. We knew the evil of crop systems prevailing in the areas where only one crop—tobacco or wheat or cotton or corn—was raised year after year for decades while the soil grew thinner and thinner and more and more exhausted. That problem did not concern us for Ohio country was given over naturally to general farming and livestock. But out of that single-crop system, out of the laxness of thousands of farmers and their wives, out of the mechanization of our civilization, had grown another abuse which played a large part in the sickness of agriculture. The old economic independence of the farmer, his sense of security, that stability which a healthy agriculture gives to the economy of any nation, had broken down, and one of the most important reasons for the breakdown was the farmer's dependence upon things which he purchased rather than producing these same things off his own land.

I had memories of the farm of my grandfather, a farm which in itself was a fortress of security. On a hundred acres he had raised and educated eight children, strong, healthy, constructive citizens. He had bought little more than salt, coffee, tea and spices. All else he had produced out of the earth he owned and cherished, and when winter came there was a great cellar stored with home canned goods, and a fruit cellar heaped with apples, potatoes and all kinds of root vegetables. In the dry cold attic hung rows of hams and flitches of bacon. In that house I ate as well as I have ever eaten anywhere in the world. I knew that he had spent little or nothing upon food for himself, his wife, his eight children, his hired man and girl and all the relations who were always staying in the big house. At the end of the year all these vast quantities of food showed up as profit on the right side of the ledger.

Opposed to that memory was the knowledge that scattered over the whole of our nation were thousands of farms where the farmer and his wife bought the bulk of their food out of cans off shelves in town grocery stores, very often in the very midst of the gardening season. The extreme examples were those one-crop area farms where wheat, or corn or tobacco or cotton grew up to the front door and the farmer's wife bought canned peas and beans in June or July or August. To our astonishment, we found during the first year of operation, that neighbors from farms, good farms, with two hundred or more acres of land, came to us to buy apples because they had not even one apple tree on their land. This happened even in our rich diversified Ohio country.

The economy of a piece of land is at once a complicated and a simple economy. The farmer's land is his capital. If he does not produce all that he can produce within economic and climatic reason, he is failing to utilize his capital to its full advantage. Whatever he buys that he is able to produce can only appear on the red side of the ledger at the end of the year.

On the point of self-sufficiency, Max's faith was less strong than my own, I think because his faith in machinery and in such economic pitfalls as the installment plan was greater than my own, and because he had never seen in this rich country the things I had witnessed and lived through in countries where there were inflation and food shortages and rationing, and discord and civil war. I was perpetually haunted by the terrible economic insecurity which a mechanized and industrial civilization imposes upon the individual.

I told Max about these things and he listened with intelligence and interest but even though he had witnessed the misery of a great depression, he never quite believed that they could ever come to rich America. Even while he talked there by the big stove in the miller's house, rationing, food shortages and other hardships were already in the cards for America. Even disorder and civil conflict were not beyond the realm of the imagination after the war. If and when such things did come, I wanted, I told Max, to be on my own land, on an island of security which could be a refuge not only for myself and my family but my friends as well. I did not want to be in Detroit or Pittsburgh or any great industrial city. I had lived through inflation, strike, violence, shortage and civil disorders three or four times in Europe and I did not believe that we, as a nation, were any more immune to the results of our folly than any other nation. But Max, like so many other Americans, did not believe that we could ever be involved in the disasters which afflicted the rest of the world.

Because he was lukewarm about the self-sufficiency angle, that part of the program fell wholly to me. I knew what I meant to do. I meant to have as nearly everything as possible, not merely chickens and eggs and butter and milk and vegetables and fruit and the things which many foolish farmers buy today: I meant to have guinea fowl and ducks and geese and turkeys which could live off the abundance of the farm without care in a half-wild state as such birds live in the *basse-cour* of a prosperous French farm. I meant to have grapes in abundance and plums and peaches, currants, gooseberries, asparagus—indeed a whole range of things which could be had for the mere planting and the expenditure of a little work and care.

One pond already existed on the farm and with the rolling land and the abundance of springs and small streams the building of ponds became a simple enough procedure. I meant to include ponds which would produce a constant supply of fish. And I meant not only to operate the maple sugar bush again but also to have bees which not only would fertilize crops but produce hundreds of pounds of honey. If there was too much fruit it could be given away, or sold at a roadside market or left to the birds and the raccoons.

I have never believed in the superficial folly of Henry Wallace's program of scarcity. There has, in fact, never been a surplus of food for the people of the world. There has always been a scarcity, with surpluses piling up in some countries and at times even in states and cities, because distribution has been abominable and because ill-managed trade relations between nations have crippled the whole system of distribution. The fundamental solution of the more grave economic problems of agriculture lies not in burning coffee and killing little pigs but in getting agricultural products to the areas where there is not only a market for them but where often enough they are desperately needed.

And thus self-sufficiency, another expression of the ultimate security, became an important and integral part of the Plan which was eventually to bear rich dividends not only for myself and my family but for all the other families on the farm.

*   *

There was another reason for the sickness of American agriculture which troubled both of us. This was the gradual disappearance, over large areas, of the family-sized farm and establishment of great mechanized farms which were more like industries than farms. The pattern repeated itself in many forms, superficially different, but essentially the same, supplanting a sturdy family by semi-industrial, often imported labor. Neither Max nor myself believed that the impulse of our times toward regimentation, centralization, mechanization and industrialism necessarily represented progress. It seemed to us and still seems to me a dangerous path with "rewards" at the end which are bought at the cost of physical stamina, human decency and the dignity and self-respect of man. We knew that the greater part of our migratory population in America—one of our most serious economic and social problems—came either from worn-out farms or from land that had been converted into factories in the fields. This roving population was one that was certain to increase in proportion to the increasing destruction of soil and the industrialization of the remaining farm lands.

We knew too that in these times the high cost of farm machinery and the necessity for it made it virtually impossible any longer for a young man to marry, purchase a farm and equipment and establish a family. If he inherited farm or machinery, he might succeed in getting along even with all the handicaps imposed by a sick agricultural economy, but if he had to buy both farm and machinery, the situation was impossible. Without efficient modern farm machinery he could not hope to succeed.

We sought a way to operate a big farm without dispossessing families. We sought a way of helping a young fellow to get started in life. We sought a way of raising the standard of living of all of us on that farm. Both of us, Max, out of his experience in this country, and I, out of my experience both here and in a half dozen countries abroad, had faith in co-operative effort as the solution to many of the illnesses of agriculture, and together after many nights by the stove in the miller's house we worked out that part of the Plan.

We took as our model the collective farm as it had worked out in Russia. We accepted its principles only in a large and rather loose way, in which I, myself, as the capitalist, was sub-

stituted for the state. Both of us had faith in the belief that some sort of a co-operative farm could be worked out under proper management so that the income and living standards of all the families involved would be as good or better than that of the average-sized family farm and far better than those of the average moderate-income city dweller.

Under the Plan each family would have a house, rent free, with light and heat, bathrooms and plumbing, all its living save only coffee, spices and sugar, as well as a salary above the average. In my role as capitalist or "the state" I agreed to put up the money on the adventure exactly as I would invest money in a factory or a business project. I would assure the finances until we came to the point where we turned a profit. From then on I should take the first five per cent as a sound but not exaggerated profit on the investment and as an offset against the salaries and living expenses of the others. Once this five per cent was paid off annually, any profits above that amount were to be divided pro rata according to the salaries paid each worker, which varied according to their education, skill and value of the common enterprise.

I was to share as well in this distribution of the profits above five per cent, my share being based upon the pro rata share of the manager of the enterprise. It was recognized that while I took the risks, I also benefited by the enhanced value of the property as we built up the fertility of the soil. The growing fertility, however, benefited by increased production; and profits the others participating in the co-operative. It was also recognized that I contributed knowledge not only of agriculture but also of world and market conditions with which my profession and political and economic interests constantly brought me in touch.

And finally there was the question of the house that was to shelter my family, I hoped, for the rest of my life. During twenty years of married life we had never really had a house of our own. We had lived for a time in houses on the Basque coast, in Switzerland, in Kensington, in Long Island, in Baroda, in Mysore. We had a liking for houses and always in a place which pleased us, like Singapore or the Indian states or Spain or Italy, we had looked at houses, planning always to stay there for a time. Perhaps we would have stayed but for children and dogs and education and such domestic matters. There had always to be a base, a center where there was a permanent establishment for children and dogs, and the vast accumulation of pictures, books and souvenirs which kept growing despite anything one could do. Once when Isabel Paterson was asked how she was going to furnish a new house she had acquired, she replied, "I've never had any trouble about that. The only trouble I've ever had was to keep furniture out of the house."

That too had always been our experience. Wherever we have lived, no matter how big the house, the attic, the outbuildings, sooner or later became crowded with extra chairs, books, pictures and toys.

The nearest to a permanent home we had ever had was the house in France and that has never really belonged to us because we could not buy it. We could only lease it for fifty years. A half century, it is true, is a long time. That old eighteenth century house was our home and base for fifteen years and we spent a great deal of time and money and work upon it until it was in all but deed completely ours. But still there hovered over the whole adventure the dread sense of impermanence and doom— that one day there would be war and perhaps the German cavalry would again quarter its horses in the ancient chapel and, as they had done in 1870 and in 1914, carry off the furniture, the pictures and books into Germany. And about that house, much as we loved it, there was no sense of real permanence, no feeling that one day grandchildren and great-grandchildren would return there to ride the pony and fish and go swimming in the little river. There was always about it a sense of living upon borrowed time in a dream which one day would come abruptly to an end. During all those years there was in every one of us, even the smallest of the children, I think, the hunger for a house of our own outside the doomed world of Europe.

In the end Mary and the children left that lovely old house as refugees. Most of the books, furniture and pictures were shipped out to safety a little while before the Germans came in. Some of them had real value in terms of a market, but all of them had rich sentimental values. Some were the gifts of friends, others of artists and writers and people of every sort and nationality. Most of the furniture was beautiful French furniture touched with that sense of immortality and permanence which the French of all people put into the things they make and build. Most of that furniture, made by fine craftsmen of the eighteenth and nineteenth centuries in France, is sheltered now in a big farmhouse in the middle of Ohio, a better fate for it, I believe, than to find itself in some middle-class house in Stuttgart or Leipzig. The love, the care, that those craftsmen, now long dead, lavished upon the chairs and tables and bookcases is still alive in a country five thousand miles away, a country which, oddly enough, was itself a wilderness claimed by the French at the time the workmen bent over their lathes and chisels carving the traditional designs of Brittany and the Valois into the beautiful walnut and pearwood.

Since the house was to shelter us as a family for the rest of our existence and perhaps to be passed on to grandchildren and great-grandchildren many things had to be considered. The same sense of uncertainty of the future which had given me the hunger for self-sufficiency and independence played a great part in the plans. The house had to be big so that it could always be a refuge for children and grandchildren and even for remote relatives and friends.

The sense of responsibility was strong in both my wife and myself for it had fallen to both of us, not always to our pleasure, to take care of the indigent and black-sheep members of our own respective families even to such remote relationships as third cousins twice removed. It was handed down to us in turn from our respective parents. All through my childhood, our house was always filled with people temporarily down and out. Remote relatives came to my mother's house when they were penniless or ill; they came there to die and be buried from our house. They were married there. Some were conceived and born there. At times whole families descended upon us during periods of ill luck. My childhood memories were filled with a sense of being crowded, of living in a moderate-sized house too filled with people, with strong and violent personalities always in conflict. It is not a good way to live.

And so, when at last it came to building a house in which we were to live for the rest of our lives, both my wife and myself were under the compulsion, born of childhood memories, of creating a house big enough to shelter all kinds of people and still provide us with a reasonable degree of privacy and human dignity. I earned much money by writing and in the background there was always Hollywood when the money ran short. As George once suggested, there should be plaques placed on each of the farm buildings announcing that "Twentieth Century Fox is responsible for the building of this sheep barn," or "Metro Goldwyn Mayer provided the money for remodeling this cattle-feeding barn." "United Artists, in payment for a short story, built this cottage."

The name for the whole farm came naturally. The bulk of the capital which went into the whole adventure came from books written about India, so it seemed only fitting that the farm should have an Indian name. We settled at last for Malabar, the name borne by the beautiful hill overlooking the harbor of Bombay and the name also of the southwest coast of India, one of the most beautiful parts of the earth, where we had lived happily for several months. Malabar Farm it became.

But the house had to be more than merely an asylum for indigent relatives and friends. It had also to be a kind of hotel where people with whom I had business dealings could visit. I had always preferred to stay at home for dinner rather than to go out, to have people come to my house rather than to go to theirs. And now in the hills in Ohio, it was not merely a question of going out to lunch or dinner; it was a question of going to New York and Washington and Los Angeles and Chicago and other places where there was business to be done. And so there had to be rooms in the new house for business agents, for political and literary people, for actors and actresses, for visiting foreigners, for foresters and farmers and professors and just plain friends.

Even in the small house in France there were always people staying with us and when there was no more room in the house, the overflow stayed at the inn called Le Grand Cerf, a little way from our house. Sometimes, on Sundays, as many as fifty people came to lunch. They came from all parts of the world, every sort of person, of every race, creed and color. All that too was in the blood. Our grandparents, our parents, had lived that way and we meant to go on living that way for the rest of our lives, rich or poor, in a big house or a small one. So long as there was money, it would be a big house in which our friends would be comfortable.

I knew, shrewdly I think, that the only way anyone could any longer lead that kind of life was in the country or on a farm where one had one's own pork and beef, milk and eggs, vegetables and fruit, even one's honey and maple syrup. It had to be a world in which there was plenty, which ration books and scarcities such as I had known in Europe could never touch.

And beyond all that was a curious sense of obligation shared by all of us, almost a kind of superstition, I think, that we should share our good fortune in life with others. We had lived thus in France among our French neighbors and friends and we wanted to live that way in the midst of Ohio, with a house which was also shared by all our neighbors and friends. That too called for a big house where dances could be held and meetings and picnics and reunions.

Altogether it was a big plan, requiring money, energy, faith, knowledge and enthusiasm. Through fortunate circumstances and some intelligent planning none of these were altogether lacking. Perhaps the most important rule we made was that the undertaking was to be carried out upon a reasonable basis without the expenditure of large sums of money. It was neither to be a plush and gold-fitted establishment of the sort in which "city farmers" once indulged nor the kind of impossibly conceived co-operative farm which had been launched with government money. Both Max and I were practical enough to know that such a subsidized venture proved nothing and did less to help solve the sickness of agriculture. Nor did we believe that such co-operatives would ever succeed either economically or on the human basis. We determined in the beginning to do nothing which the average farmer could not afford to do. Whatever experiment we made, whatever building we did, whatever restoration we undertook would be in the terms of ordinary farming and within the economic possibilities of any family-sized farm enterprise.

We sought to prove that run-down land which had become virtually an economic liability to the nation could be turned into an economic asset and that farming, done properly and managed intelligently, could provide an excellent investment for capital. We were aware of two advantages over many small and all submarginal farmers. Backed by the proper capital, we should never be forced to sell in a bad market in order to pay interest or taxes. We could, often enough, be able to deal with the ruinous middleman on our terms and not his.

I think what all of us were trying really to find was the old spacious comfortable life which farmers and landowners once lived. We believed that it was possible to live that way again— the best life, I believe, that man can know—if intelligence and skill and hard work were employed in building and carrying out the project. We were building on a fairly large scale, but scale, we believed, had nothing to do with it. A man could have that good kind of life whether he had fifty acres or fifty thousand. Whether we failed or succeeded was important to us, but not so important as the adventure itself.

None of us held the illusion that in order to be a "dirt farmer" we had to be louts who lived in the squalid conditions of "Tobacco Road." That illusion, that legend, was in itself a sign of the sickness of American agriculture. Max's father had not lived like that, nor my grandfather, nor the greatest of farmers and Americans—Thomas Jefferson. We all believed that in the soil could we find not only security but the best life in the world.

A Year at Malabar

After the land was acquired, "the Plan" created, and the "Big House" built—it turned out to be thirty-two rooms, made to look like an old Western Reserve farmhouse with step-back wings added onto it over the generations—life at Malabar could begin in earnest. That it was rich and amusing and fulfilling and peopled with an astonishing number of odd and appealing individuals, both human and animal, is most affectingly revealed in the "Malabar Journal" chapters of Malabar Farm, Bromfield's sequel to Pleasant Valley.

There are five such journal chapters, with dated entries spanning 1944–45. To reproduce one of these chapters would lose the seasonal flavor that they possess when taken together. Therefore a selection of entries has been made from all five chapters to represent, in the length of a single chapter, a Malabar year.

Here you will meet the famous boxer dogs, a good many famous people (though the fabled marriage at Malabar of Lauren Bacall and Humphrey Bogart is still a few years away), a lot of farmyard brag and some fact, a fair sampling of Bromfield's iconoclastic political views, and the true feelings of a man who loves the land and the people of the land. The "Bob" referred to in these entries is Bob Huge (hew-ghee), who took Max Drake's place as farm manager after Max resigned to take another job. Kenneth Cook is a farmer and mechanic at Malabar.

Autumn 1944

We are but farmers of ourselves; yet may
If we can stock ourselves and thrive, uplay
Much, much good treasure for the great rent day.

John Donne

S*eptember 3:* Yesterday and today had better be entered as one day since they are hopelessly mixed up in a procession of people and work. In the morning Mr. Harrison of the Redpath Bureau appeared with the joint purpose of seeing the farm and inducing me to sign up for lectures with his bureau. He was a very sympathetic and agreeable salesman and an intelligent and good companion. We didn't talk lectures until the last minute and then it did no good because I despise lecture tours. By the time we got round to business after three hours on the farm, we had become old friends and it was not difficult to make him understand how I felt.

I don't dislike people or talking or even making speeches but I can't make lectures to audiences who have paid $1.50 to come and see a show. I like political speeches and talking to farmers and businessmen and to people who share common interests. I tried to explain this, saying that I make a hundred or more speeches a year for conservation, for political reasons, on soil, on gardening, even at times on Europe and India. I get paid little or nothing for all this and turn over the proceeds to the Friends of the Land or to charities. Usually I pay my own expenses. Happily I can afford to talk when and where I please and about what I please. I explained that I could make more money by staying at home minding my farming and writing than I could ever make on a lecture tour, even at the high fees suggested, and I keep my independence and freedom and am not bored by repeating over and over night after night the same speeches.

The interesting part of Mr. Harrison's visit was entirely devoted to horticulture and agriculture. I think his real interests were his fruit farm in northern Michigan and his wheat ranch in Texas. The valley looked beautiful after the big rains and several shades greener than a week ago. I was proud of how well our crops looked and how well our springs flowed after nearly fifty days without rain. Mr. Harrison promised to send us a crate of his best cherries next July.

The car that took Mr. Harrison to Mansfield brought back Dalpeggeto and Herbert Spencer, two young ensigns and friends of Hope's, who have been at the University in a special Navy course. They have been spending week ends here during the summer. Nice and very smart kids they are. If the whole of the younger generation is as good, the future of the country is safe.

A Mrs. Johnson called from Antioch College saying she was from Connecticut and was interested in the soil program we had here in relation to human nutrition and in the co-operative side of the farm. I told her to come and reserved a room at the hotel in Mansfield. I have learned a certain caution about strange visitors. Sometimes they turn out to be charming and intelligent and stimulating people and sometimes they turn out to be bores and cranks. If they turn out all right they're moved from the hotel to Malabar.

We have had strangers come to pay an hour's visit, remain for lunch, then the night and finally stay for a week or ten days. That is what happened with the Robertsons from South Africa. He is the editor of *Libertas,* a South African publication resembling our own *Life Magazine* and a great advocate of American soil conservation methods. South Africa has suffered devastation by erosion, both wind and water, even greater than our own, if this were possible. Dr. Bennett of the U.S. Soil Conservation Service is making a trip there this winter at the urgent request of the South African government. I made several talks on the subject by short wave radio for the OWI [Office of War Information] during the war at the request of South African government officials, *Libertas* and the Johannesburg newspapers. I hope to follow Dr. Bennett's route during 1948. Countries all over the world are turning to our Department of Agriculture and principally the Soil Conservation Service for aid and instruction in the New Agriculture developed here. This is a little-known fact in which Americans should take pride— that out of the widespread ruin of our originally rich virgin land we have built the principles of a New Agriculture of great value to every nation in the world.

Before supper the boys and I gathered two bushels of yellow and white tomatoes, carrots, onions, and celery from the garden. After supper Nanny and Tom made it up into a drink which we worked out for ourselves and found much more interesting and stimulating than ordinary tomato juice. There is no water involved, only the juice of the tomatoes for a base with half a peck of onions, two dozen carrots and eight big bunches of celery, tops and all, the greener the better. Sometimes spinach is added, and always three or four cloves of garlic, parsley, bay leaves, celery and mustard seed, salt, pepper and a dash of Cayenne. When boiled and strained it looks and tastes like the finest consommé; jellied it is wonderful in hot weather; served hot, it is a delicious, clear soup. You can also drink it as you drink orange or tomato juice. We whipped it up as an experiment two years ago and have put up several dozen bottles of it each year since then. Nanny calls it "Doctor Bromfield's Special Vegetable Compound and Celery Tonic." The chief difficulty is to stop drinking it.

After supper the two ensigns, Dal and Herb, and I went plowing while there was still light. We used the Ford-Fergusons—which make plowing a pleasure. In fact I know nothing that gives me more pleasure or satisfaction than turning over rich soil, mixing sod, manure, rubbish of all sorts into the earth to raise big crops. The field was on the Fleming Place —the same field I described the day of the walk in the rain— and presented a tough job. It was a steep field which before we got the farm had been used to grow row crops in the old-fashioned up-and-down-hill method, which had allowed the top soil to be washed off the slopes by the time we arrived on the scene. The rain had softened up the ground and plowing was easier. The boys were fascinated by the power and maneuverability of the neat little Ferguson tractor.

We had hardly gotten started when George came down to say that Frank and Jane Lausche were at the Big House and I left the plowing to the boys to go and see them. Two nicer or finer people do not exist. Frank is the Democratic candidate for Governor and had been campaigning in the southern part of the state. He wanted to talk about his campaign. He was a little discouraged by what he felt was the "isolationist" feeling he had encountered. I tried to persuade him that he had not gotten a fair picture of Ohio during his trip since he had visited only five or six counties, strongly German in ancestry and in open rebellion against the New Deal, where Gerald Smith, Father Coughlin and their friends had taken advantage of the discontent to muscle their way in. In one of the counties a faction of farmers, in open rebellion, smashed up the OPA [Office of Price

Administration] and the AAA [Agricultural Adjustment Administration] offices and burned the records after seizing a cornpicker without a WPB [War Production Board] priority.

Frank and Jane stayed late but would not spend the night. They had to return to Cleveland as the Graphite Bronze Company, one of the most important war production plants, is in the throes of one of the most irresponsible and shameful strikes, and Frank wanted to return and do what he could as Mayor of Cleveland to end the situation.

After they left everybody went to the kitchen and finished bottling the "Vegetable Compound" and as usual the evening finished with us—everybody from Patti Aldrich and Ellen and Sigrid Meisse who are twelve to Ma who is eighty-three—sitting around eating cantaloupe from the garden and drinking milk and talking about the war and India and international politics. Dal and Herb displayed remarkably sound grounding in all subjects and offered some good contributions concerning the past, present, and future of this wretched world.

Finally to bed after hearing the midnight news that American troops were in Belgium and near the German border. In bed, read an excellent article in *Fortune* on political monkey-business that went on at both party conventions in Chicago. I saw them both from the inside and certainly neither one was an especially elevating spectacle.

Sunday Morning: Rose late after a night interrupted a couple of times by the exit, entrance, and barking of the dogs going courting with Bob's bitch Kitchee. Yesterday Bob was boasting how he had fixed them by keeping Kitchee locked in the garage but this morning he admitted that the dogs (and nature) had won out by making sleep impossible and by Kitchee's rescue and escape from the garage, aided by Prince, Baby, and Smokey, who simply chewed and tore a big hole in the garage door. This morning Kitchee was all smiles and wriggles. At times the fertility of this place, like that of India, becomes terrifying.

Herb Spencer drove to Mansfield to fetch the mysterious Mrs. Johnson, and Dal and I and the dogs drove to the Bailey farm where Kenneth Cook and his boys, Bob and Jim, and Bob Huge and his brother-in-law were busy with the tractors, fitting* the ground and drilling rye in the sixty-acre field above the house. It will be good to see those hills green once more. The worn-out soil has been bare for too long.

The longer I watch the operations and co-operation involved the more it seems to me that co-operation in one form or another is the solution to many problems afflicting agriculture today. Nobody asked the boys to work on Sunday; they did so on their own because it was to everybody's interest and they did it as a kind of lark. Kenneth's boys, Jim and Bob, work in a factory during the week and on the farm evenings and Sundays, laying aside money for their education. No one would have worked on Sunday save that we are, like all farmers, desperately short of help. We need four farmers and two hired men and actually we have only three farmers—Bob, who manages things and works like a dog in the fields, Harry who has thirty head of Guernseys and 1200 chickens to care for, and Kenneth who has all the machinery to keep in order, in addition to the bulk of the actual farming. This year we haven't even been able to find a man or boy to cut weeds. The three high-school boys from Cleveland— Johnny Rudhuyzen, Dave Stamper and Jimmy Caddick were whirlwind workers during the day part of the year but they had to go back to school. This, their second year, they did the work of full-time hired men and were a lot more intelligent than the average hired man.

On the Bailey Hill we again picked a shirtful of mushrooms, many of them growing out of the bare clay on poor ground which seemed to indicate that fundamentally the apparently worn-out soil was better than it seemed.

Went through the corn originally planted for silage, and if we have any luck with the frost holding off, we shall have a good crop of corn despite the drought. Luckily we had the sense to put the half-ruined corn crop into the silo and let the silage corn benefit by the rain that came at last. The drought was very nearly a disaster but out of it we have learned many valuable things about soil and crops, most of all about the priceless value of humus and organic material as a means of soaking up and preserving moisture.

*"Fitting" means preparing the earth for seeding.

Mrs. Johnson appeared and turned out to be very intelligent, having had many years of experience working along dietary and nutrition lines. She was very interesting about her experiences with the dreary Okie camps in California during the bad years. She agreed that after the post-war boom dies down, we shall have the armies of migratory workers, dispossessed from poor, worn-out land, back on our hands, a liability, not only in relief and taxes but a moral, physical, and spiritual liability to the nation. The economic-human problem of the "poor whites" and "Okies" is an extremely complex one which in the end can be solved only be dealing with fundamentals—soil, diet, and education in that order. Poor, worn-out soil produces specimens handicapped physically, mentally, and morally from the very beginning. Food grown on such soil from which calcium, phosphorus, and other vital minerals and elements are exhausted can only produce sickly specimens, both humans and livestock. Wretched diet aggravates sickliness, and poor, undernourished, stupid people make bad farmers who only destroy the soil still further. Education comes third because it is useless to attempt education with people sick physically and mentally from deficiencies of vital minerals. It is no good trying to solve the problem by taxes, WPA [Work Projects Administration], charity and relief, although these may be necessary in time of acute crisis.

Reba is off for the week end in Mt. Vernon so Tom and Nanny cooked lunch aided by bits of advice, some corn-husking and potato-paring by the rest of the family. And a good lunch it was—young White Rock broilers, mashed potatoes, gravy, cauliflower and sweetcorn fresh from the garden, quantities of fresh butter churned Thursday, tomatoes like beefsteak and the first limestone lettuce, newly made peach butter and freshly made pickles put up by Nanny and Jenny Oaks, ice-cold cantaloupe watermelon, big bunches of Niagara and Concord grapes and fresh peaches, ice-cold glasses of Guernsey milk or fresh buttermilk with little globules of butter still floating in it. Everything on the table was produced on the place.

We were fourteen in all in the Big House—from Butch who is seven to Ma who is eighty-three. It reminded me of the meals of my grandfather's farm long ago when farmers somehow lived better than most of them do today. I believed it could be done and it has been done, but best of all every other family on the place was having the same kind of meal. Today the acres of Malabar support *more* people than ever before in their history. And the families live better, having more comforts and a higher standard of living than any living on the same land in the past. We have dispossessed nobody. On the contrary we have been able to make much of the land, poor and run down when we took it over, do a better job than when it was virgin soil, freshly cleared of forest.

As we left the Sunday dinner table three cars of people—men, women and children—arrived from Wooster to go over the place to see what we had accomplished. Two of the men and one of the women were doctors. I had met them all when I went to Wooster last spring to speak under the auspices of the Izaak Walton League and the State Agricultural Experiment Station.

The farm was in an interesting condition, its springs flowing despite the drought, its corn and beans and pastures greener than those on most farms, part of it plowed for wheat, part of it "trash-farmed" without a plow in order to conserve moisture. The cattle, despite the drought, were looking sleek and well from a summer on bluegrass and white clover, supplemented by corn, soybeans and alfalfa, and the calves fat and happy. The story was all there—the results spread before the eyes of any who wanted to see. The "new fangled" ideas were paying big dividends.

In our old Ford station wagon there were six dogs, Mrs. Johnson, Ma, the two ensigns and Ellen and her two friends. We finished up in the big spring house at the Bailey Place where a whole brook of ice-cold water flows out of a crevasse in the sandstone. It was a hot day and never did that clear, cold water taste so good.

When the Wooster party departed, Charlie Schrack and his son Hilbert arrived. Hilbert has been nearly four years in the Army—four of his best years as he is now twenty-eight—for the idiotic reason of war. This time Hilbert brought back a wife and year-old son his parents had not seen before. He is bringing them over tomorrow.

Managed to get a half hour off and went to the swimming hole in the Jungle. No ladies this time so we went in the good old-fashioned way—George, Butch, the two ensigns and myself. The day was hot but the spring in the bottom of the pool made the water very cold. On arriving back at the Big House found Todd and Sadie Chesrown. I know of nobody I love more than Todd and Sadie. Todd went to school with me and last year won the award of the Cleveland City Farmers Club for having done the best job in restoring a run-down farm to productivity. They have built up their farm and raised eight children and are giving them all college educations, without asking help of anybody. It's a damned shame there are fewer and fewer Americans with that spirit and more and more who want the government to take care of them. I don't know any happier couple. They gave us the guinea fowl which insist on roosting in the big catalpa tree just outside the bedrooms and make the most god-awful noises when any intruder comes within five hundred yards of the place. But they are wonderful eating in the winter—all breast and white meat with a delicious wild flavor because they live wild, like pheasants, roaming over the farm all the year round. Roasted and basted with butter in which celery, parsley, and dill have been chopped, and served with bread sauce they are better than any pheasant. Todd and Sadie have one of our Boxer pups which they love with the same passion which afflicts all owners of Boxers. Mr. Hunter, superintendent of the Ashland schools, his wife and grandson, came with Todd and Sadie.

The supper bell rang and Todd left saying the American Legion Band wanted to come over some Sunday evening before the end of September for a picnic and serenade. We decided on the twenty-sixth as I have to be in New York next week end.

Usual Sunday night supper is by co-operative effort in the kitchen and pantry. After supper Mrs. Johnson and the ensigns left, one for California and the others for Columbus, and my cousins Catherine, Roy, and Johnny McGinty arrived. Catherine brought a lot of old photographs and daguerreotypes of our common ancestors on my father's side of the house. It gave one an extraordinary feeling, going back and back into the past to great-great-grandfathers and grandmothers sitting primly before the camera. Some of them whom I remembered only as very old people were remarkably handsome and beautiful as young people. It gave one an intense feeling of the continuity of life and of immortality. All of them are Ohioans. We came here in the very beginning and are still going strong.

Catherine brought a big watermelon, and, in return, we gave her a bushel of tomatoes for canning and a half bushel of the little yellow and orange tomatoes for making tomato butter. Roy is having fire-blight in his one Bartlett pear tree.

The dogs all got in their chairs and went to bed early. They had had a hard day, covering miles of hunting while we made the farm tour. Prince got a groundhog, his second this week, and tried proudly to bring it into the crowded station wagon and had to be restrained by force.

Marshall Bullitt wired and asked me to stay at Oxmoor while in Louisville. It is one of the oldest and most beautiful houses in Kentucky. He has a famous herd of Jerseys and is immensely proud of the thick yellow cream.

Winter 1944–1945

> I return to farming with an ardor which I scarcely knew in my youth.
>
> Thomas Jefferson,
> in a letter to George Washington

November 19: A long gap mostly spent in traveling. The election is over and thank God we can live in peace again. The first real news is beginning to come in from France. Annie Chamay has had word that her husband, who was missing, has turned up after having been twice seized by the Boches and taken to Germany, once halfway to Lublin in Poland. Twice he managed to escape and is now a Captain in the Resistance Movement.

I have had a long letter from my French publisher, carried by someone to England and posted there. He tells me that he was able to turn over to the Underground and to French soup kitchens a considerable sum in royalties belonging to me. It was done through Denise Clairouin who came here in 1941 on a passport secured for her by one of the Underground working *inside* the Vichy government. I saw her and gave her an order to my publisher to turn over the money to the Underground. This he managed to do since the transaction was between two French citizens. Otherwise, the money would have been frozen or seized by the Germans, who prohibited the publication of my books after they took over France. Long before that I was a proscribed writer in Nazi Germany. Delamain writes me that Denise Clairouin was finally caught and arrested and has disappeared.

Also heard again last week from Jean de Sourian who has joined the American First Division as a liaison officer, how I do not know, as he is a French citizen. His mother is English and he speaks English perfectly. In any case he is, as an American soldier, allowed to write, and we have had much news from him. He and all his family lived during the war in a workingman's villa near his father's factory in order not to attract attention. He dared not go on the streets of Paris in the daytime for fear of being picked up by the Germans and shipped to Germany to work in a factory. This war has produced fantastic stories. It is remarkable the number of people who, like Denise Clairouin and Annie's mother-in-law, have simply disappeared.

The beef cattle are all in the barns as the pasture ran short owing to the drought. The dairy cattle are still out in the daytime feeding on rye and vetch and ladino. Fortunately it has remained warm.

Tonight it is raining—badly needed rain although the wheat never looked better to go into the winter. Just before I sat down to write, the dogs and I went out to put the cattle to bed in the big barn. It is one of the keenest of pleasures to see them looking fat and sleek standing in clean straw, their bellies full of silage and good mixed hay. There are about fifty big weaned beef calves in the feeding shed. I go out every night and put back the hay they throw out of the mangers while eating. Tonight they were so full that they simply nosed it over, making only a pretense of eating. They are a beautiful, uniform lot of blue-roans, sleek and black and hornless, save for a red maverick with horns for which we have never found any explanation save that he must be a throw-back. He has a faint wild look of Highland cattle and may have been the result of inbreeding which will often produce throw-backs.

Charley Kimmel, the Game Warden, and Fanny Copeland dropped in and stayed for Sunday noonday dinner. Charley, like myself, is interested in the new dam proposed at Lexington. It will help the industrial water supply of Mansfield and create a beautiful new lake four miles long on the upper Clear Fork. People are beginning to make sense about the water supply, but only, I think, after they have been scared into it.

Made two speeches on conservation yesterday at York, Pennsylvania, one to the women in the afternoon and another in the evening to a mixed audience of 1600 businessmen and farmers. It is remarkable how people are becoming interested in these things—a very hopeful sign. If we can overcome the evils, economic and social, which industry and great cities have brought us, we shall be making progress. That is the frightening element in the recent elections. A growing urban proletariat without economic security can wreck everything that America has been in the past and darken the whole of her future.

I have been reading Darwin's *Voyage of the Beagle*. It is the best escape literature I know, taking you completely out of the confusion and anxiety of the times in which we live. Darwin's books are filled with interesting observations which tie in with our own experiences in the crossbreeding of animals. In his day his great mind held intimations of discoveries which many scientists of today have not yet suspected.

December 31: The last day of a year which can go without regrets so far as the world is concerned. I have had much to be thankful for in my personal life and the life of Malabar, most of all the great progress that has been made during the last year toward the goals which were set up in the beginning and I have been very lucky indeed in friendships far and wide.

There are times when I am very grateful for having spent so many years outside America, in Europe and the East, not only because it helped me to understand the stupendous things going on in the world but because it has made America a new country to me, which I will never again take for granted as so many Americans do. Out of the countless letters I get from overseas, I gather that the experience of the war has made thousands of young Americans understand and appreciate this country as they could not have done without having seen something of the rest of the world. It seems to me that this country is inexhaustible in its variety and beauty and in the variety of its people. The Sinclair Lewis philosophy, like most of the thinking of the twenties, was superficial, especially in its assumption that Americans are standardized. A Texan and a Bostonian could scarcely be further apart and still belong to the same race and nationality.

Perhaps most of all I am thankful for having been born in a country which, after an absence of twenty-five years spent all around the world, I found I would have chosen to be born in, if I had had the choice. Its woods, hills, streams, fields, and springs suit me. They have the fertile, half-wild, well-watered beauty which seems to me to include almost everything. I suppose everyone in the world feels that way about the country in which he was born, but the feeling is doubly important and sound after one has actually put it to the test against other countries and landscapes over most of the world.

Today it is raining instead of snowing, but the snow is so deep that the thawing rain has made little impression upon it. Very little rain is running off. It is being soaked up by the snow and carried on down into the earth. Sometimes the snow goes quickly and the streams turn to torrents, the water rushing off the land to create floods downstream. This time all the deep snow and the rainfall is being soaked up by the soil beneath, a good thing after the long, hot dry summer. The underground reservoir will need filling up after two dry years. Thus far the weather has been wonderful for the wheat and the meadow seedings. The ground beneath its deep cover of snow is scarcely frozen at all and is protected from the devastating heaving process caused by alternate freezing and thawing.

The deep snow has brought numbers of birds close in around the house and the suet and grain box outside my window is covered all day long by a wide variety of them. I am very ignorant about wild birds, but in the next year or two I must repair the deficiency. It would add greatly to the pleasure of watching birds and understanding their actions. Heavy snows like this one often drive in rare birds, which in my ignorance, I do not recognize.

I do know the mourning doves, which strangely do not migrate but stay with us all winter, and the jays and a variety of flickers and woodpeckers, and of course many of the migrating beauties like the Indigo bunting, the Baltimore oriole, the kingfishers, the goldfinch, and the shy and dazzling scarlet tanager which one sees only in the deepest part of the woods and the Jungle. And in winter the cardinal is very common when he comes in close to the house to feed. Our native Ohio birds can be surpassed in color and beauty only by the birds of India. One of the sights of the world is the assortment of brilliant-plumaged birds to be seen in Crawford Market in Bombay.

The sparrows are always with us of course, very close in about the house, for they seem to prefer people and bustle and sociability to solitude. They are noisy and thieving and at times when they build their big, shaggy, disreputable nests among the grapevines or in a roof gutter or behind the statue of Ganesh over the front door, I would like to be rid of them. Jane Francke, who is a great bird expert, says they drive away other more rare and timid birds but I do not find this so. She advocated shooting or poisoning them but that I cannot bring myself to do. It is true they drive shyer birds away from the feeding table but once they have had their fill they go away and the other birds take their turn. They never want for food because they are brassy and fearless and feed out of the corn cribs or on the barn floor and even inside the cattle feeding sheds. In winter they sleep in the thick evergreens which are warm and dry and windless. In summer they like the grape arbors but I discouraged them last summer by turning water on them from the garden hose every evening. One little hen sparrow slept every night for three winters on a ledge inside the portico covering the front door. Even when you turned on the light she did not go away but watched you very quietly with bright little eyes. This year she is gone. I am only afraid that Pete or one of the other big barn cats got her.

Spring 1945

Have you become a farmer? Is it not pleasanter than to be shut up within 4 walls and delving eternally with a pen? . . . I have proscribed newspapers . . . my next reformation will be to allow neither pen, ink nor paper to be kept on the farm. When I have accomplished this I shall be in a fair way to indemnifying myself for the drudgery to which I have proved my life. If you are half as much delighted with the farm as I am, you bless your stars at your riddance from public cares.

Thomas Jefferson,
in a letter to Henry Knox, Boston bookseller

March 1: A long gap, but there seems no end to demands on time. The deep snow has gone and the spring came suddenly in two or three days with brilliant sun and a few showers. I hope it is here to stay. The suddenness put a quick end to sugar-making. Good maple syrup weather means cold freezing nights alternating with warm, sunny days. The nights have been mild, almost hot and all the sap has rushed up out of the ground into the high branches and twigs, swelling the buds and casting a faint cloud of pinkish green over the whole of the woods. While the sugar run lasted, the camp became as always the center of farm life. Even Ma had to clump through the mud with her cane. It brought back very old memories of her father's day. On Sundays neighbors and people from town kept coming and going all day. It was like a festival marking the wakening of the New Year. Certainly it is one of the most pleasurable ceremonies and in these times of sugar shortage it is good to have the storeroom full of maple syrup and honey.

Chris Hugert, who has taken care of the bees for years, gave it up this year to go permanently to live in New Mexico because of his health, and Sunday his cousins came to take over the job—a pair of big, hearty countrymen, very different from poor asthmatic Chris. They went over the hives and found that the bees in four of them were dead. It has been a hard winter for bees with the snow drifted high up around the hives and the temperature always close to zero with many blizzards. There seemed to be plenty of honey for them still to feed on. The shortage was in pollen but the quick turn to spring has brought out all the catkins and crocuses and all around them the air buzzes with the sound of wings.

I would like to care for the bees but it is one of the most complicated professions in the world. The person who thinks that all one has to do to have honey is to put up a couple of hives has much to learn. There is a book—a very thick one—called *The A.B.C. of Bees,* but to me it is more confusing than a book on advanced mathematics.

Today Kenneth, Bob, and I built fences between the lower bluegrass pasture and the cemetery field. It was a brilliant day and that corner of the farm is one of the loveliest spots—a kind of bowl with the big trees of the virgin forest on one side raising their top branches a hundred feet and more above the sugar camp. A spring stream wanders through the pasture with ox-bow ponds filled with young fish and bordered by water cress, marsh marigold, and skunk cabbage. The steep cemetery field is planted to wheat which has grown prodigiously in a few warm days and looks like a carpet of emerald green velvet. All the dogs—Prince, Baby, Gina, Susie, Folly, Kitchee and Smokey—played in the fields and chased squirrels and lay flat in the shallow water when they grew hot and tired. George Cook came down when the school bus dropped him off, his pockets filled with marbles, another sign of spring. Jim hauled manure out of the Fleming barn on to the small garden to make it ready for plowing. Charlie already has onions, lettuce, radishes and beets planted. Yesterday he was in a rage because Charlie Schrack's big red sows broke out, traveled down the creek and rooted up part of what he had done. I don't blame him.

The lower fish pond came to life today with a vengeance. It was filled with fingerling bass and mud-turtles were scuttering about. I saw forty or fifty bass a foot to fifteen inches long. They are out scouting for nests in the shallow water covering the sand and gravel. The bluegills have not yet made their appearance. Taking the giant bass out of the pond last year was a good idea. They are cannibals and were eating up all the young. The increase in the number of fish is very apparent this year. There are still some big ones to be cleaned out.

The dime-store goldfish the children dumped into the pond five years ago have grown monstrous in size and vivid in color. I saw several females today, enormous with roe. The goldfish never increase in number—still the huge, venerable brilliant-colored originals. On the edge of the pond the first red-winged blackbirds have appeared in numbers, looking for nesting sites on the hummocks of grass and among the cattails. The big gray Toulouse geese are fussing about on the islands making nests. I must take down a couple of straw bales tomorrow for them. I hope we shall have better luck this year with the goslings, now that we caught a giant snapping turtle offside in the pasture last summer. These geese can drive off the foxes but the snapping turtles get the goslings. Nor do the guinea fowl ever lose a single chick from the foxes. I think they put up such an ungodly racket they drive them off.

The upper pond at the Big House stayed frozen over all the winter and many of the fish died, from lack of oxygen and sunlight I suppose. When the ice melted there were several big dead bass, about four or five pounds each, a dozen bluegills and a huge carp, about fifteen to sixteen pounds, the only one in the pond. The children caught him in the Clear Fork as a young fellow and dumped him in. I thought carp could survive almost anything, but apparently this is not so.

Louise Reese came to lunch today before leaving for Florida. She may stay there or she may come back. I hope she returns. She is a merry companion, a great fisherman and has done as much for hunting and fishing, soil conservation and forestry as anyone in the county. She is one of those who realizes that if you create proper and natural surroundings you will have all the fish and game any sportsman could wish. She is not the fish-hatchery, pheasant-hatchery kind of sportsman. We shall miss her. I know of no man who finds more delight in the fields and streams and forests than Louise.

May 14: Another long gap with abominable weather. Never can I remember a worse spring. The fantastically warm weather of March brought out everything—alfalfa, bluegrass, ladino, fruit blossoms, garden flowers. The alfalfa and ladino were frozen back. All the new growth of the grapes froze as if it had been scalded. What magnolias the rabbits did not girdle and kill, froze in full flower. Even the dogwood is pinched and frozen-looking and the wild crab blossoms singed and without the wonderful perfume they usually have. The bluegrass and the wheat have turned yellowish.

Added to all this were cold and torrential rains. By industry and luck we managed to plant 60 acres of oats which are flourishing although there has been too much rain and cold even for the oats which usually like that kind of weather. But we are much more fortunate than most for our well-drained glacial hill land permits us to plow in almost any kind of weather. Despite the awful season we are almost ready to plant sudan grass and soybeans when the frost is past. Even in this county only 25 percent of the oats has been planted. In the flat country none is in the ground, and by the time the soil is dried enough to plow, it will be too late to put it in. This will have a serious effect on feed supplies for the condition is not confined to Ohio but in general all through the richest part of the country. I hope this is not the "bad year" agriculturists have been fearing. We have had enormous luck with weather during the war. A "bad year" would be disastrous and affect the history of the world for generations to come. We have never been so short of food and the needs for ourselves and all the rest of the world have never been so great.

Margaret Reed, who is always cheerful, pointed out that the late and violent freezes may do good by killing millions of insect pests which otherwise would have survived the mild snowy winter. Deep snow lay on the ground from December to March with the ground scarcely frozen—a condition which is usually followed by hordes of corn borers, chinch bugs, grasshoppers, aphids and other pests. The spittle bug has already been working on the alfalfa.

VE day has come and gone with few but the fools using the occasion as one of celebration. There is indeed very little to celebrate. Here we celebrated it by plowing all day—as good a way as I can think of. There is a particular delight in plowing this year especially in our bottom land in the Muskingum Conservancy. It is our only really flat land—two great fields, one of 90 acres and one of 70. Most of it is fine gravel loam that turns beautifully under the plow, but it was worn out by generations of hog-greedy farmers and very nearly abandoned until we rented it. To bring it back we have been practicing a rotation of corn, oats, and sweet clover. It was Bob's idea and a sound one, for the land is too far from the barns to haul manure to it.

This year the "catch" of sweet and mammoth clover which followed liming is thick and lush and green—so beautiful that farmers came from all around to look at it. When you pull up a plant the roots are thick with nodules taking nitrogen from the air and fixing it in the worn-out soil. It is worth countless dollars per acre in expensive nitrogen fertilizer which we cannot buy today even if we could afford it. And the green tops plowed under will put back huge quantities of nitrogen and tons of the humus that the starved land needs so badly. No wonder that all of us look backward over the plow to watch the crumbling soil swallowing up all that richness. We came home at night with stiff necks and crooked backs from leaning over to watch.

We have been trying a lot of experiments with the big field —shallow plowing, deep plowing, burying all the green stuff and also setting the plows so that they do not completely bury it but set it on end mixing it *into* the earth. One strip we are Faulk-nerizing—chopping it all *into* the earth with "bush-and-bog" harrows which are really heavy, super-disks. It will be interest-ing to see what the results will be after the corn is planted. It is the sort of thing which makes farming a fascinating occupation and a "live" one.

Gradually we are becoming able to grow more and better corn on half the land. Perhaps presently we shall grow as much on a third of the land as we once did on all of it. Then we shall be approaching the goal of making every acre produce 100 per cent of potentiality without loss of fertility, perhaps even, as in parts of Europe, with a gradual increase. The sweet clover is doing it with its wonderful capacity for translating sun and air and water into nitrogen and organic material. One thing I noticed this year while looking backward over the plow was the great increase in the population of earthworms. That is a good sign.

The crows followed us as we plowed, unfortunately gob-bling up some of the earthworm population. They are birds with scarcely a redeeming feature and in the Conservancy land they are a pest, for it is surrounded by wild country and forest which gives them cover, where they gather in great colonies. Once the corn has begun to sprout they descend on the fields and tear it up grain by grain. We finally put an end to that by using some-thing called Crow-tox applied to the corn before planting. It does not kill them but produces a burning sensation in their gullets and, being very shrewd birds, they soon connect the cause and effect and leave our fields alone. Clem Herring told me that he used to rid himself of them by using hen's eggs into which he had injected strychnine through a small hole at one end sealing the hole afterward with paraffin. These he scat-tered about the fields. On several occasions he killed foxes in-stead of crows. Both are pests in our country and both are crafty and maddening. If you have a shotgun, they will come nowhere near you, but if you are unarmed, they become as bold as Moses.

While we were plowing the Conservancy land all seven dogs were with me and the crows tormented them all afternoon, descending quite near to them in a tantalizing way, only to leave the ground just as the maddened dogs came within a foot or two of them. They would chase the crows for an hour and then go down to the Clear Fork and throw themselves into the water, swimming about and lapping the clear, cold water greedily, and then return to the futile chase. They seemed to enjoy it although they got not so much as a crow feather as a reward.

The Clear Fork Valley is unbelievably beautiful with the steep wooded hills all about it, the lake mirroring the blue sky and the trees ranging in shade all the way from the black-green of the hemlock against the red sandstone cliffs through all the soft pastel shades of green, some of it pink and yellow and pale red. The young foliage of the red oaks is a deep pink so that it makes the tree appear as if it were covered with deep pink blossoms. The white dogwood and the pink wild crab grow all along the edge of the forest above the water, and through it all runs the wide thick carpet of pale emerald-green sweet clover, slowly turning to brown as the earth swallows it up behind the tractors that move across the field like shuttles on a gigantic loom. There is no smell quite so good as fresh-turned sweet earth, and all afternoon it was tinged with the vanilla-like smell of sweet clover being crushed by the moving wheels of the tractor.

Ma came with me and the dogs in the old Ford station wagon and sat there with her sewing all afternoon watching the plowing. She brought a gallon jug of fresh buttermilk which we kept cool in the running spring water and drank when we grew thirsty. It was buttermilk made of sweet cream with little flecks of golden bluegrass butter floating in it.

Once during the afternoon, I thought, "Paradise must be like this."

After supper we returned to the plowing and Harry and Naomi joined us with their three small children. Harry entertained them by carrying them in turn on his lap as he drove the tractor. In the old days they would have ridden on the fat back of a Percheron. It is remarkable how much children like machinery on a farm. One of our worst problems is to keep them off it. Even "Butch," George's nephew, and George Cook who are only seven have figured out how to drive a tractor and get aboard the moment you turn your back. They aren't afraid of tractors as they sometimes are of horses.

We stayed out until nearly dark—Jim, Kenneth, Harry and I—plowing, until a wild thunderstorm came up. We tried to beat it in a race back to the house but lost the race and came in drenched.

June 17: Back again from selling War Bonds in Indiana and New England. I know of no tougher work—beginning every morning at nine o'clock with a municipal breakfast, then schools and colleges till noon when big lunch comes up. Then women's clubs and civic organizations all the afternoon and a big public dinner in the evening followed by a meeting of thousands in the largest available auditorium. Then a late train, rarely on time, to the next town. Thousands of people, dozens of speeches, handshaking by the hour, banquet food, sketchy train connections and not even five minutes rest all day. And worst of all perhaps is the doubt that maybe I'm selling something that may not turn out so well. The war *has* to be carried on and to carry it on money is necessary. But I'm not too confident about the future if enormous taxes, scarcities, and inflation continue. If I had not lived through two wars and watched the sagging economy of every country in Europe, I might be less concerned.

The weather continues to be abominable. Frost on June 6th and 7th with two or three days of terribly hot weather, followed by rain, rain, rain. There will be damned little corn "knee-high by the Fourth of July" this year. Our own may be but we are used to having it hip-high by that time. If it doesn't stop raining the weeds will be knee-high but not the corn. We have mowed ten acres of beautiful alfalfa-brome grass hay which has been rained on steadily for nearly a weak. It is a total loss. The beef cattle may pick up some of it but it is really only fit for bedding.

In the flat country the corn is being drowned out and much of it is not yet planted. According to Director of Agriculture Hodson only about 30 per cent of the oats was planted in Ohio. On flat land even that is being drowned out. With the food shortage a reality and half the world starving, the prospects

are grim. The Black Market is practicing wholesale. With little or no poultry in the market and people standing in line to buy two or three eggs and getting none at all, Black Marketers and even legitimate dealers are buying up laying hens, thin and tough, at three and three-fifty apiece. One farmer I know was offered $3500 cash for 1000 skinny leghorn laying hens by a man who drove up in a truck ready to carry them off. These same poor hens will sell for five and six dollars apiece in city Black Markets.

The whole of the food situation was inevitable. The theories of administration economists could produce nothing but the present tragic shortages. It is impossible to regulate food production unless ceilings are placed upon every element concerned with food—the producer, the feeder, the processor, the distributor—and those ceilings must be adjusted at least monthly in order to keep pace with the value of the dollar which inflates in time of scarcity and easy money despite anything government bureaucracy can do. None of these things has been done and the result has been first gluts and lowered ceilings and checked production and then bitter scarcities. The end is not yet, nor is improvement in sight. Those of us who predicted the shortages and Black Markets two years ago, even so wise a man as Mr. Baruch, were mocked at by the "bright young men" who have today become discredited. Once price controls are lifted and supply and demand again operate, the public will forget shortages and Black Markets quickly enough. I am not so sure of prices; there is too much money in circulation.

Unfortunately the results of malnutrition arising from deficiencies of a protein diet are not immediately perceptible save in terms of lowered vitality and efficiency and an increase in absenteeism in factories. The results, however, linger long afterward in children and young people. The protein deficiencies of the First World War are still evident in the physique of mature Europeans of today. Some day people and governments will come to realize that physically and in so far as diet is concerned, there is little difference between people and animals—except perhaps that animals have more sense. If you put before a hog all the ingredients of a perfect diet he will balance it perfectly himself, choosing something of this and something of that. If you did the same thing for many a city stenographer she would still lunch on an ice cream soda and a pickle. If you offered the "poor white" a perfectly balanced diet he would be likely to turn instead to his hominy, sow belly and turnip greens grown on worn-out soil, devoid of calcium, of potassium, of phosphorus —indeed of practically everything—and containing nothing to make either a strong or an intelligent or an energetic human being.

This winter we made a record in the laying house. Seven hundred leghorn pullets produced over six hundred eggs a day for six months. Even now after eight months of laying they have only fallen to around 500 at the lowest. There has been *no* cannibalism and no range paralysis.

The trace mineral feeding has great results here as elsewhere in the feeding of livestock. I am delighted to see the laying mash largely done away with, for it brought us about five different kinds of noxious weeds which we have never had before on the farm, among them quack grass. The seeds were distributed through those parts of the vegetable and flower gardens where only chicken manure was used. The check is absolute. There is no doubt as to where they came from.

I mowed hay on the Ferguson Place until twilight. It was good clover and alfalfa mixture, so thick that it was hard to get the mower through it—a wonderful sight, some forty acres of it on the top of what was once a bare, bald hill where even the scanty weeds were sickly. I remember well the first time I saw that particular field—a gullied, bare cornfield unprotected during the whole of the winter and covered with a stubble of puny cornstalks. Today there is not a gully an inch deep on the whole of the Ferguson Place, or the whole of Malabar for that matter. It is a real hill farm worn-out and abandoned only five years ago. Today it is raising wonderful alfalfa and bluegrass and white-clover pasture that looks like a beautiful English lawn. In fact, after the pasture is mowed the whole place looks like a lovely park with the springs, the big trees, the cave and the waterfall where the water comes in trickles out of the overhanging sandstone. You can stand under one of the streams and drink the icy water merely by tilting your head and opening your mouth. Baby, one of the Boxers, has learned the trick and always drinks there. It is odd how all animals prefer cold, clean, *living* water if they can get it.

While I mowed this afternoon a whole army of fat, half-grown young rabbits kept coming out of the alfalfa ahead of the mower. There is something very engaging about them. During the morning I uncovered a woodchuck lair and as I came round the second time, I noticed something moving beneath the fresh mown hay. It was the young woodchuck himself returning home. Evidently I had caught him out and he was creeping back under cover of the hay. I stopped mowing until he was safely home again. In a week or two the alfalfa will be grown up again to give him cover. They are odd beasts, full of charm, always fat and always a little lazy. They seem to get all the water they need from the clover and the dew for many of them choose to dig their homes high on the hills away from water. On the other hand the marshes next to our corn land in the Conservancy are filled with woodchuck holes. Often enough, when the lake level rises they are flooded out and have to dig new homes on higher land.

Three times this spring I have had puzzling experiences with wild animals. Early in the year we found a woodchuck in the fork of a sapling a good ten feet above the ground. He lay there resting on his elbows, showing no alarm, not even stirring when I poked him with a stick to make certain he was not caught in the fork of the sapling. He seemed very sleepy. I do not know whether he had just come out of hibernation or had climbed the tree to die in peace. The next day he was gone. I have never before heard of a woodchuck with tree-climbing habits. In June, I encountered another woodchuck in the middle of the road below the Big House. He showed no inclination to run away and when I turned the old Ford slowly toward him, he held his ground and gnashed his teeth at me. At last I drove off leaving him there but when I returned later the same day he was lying dead in the road, the victim of some driver more bloodthirsty than I.

Yesterday in the Bailey barnyard I came on a young rabbit feeding on the spilled corn from the old crib we tore down. He showed no fear and paid no attention to me, except to move away about ten feet. As I moved toward him he kept just out of reach, stopping and turning now and then to regard me without fear but with curiosity. I talked to him for a time and he seemed to like the sound of my voice. I went away and he returned to the scattered corn. Fortunately the dogs were not along.

The only time they do not go with me is when I go out with the power mower. They have learned that the mower means long hours of boredom and heat for them while I go round and round a hay field. And I think they don't like it because they cannot *ride* on the tractor.

Evening on the Ferguson Place has a beauty that is almost unbearable. The whole farm lies against the sky with a view of thirty miles across Pleasant Hill lake and a panorama of hills and valleys, woodland, and farms. It is like the lake country of England on a much bigger scale. Last night Anne went for a walk just before dinner and was caught in a wild thunderstorm. When she did not return I took the power mower and went up to the Ferguson Place, thinking she might have gone to the cave to collect some of the fungi and the pre-glacial moss and primitive plants that grow there. The cave lies at the head of a wild, deep ravine and there is always danger of falling. When there was no sign of her I stayed up there and mowed pasture.

The whole place was wet and green after the thunderstorm. Even the light seemed green and while I mowed, the shadows in the valley turned blue and the mist began to rise from the soaked earth into the air, chilled by the storm and the heavy hail that had fallen in the northern part of the county. On the top of the hill the shadows of the trees grew longer and longer and bluer and bluer across the emerald-green of the bluegrass and clover. Presently the cattle came up to the top of the hill, their favorite feeding spot in the evening when the air begins to cool. In the heat of the day they stay deep in the bottom of the ravine in the shade of the great trees where a spring stream and the damp sandstone keeps the air too cool and moist for flies. Indeed the whole Ferguson Place is a kind of paradise for cattle with the deep-wooded ravine, the cold water, the springs, the bluegrass and white clover and when that grows short in August the whole of a field of knee-deep alfalfa and ladino to replace it.

Few things are more pleasant than to sit watching the herd. The big white bull is a docile fellow who pays you no attention. At first the cows and calves will gather round you to study you for a while. If you sit quite still and the dogs are not along, they will come quite close and nuzzle you, and then, presently, they will go away again to eat lazily. But the young calves stay around, skittering off in mock alarm if you make a sudden movement, only to return in a little while to watch you like children daring each other to come closer and closer. As you lie on your back in the thick bluegrass looking up at the sky you can hear all about you the "whisk-crunch" as they eat their way across the meadow.

The herd seems to lead a very ordered existence, always remaining together and the cows feeding their calves at prescribed hours—morning and evening. During the day they will put all the calves together in a kind of kindergarten well hidden in a copse while the herd goes roaming. If you stumble upon the kindergarten, the calves will lie quite still at first but if you disturb them at all, they will set up a bellowing and are answered at once by the mothers even if they are a mile away on the opposite side of the big pasture. The calves will high-tail for their mothers who come running anxiously from the opposite direction.

The other herd, of Shorthorn cows on the Bailey Place, are ruled by Blondy, the patriarchal coal black Angus bull. He takes his paternal responsibilities more seriously than the white bull, Elmer, and will always stay behind to guard the kindergarten although he is never alone but accompanied by two or three of the cows on watch. I do not know how he selected the honored ladies-in-waiting. I wish I did.

Just at dark Anne appeared, flushed from the long climb up the hill through the woods to tell me she had been found. She had gone up the road toward Hastings and stopped in at the Areharts when the storm broke. She "visited" after the storm and forgot all about dinner. She stayed with me for a while clearing fallen branches out of the path of the mower. The dogs came with her and were glad to see me but disappointed at the sight of the mower. When Anne left they did their best to make me return home too, barking and jumping and carrying on generally. Prince came back twice after Anne started down the hill and finally gave up and went home with her.

Finally, while I mowed, a blue-wet darkness came down and the valleys and woods and farms faded out first into a blue mist and then into blackness, starred with the distant lights of farmhouses and the comets of moving light made by cars on the road far below. I turned on the tractor lights and kept on mowing and the whole herd found a new curiosity in the lights. The calves frisked round and round me as I mowed and even the cows would stand in front of me staring at the lights until the last moment. When I yelled at them they would frisk off kicking their heels high in the air, their udders bouncing about ludicrously, giving that "rabbit-punch" kick which can break your leg if you come into contact with it. Altogether they enjoyed the evening, I think, as much as I did.

About ten-thirty I gave it up and set out for home down the steep, rocky lane that goes through a tunnel of woods bordered by ferns and laced with wild grapevines. All the way down I had an eerie feeling that I was being watched by the eyes of wild things—foxes and raccoons and mice and owls. Once, near Jim Pugh's cabin the lights caught a pair of green, phosphorescent eyes that may have been one of the catamounts that live on the hill opposite the Big House. Or it may only have been a fox or a raccoon. In any case the goose pimples rose all over me and my hair stood on end like the hair of a dog.

Smokey and Baby stayed at the house last night instead of going down to the barracks to sleep with the boys who have come to work on the farm during the summer. Usually they spend the day following Charlie who feeds them or following me while I am plowing or working in the fields. With Charlie and me both away they were lost and deserted my room for the company of the boys. Prince still slept in my room with Dusky, the Cocker. Both Gina and Folly were at Dr. Wadsworth's—Folly to be bred. Gina not to be. While Charlie and I were away Prince, Baby and Smokey fought incessantly, once knocking Ma out of her chair onto the lawn.

Boxers are strange dogs. They have no tramp habits and will not go fifty yards from the house unless they have human company. They are affectionate but never groveling. In fact, I sometimes find myself groveling to them, especially to Baby, who is a clown and a ham actor, but still possessed somehow of an immense dignity and indifference. If you do anything foolish or unworthy, they know it and do not hesitate to let you know.

This year the boys are living in a Quonset Hut, given us by the company which manufactures them, to discover farm uses for them. The four boys working on the farm, Eddie who is

working in the big garden, and Jim and Bob Cook all live there
—Army fashion. It is cool and airy. There is a weird assortment
of beds, ranging from army cots to brass and iron beds. Nowadays you have to take what you can get. Most of the boys come
from Cleveland but Craven comes from St. Louis and Eddie
from Tiffin, Ohio. It is remarkable how well they turn out, considering the fact that we have seen them at most only once before and some of them not at all. There has never been one we
had to send away. Two or three times we have had boys who
didn't work out very well at first but always they developed into
good responsible workers. Most of the older ones have gone into
the Service as they reached the age of eighteen. Without them
we should have to curtail farming operations or shut down altogether. They help with hay-making, straw-baling, fence-
building, lime-spreading, and corn-cultivating. It is a good
summer life.

With mechanization they don't go to work until eight
o'clock and are finished at six with all the long summer evenings free. There is swimming, fishing and riding. What they
like best is tinkering with the old cars and motors in the farm
repair shed. They turn out some mechanical monsters, made up
of parts drawn from a half dozen old cars, but they seem to run
somehow.

Jimmy Caddick, who has graduated as a veteran to the
position of foreman, bought Johnny's and Dave's old jalopy when
they went into the Army. It is a 1930 Ford with flags and foxtails
flying, painted bright yellow. Jimmy is, like Johnny and Dave, a
remarkable fellow—conscientious and capable as a grown
man, with a wonderful sense of humor. Like the other boys he
came here in summer to keep in training for football but in the
end he and all the others decide to take up agriculture, in one
form or another. I think it is because they find here how fascinating and how profitable agriculture can be, but most of all
they like the life and the deep satisfaction of soil and animals
and trees and wildlife. Bob is largely responsible for this interest for he seems to make everything on the farm take on an
added zest. The boys have a real sense of *participation* in what is
a fascinating job of restoration and soil management. That is
also the reason why all of us get on so well together. It is not a
question of hired labor or of merely working for a living. Every-

thing that happens is I think charged with interest and a sense of achievement and satisfaction. Emma, Tom's wife, cooks for the boys. They eat at the miller's house, where Ceely Rose murdered her whole family, and do their own washing in Bob's basement with Virginia's washing machine.

When the war is over and we can buy or build what we need, we shall probably take on fifteen or twenty boys instead of five or six. The waiting list is already far beyond our capacity to handle. Vane Close has two boys from Cleveland helping him this summer. They come over frequently on Sunday and in the evening. The kids like all the machinery and seem to prefer the life to that of a vacation in a summer camp. Also they earn money which most of them put away for college. Meanwhile they have contributed mightily to the food supply in wartime.

The week end was terrific. The four Texans came back with us from the Cincinnati conservation meeting sponsored by the Junior Chamber of Commerce. Also Roy and Marie Ballinger. So the house was full. The Texans are Victor Schoffelmayer, agricultural editor of the Dallas *Morning News* who, with Mr. Dealey and his son, the owners, make up a strong force for good agriculture in the whole of Texas and among the best in the whole of the United States; Dave Reed, R. C. Schmid and Gilbert Wilson. Reed is a big oil operator and owns hundreds of thousands of acres in Texas. Schmid, born in Switzerland, is his manager and Gilbert Wilson is the man who invented the sweet potato dehydrating process which has played a large part in the war effort. All four are filled with Texas gusto and the week end was gay and filled with laughs. Schoffelmayer is the most serious of the lot and a fine musician as well. He lured Reed and Schmid up here to convert them to better uses of the huge agricultural holdings owned by Reed. Schmid is a dynamo, and Wilson the slow drawling kind of Texan, who couldn't keep up with the volatile Schmid but when he found an opening in the conversation scored heavily. Reed has about as much gusto as I've ever encountered. Nobody is more charming or better company than the Ballingers.

On Saturday night Billy Foster and his band came up from Delaware for the annual square dance before the big barn is filled with hay. Bob, Kenneth, Harry and the boys spent two days cleaning the big mows and arranging bales of straw as seats all around the edges. We furnish the music and the soft drinks and everybody brings box lunches. Each year the dance gets bigger. This year there were about seven hundred, mostly from Richland and the neighboring counties, but there were people from all over the state. The boys acted as traffic police-men and had a Ferguson tractor on duty to haul those who got stuck out of the mud. I think everybody had a good time. The party lasted until well after midnight and then broke up into other parties—one at Jim Pugh's cabin and one in the Big House with Billy Foster, his band and friends, having a couple of drinks for the road. There is no better square-dance band in the world and no better caller than Billy Foster. I think the prize for dancing went to Jeff and his wife. They are sixty or over but he can throw her high in the air on the turns. It is odd how much square dancing done with gusto resembles modern jitterbugging—the same zest for pure dancing without much sex thrown in.

Summer 1945 (1)

> The proper caretaking of the earth lies not alone in maintain-ing its fertility or in safeguarding its products. The lines of beauty that appeal to the eye and the charm that satisfies the five senses are in our keeping. . . . To put the best expression of any landscape into the consciousness of one's day's work is more to be desired than much riches. . . . The farmer does not have full command of his situation until the landscape is a part of his farming.
>
> Liberty Hyde Bailey, *The Holy Earth*

July 13: It was good to be home again. I think sometimes that the farm is becoming an obsession to the exclusion of all else, which is bad; but there is in it so deep and so fundamental a satisfaction, which is difficult to control.

I have come to the conclusion that of all farm implements the mower is the greatest and most important. Certainly it is in our hilly country where hay and pasture are of so much impor-tance. We keep a mower on one tractor all through the summer to cut hay and mow pasture and weeds on fallowed ground. On the Bailey Place, where the soil had been reduced almost to the texture of cement, a year or two of fallowing in legumes with lime, mowing the legumes and letting them lie on the surface to mulch the hard ground, retain moisture, and finally to be mixed in the soil, has increased production in a year or two by as much as five hundred to a thousand per cent.

All the way to Battle Creek and back I saw not one blue-grass pasture a tenth as productive as our own at this midsummer period of the year. Nearly all were burned out, dormant, weedy, and dry while our own pastures are green and almost lush. Lime, whole fertilizer, and mowing, which lays down a constantly increasing layer of humus mulch and preserves the moisture, have done the trick. Some day all livestock farmers will understand that pasture is one of their most valuable crops and do something about it.

This afternoon while I was mowing a fallow ground, I flushed a whole family of baby rabbits and their mother. They could not have been more than a couple of weeks old and too young to know how to save themselves. They just hopped about in aimless circles. The dogs—Gina and Folly—were with me and behaved very well. At my command they simply stood still, trembling, and let the rabbits hop away into the thick oats of an adjoining field.

The pheasants seem to be increasing in the valley fields, away from the foxes which haunt the hills. I flushed two families yesterday. And despite the snow of the winter, the quail are more abundant than usual. They seem to be everywhere and very tame. It may be that they are attracted to our fields by the abundance and by the presence of minerals that have been restored to the land.

Last night Bob ran down a fox with his car in the lane leading up to Jim Pugh's cabin. The legislature has now declared an open season on foxes and permits County Commissioners to offer bounties. Foxes have become a serious menace to other game as well as to poultry. Last summer they took more than a hundred of Walter Berry's pullets on range in broad daylight and when we mowed the hay in the field next to his, we found it littered with the feathers of young leghorn pullets. With all the crevices and caves and thick cover in this country they are very difficult to exterminate.

Tonight Bob and I drove to the Conservancy fields to look at the corn. I have seen no better field anywhere in the Middle West, even in Indiana or Illinois. It is a deep, luscious green, even and solid over the whole 80-acre field, with the leaves extravagantly ruffled. If we have enough rain it should bring in a hundred baskets to the acre, easily. No matter how worried or depressed you may be, a sight like that drives away all depression.

Bryce Browning, Secretary of the Conservancy, is coming tomorrow with six farmers from Tuscaroras County and a young soldier is coming up from Dayton to look over the place and get some advice about setting up as a farmer.

Friday, the 13th: What a day! The farmers turned out to be twelve instead of six. We spent three hours going over the fields. I was very proud of the appearance of the crops and animals. We are going to save out a couple of thin, gullied acres on the Bailey Place as a museum piece of what the farm looked like when we took over.

Noble Crane came up from Columbus to go over the "Prosperity from the Ground Up" plan which aims to bring farmers, industry, and labor into closer and more friendly relations. Also to restore the farmer to that position of authority and dignity which was largely lost in the madhouse industrial scramble of the past fifty years.

Two American Field Service boys on leave drove down from Cleveland—one back from Burma, the other from Africa. The boys certainly get around nowadays. Pete, our former dairyman, sent a picture of himself yesterday taken in the garden of our house in France!

Just after lunch a taxi drove up with a strange woman in it. Wishing to keep the taxi to take Noble Crane back to Mansfield I went out and asked, "Are you keeping the taxi?" To which she replied, "Oh, no! I've come to stay a few weeks. I had a lot of troubles and thought I might get them straightened out if I stayed with you a while."

She returned with the taxi, and a large suitcase obviously packed for a long stay. We've had some other screwballs from time to time. The old man who arrived with all his baggage to make his home with us, the old woman who wanted to stay for a time because she felt I could help her commune with her dead husband whom she saw from time to time "through the cleft in the Rock of Ages." Almost every week there are two or three in addition to about twenty or thirty letters from crackpots of one sort or another, either filled with obscene abuse or containing thirty or forty pages of the one and only plan to save our economic system and humanity. A good many of them are nebulous versions of "the Common Man" philosophy. Sometimes I think we produce more nuts per acre in this country than any country in the world.

After the unexpected visitor left, another lady, younger, all dressed up and wearing high-heeled shoes appeared coming up the road. She had hitch-hiked from Mansfield and wanted to know how to write. Of course there isn't any recipe except to have something to say and to learn how to say it. Nearly always the people who want to "know how to write" want to be writers not because they like writing or have anything to say but because they think it's a free and easy life with a lot of money— which it isn't, God knows! But it's a poor basis on which to build any success. As Henry Ford once said to me, "Most successful people want to do something passionately. They know what they want to do and stick to it. The money takes care of itself. Usually you can't keep the rewards of money or recognition away."

The longer I live the more it seems to me that most people never get on as far as they should because they never make up their minds what they want to do and never stick to it. They're always looking for "breaks" and always suspecting others of double-crossing them. The energy spent in trying to take advantage of a "pull" and "breaks," if spent directly, would carry them a great deal farther. The person who is just "looking for a job" never gets very far, either materially or in living satisfaction. I suspect this is the group Henry Wallace refers to as "The Common Man."

After supper, mowed all the near-by marshy ground out by the "Stoll Field." There is about three acres of it, fairly weedy, but very moist all through the hottest weather. Am certain it can be turned into the best ladino-alsike pasture for the dairy cows.

I like the natural names that places acquire in the country. "The Stoll Field" has its name from an eccentric Pennsylvania

Dutchman who built a cabin there about a hundred years ago. Of course the various farms are known as the Anson Place, the Bailey Place, the Fleming Place, and the hilltop farm is "Up Ferguson Way." Then there is the "Cemetery Field," the "Bottom Pasture" and the "Lower Bottom," the "Bailey Hill," and the "Hog-lot Field."

A kind stranger enlightened me the other day by letter concerning the curious name of "Steam Corners" bestowed long ago on one of our crossroad villages. It appears that after the first county roads were laid out bisecting each other at right angles, small settlements grew up at each intersection. The first buildings were usually placed on the four corners and among them was the first steam sawmill in the countryside. The crossroads became known as "Steam Corner," later corrupted to the plural.

I still haven't been able to run to ground the origin of the curious name of "Pinhook," another crossroads near us.

Among other things the day was marred by two heroic dog fights both staged within five minutes involving five dogs on one side and seven on the other. Prince, Baby, Gina, Folly, Smokey, Susie and Dusky were all with me when I stopped at Harry's house to inspect the improvements he was making. Laddie, his big St. Bernard, came running out, followed by Sandy, the Border Collie who has ten new pups, Penny, Harry's Boxer, and the St. Bernard pup.

It was a real brawl with all the ladies joining in a hair-pulling match—six Boxers and a Spaniel on one side, two St. Bernards and a Border Collie and a Boxer on the other. We just managed to separate them and lock the Hellers' dogs in the house when one of the children opened a door at the back of the house and all of them came galloping out to renew the battle. The big St. Bernard seemed to have been the chief casualty. Prince got hold of his big floppy ears and wouldn't let go.

After two years we are still "mining" the manure out of the Bailey barn and barnyard. We can use it to advantage in restoring the bare Bailey Hill to fertility. I doubt that it has seen manure of any kind, green or barnyard for at least twenty-five years, perhaps never.

I suspect from the sounds that the field mouse which haunts Mary's and my bedrooms has built a nest inside the radio beside my bed. The dog doesn't seem to mind so I don't. He is a pretty little fellow with very bright eyes and enormous ears and sits up like a kangaroo.

Harry and Jimmy are amassing a small fortune by working the haybaler on custom service on Sundays and during the long summer evenings in the neighbors' fields. The arrangement satisfies everybody—ten cents a bale, split fifty-fifty with the farm for the use of the baler—and the neighbors, terribly short of help and machinery, are getting their hay in. They work as a team and have arrived at a high state of efficiency, Harry pushing the wires and Jimmy tying. It is a comical sight to see them crossing a rich hayfield with the baler running about fifteen miles an hour tossing off bales like a carp spawning. They made twenty dollars apiece last Sunday. Harry wants money to buy a new car and Jimmy, who is seventeen and foreman of the boys, is saving up to buy a farm. It is fairly light work and, except for the dust, one of the most pleasurable jobs on the farm.

Observation: When some silly woman asks Mary, "But don't you get lonely on a farm?" Mary answers, "Spend a day there some time and see how lonely it is!"

Summer 1945 (2)

> I was tired of the idle and turbulent life of Paris: of the crowd of *petits maîtres,* the bad books printed with official approval and royal patronage: the cabals of the literary world.
>
> Voltaire, at Ferney

August 20: Back from two days in Detroit where we went for agricultural reasons to talk with Roger Keyes and others at Harry Ferguson, Inc., concerning new agricultural implements for the New Agriculture and with officials of the Stran-Steel, a subsidiary of Great Lakes Steel Corporation, regarding their plans for farm buildings. Growing production has swamped us and we need new dairy buildings to house a bigger herd, new feeding barns for more beef cattle and poultry buildings for several thousand more chickens or turkeys. Harry is enthusiastic over turkeys but I remain cynical and dubious. They represent a big investment, a low will to live—less even than sheep—and a brainlessness that is virtually unexcelled. Incidentally, it would appear in the case of many animals that the will to live is somehow related to intelligence and to a greater *internal* resistance to illness and death. A ewe or a turkey, both stupid creatures, if it feels badly, will simply lie down and die with serenity, almost with pleasure. The hog, perhaps the most intelligent of farm animals, will fight with all its wits and spirit against illness and death.

The steel dairy units, standardized but flexible enough for adaptation, have immense possibilities on the grounds of fire resistance, durability, moving and general convenience. In a short time we have evolved plans for a really modern and practical dairy unit, in which the cows would run free in covered feeding sheds, partly open all the year round for health's sake, with a milking-parlor where they would be fed silage and grains. Hay would be fed actually in the mow or storage room itself where they would be walled in by the bales of hay and straw. It would of course be a one-story, ground floor mow and as they consumed the hay the cows would gradually eat their way out until spring pasture was ready. We had the idea of using movable hayracks so that as the bales were consumed the racks could be moved back and out. Thus they would always be exactly next to the hay so that no carrying and little labor would be involved. All the mow and feeding shed would be kept bedded all winter and the manure removed as the occasion permitted. All of this plan has its origins in the mind of H. E. Babcock of Cornell University, perhaps the best, most co-ordinated and comprehensive mind in American agriculture.

If our plans work out we shall put the new dairy unit on the plot next to Bob's house at the crossroads by the red school house. It will make an interesting contrast with the older farm buildings of the Beck Place just across the road—the one steel, fireproof, practical and completely modern, the other modern, somewhat old-fashioned, subject to fire and wasteful of labor. It seems to me that the need for two- or three-story farm buildings has largely disappeared. So far as we are concerned, baling is the only practical way of handling hay and straw, and forage in bales can be stored much more easily on the ground level than overhead in the huge, high, old-fashioned mows. This is especially true when the bales are kept, as we plan, exactly next to the cattle and actually form a part of their shelter. Few things can increase the profits and efficiency of a farm so much as modern buildings conceived and planned for saving labor and with consideration for modern machinery and feeding methods.

Dr. Borst of the Zanesville, Ohio, U.S. Soil Conservation Station, who discovered and developed the use of alfalfa as a poor-land crop, spent all of Sunday with us. We went over the whole farm, field by field, and showed him with a good deal of pride the fine thirty-acre field of alfalfa high up on the top of the hill on the Ferguson Place on what was only four years earlier a barren, eroded hilltop. Also the fine two-head-per-acre bluegrass—white clover permanent pasture next to it established on the same sort of land.

We found a lot more evidence of the ecological fact of the effect of minerally balanced soil and abundant organic material in relation to disease and insects. The only alfalfa attacked by leafhoppers is on spots, usually on the flat spots, where the terribly depleted topsoil remains. Here even our concentrated efforts have not yet been able to restore the soil to full life and strength. The leafhoppers simply do not attack the healthy plants on good, well-balanced soil.

The same evidence showed up brilliantly in the vegetable garden where a large plot given over to tomatoes, cantaloupe, sweet pepper, cucumbers, and late sweetcorn exists, in abundant health absolutely free from insects, blight or disease although *no* dusting or spraying has been done. The melons are absolutely free from the blight which usually attacks them. For the first time in our experience we have not lost a single cantaloupe plant after germination, and this in a patch representing about a third of an acre.

Most of the time with Dr. Borst was interrupted by farmer visitors, some of whom stayed with us to complete the tour. It was the first Sunday without gas rationing and visitors descended like locusts upon Egypt. Some came simply out of curiosity but a good many were farmers or soil men whom I always find interesting and am glad to see. Very often I learn much from them. One party which I found the most interesting was made up of three boys from Clark County, more than a hundred miles away, with their girls. They were all under eighteen and very much alive, intelligent and full of ideas. They stayed with us all the afternoon and at the end asked shyly if I would come down to Clark County during the winter to talk to the 4-H Clubs and the farmers. It is clearly evident that the future of our agriculture, and therefore the future of a large segment of our complex and interlocking economy, lies in the hands of our young people. With them the land-grant colleges, the extension service and the soil conservation service are doing a wonderful job. Very likely the government money spent on their education is the best investment made of government money and its good results affect us all, even in the congested areas of our unhealthy cities—a fact which too few people understand.

One of the striking things we have discovered slowly is the relation between animal secretions and droppings and the germination and vigor of meadow seedlings. Without exception, in the fields where cattle and sheep were allowed to wander the germination and vigor of seedlings is much higher than in the fields, even with much better soil, from which they have been excluded. This fact is also true on the poor areas where barnyard manure has been used. The most striking example, which caused Dr. Borst to whistle and say, "Jehosaphat!" was the cemetery field, once perhaps the poorest field on the Fleming farm, mostly steep and rough, which had been destroyed by row crops and erosion. Lime, a mixed legume seeding, and turning over the field to cattle for two years achieved a miraculous result. The seeding, even on the poor, bare, mound-tops and steep slopes is fantastically thick and vigorous. It is a mixture of ladino, alfalfa and brome grass. As we stood in the deep growth talking about that particular field, Dr. Borst said, "We still know practically nothing about these things." I do know that if virgin leaf mould topsoil out of our virgin woodlots is used alone in the greenhouse or in window-boxes, the plants grown in it are feeble and spindly. A little lime and a little barnyard manure completely alter its character and the resulting germination and vigor of growth is astonishing.

During the middle of the day we, with the help of the kids and visitors, drove the Shorthorn herd with Blondy, the Angus bull, from the Bailey Hill pasture to the Ferguson Place to join the blue-roan herd running with Elmer, the white Shorthorn bull, a distance of about a mile and a half, mostly along highways. Everything went wrong—calves got lost, one ran back up to the 120-acre Bailey pasture. One of the cows was in season which added to the confusion. In order to rescue one little two-day-old calf, we had to drive the whole herd back so that his mother could find him. Each time we sought to round him up, he high-tailed it up over the hilltop where he found a clump of bushes or a patch of blackberries to hide in, staring out and watching us with comical, very bright black eyes. When we tried to surround him, he would break through and with his tail straight up in the air take up over the hill. I am sure the little stinker enjoyed every minute of it. It was a hot day and all of us felt like killing him but we couldn't help laughing.

As we passed the bottom pasture all the yearling beef cattle crowded up to the fence bawling with curiosity and sociability, perhaps recognizing their mothers of last season or wanting to meet their brothers and sisters born this year. In the uproar and confusion a white calf got through the fence to join them and Jimmy, the high-school athlete and Harry ran him down on foot and finally returned him to the herd. Harry put him in the back seat of Jimmy's car and sat on him to keep him quiet.

Once we reached the Ferguson Place, Blondy and Elmer engaged in a first class bullfight surrounded by admiring and very vocal cows of both herds. Blondy, the big Angus, is heavier and older but Elmer had the advantage of having horns. They pushed each other around, bellowing and pawing for a long time until Blondy decided he had had enough. He wanted to quit but Elmer pressed the issue and finally Blondy simply broke down the heavy gate and set off down the Ferguson lane through the thick woods with Elmer behind him. The chase continued all the way back to the Bailey Place along the highway and over and through fences, to the elation of the Sunday tourists on the road.

Finally we gave up and simply put up the gates, leaving the two gentlemen in the big Bailey Hill pasture. The pursuit continued at a slowing pace until dark. We could see them from across the valley—big, black Blondy walking ahead, willing to call the whole thing off and followed at exactly the same speed by Elmer about ten feet behind. In the morning when we passed the Bailey pasture on the way to Cleveland, they were eating peacefully side by side without their harems, who, with all the calves, were eating rich alfalfa and clover on the high, distant Ferguson Place.

The two bulls have always run together before with the combined herds after breeding season, but up till this year Blondy was the pusher and kept the younger Elmer in his proper place. Apparently Elmer considers himself grown up now and will take no more pushing around. Of the two, I am afraid that for reasons of personality and charm my sympathies are with Blondy, the Angus. He is a very gentle fellow with great dignity who allows you to come up and scratch his ears in the open field. Elmer, the Shorthorn, has always been a little dumb and shy.

Spent Monday in Cleveland for a meeting of the Mayor's Committee on the new farm Cleveland plans to set up on the lake front in the very heart of the city about two minutes from the public square. It will be a real farm of about 160 acres—a unique development among farms and cities in that it will be in the heart of the city itself. It will provide a spectacle of great interest to city folk, especially the children, and do a good deal toward bringing about some degree of understanding between city and country people. It is planned also to have exhibitions of farm machinery and products of all kinds—in other words, to make an agricultural center in the heart of a large area which is one of the richest agricultural and industrial areas in the world.

I have also been made Vice-President of the new association which is establishing a new international horse and livestock show in Cleveland. It will fall in the week between the Toronto and Chicago International and permit exhibitors to show during the intermediate week instead of having to lay off. Cleveland has great advantages with its auditorium and exhibition hall in the very middle of the city adjoining the proposed site of the farm, with railway sidings only five minutes away. The site of the Chicago show is more than an hour's drive from the center of the town. I am honored by the two appointments as I am not a Clevelander but live 75 miles away, down in Richland County.

We shall be a full household over the week end with

Ramona Herdman of Harpers, Freddy Spencer convalescing after illness in the Navy hospital in Washington, Mimi Rand and Muriel King motoring east from the Pacific Coast and Mac coming down from Detroit for Saturday and Sunday.

The Story of Kemper's Run

The business of farming begins with the land. And on the farms that Louis Bromfield acquired to make up Malabar, the land had been abused for a hundred years, partly out of ignorance, partly out of thoughtless greed. And yet, the land can heal itself, if given the chance. In this chapter, the story is told of how Kemper's Run was "murdered" and yet came back to life. In the process, Bromfield provides a vivid description of the history and natural features of the landscape in the neighborhood of Malabar Farm.

T his is the story of a creek called Kemper's Run. It runs along the middle of a valley that lies wide and flat between the cracked and slowly disintegrating shoulders of a pre-glacial sandstone canyon about two million years old. The first great glacier, acting like a gigantic bulldozer, filled up the canyon with scrapings of rock and earth pushed before it all the way down from Northern Canada. The second great glacier came to a slow stop about on the line of the filled-in canyon and started melting, leaving behind as it slowly withdrew northward great heaps and mounds of glacial drift.

This residue, made up of gravel and loam, was rich stuff and presently there sprang up on it the finest hardwood forest in the world—a forest of oak, chestnut, maple, ash, beech, and hickory. For a million or more years these trees shed their leaves, grew, and died, fell, and returned their substance to the earth in the form of an incredibly black and rich topsoil. This topsoil, covered by virgin hardwood forest, was what the first trappers and settlers found when they came into the valley.

During all that time Kemper's Run wound its way through the bottom of the rich valley between the ancient shoulders of the pre-glacial canyon. It was a crystal clear stream, here and there bordered by marshes filled with game—mink and beaver, bears and deer, muskrat and otter, wild duck and geese, flocks of carrier pigeons that darkened the sky, and thousands of other birds. The creek was fed by springs gushing out of the hillsides and the sandstone rock that bordered the valley and its clear waters were filled with cress and other vegetation. Now and then after torrential rains lasting two or three days, there were floodwaters which raised the height of its flow a foot or two, but the floodwaters were clear and never of a violence to tear out the vegetation in the stream, which fed and gave shelter to myriads of bass and crappies and bluegills and sunfish.

The valley was a paradise for the Indians who lived in the country. They grew corn and squash and beans on the rich lowlands that bordered the marshy land and there were unlimited supplies of game from the woods, and fish and crayfish in the clear water of the little stream. That is a fair and accurate picture of the valley when the first settlers came into it about the beginning of the nineteenth century.

They claimed the rich, glacial, forested land in sections of 640 acres. The bottom land went first and then the gently sloping hills on each side and finally the top land, and as rapidly as they could the settlers began clearing away the forests, heaping the tree trunks of oak, beech, ash, maple, chestnut, and hickory in great piles and burning what they did not need for building barns and houses. They were eager to get at that deep, black, rich topsoil laid down on top of the minerally rich, deep, glacial drift. The grain and the cattle they could grow were urgently needed by a nation at the beginning of the great industrial revolution with a population rapidly growing not only from the steadily increasing birthrate but by hundreds of thousands of newcomers from old, oppressed Europe where there were too many people and not enough land.

That was the beginning.

I first remember the valley about 45 years ago when I went there fishing with my father at the age of five, about a century after the first settlers had come in. I knew it intimately for the next ten years through fishing, hunting, camping, and friendship with most of the valley people. At that time it was still a beautiful valley and still fairly productive. There were still lots of fish in the creek although their numbers and size were diminished. The marshes still existed on the borders of the bottom farm lands. There were deep holes in the creek that provided both swimming and big fish. There were three old mills with big millponds that held back the water and made breeding places for fish. It was the best hay and pasture country in the world and the farmers were making big incomes from the timothy hay they grew on the slopes of the glacial drift cleared of the forest. Every year they shipped out thousands of tons to feed the draft horses, the carriage horses, and the saddle horses which existed by the millions everywhere in the country.

There wasn't much corn grown there—only enough to feed the few hogs—and the hills and the bottom lands grew hay or pasture or wheat and oats planted largely to get the land back into meadow seedings. About 40 per cent of the forest land remained although it was pretty badly cut over and coming back with second growth. There wasn't much erosion and very few floods and even those weren't big enough to flood the bottom lands to carry out the mill dams. There wasn't much chance for the water to rush across naked fields carrying off topsoil because most of the fields were covered by sod in pasture or meadow.

But the land was being "farmed out." Few of the farms in the valley put back enough to recompense for the tons of fertility in the form of minerals which each year were carried off out of the valley into the cities in the form of timothy hay. Some of the farmers even dumped the manure out of their stables into the creek itself to be rid of it. Some regarded the creek as a great asset for that reason—it was an easy way of *getting rid* of manure. But already on some of the hilltops and higher slopes, the soil wouldn't any longer grow timothy either in quantity or quality, and those farms began to go to pieces. They didn't produce enough, and roofs began to leak, buildings to go without paint. Taxes became delinquent, and fences began to rot down or rust out without replacement. On the high land there were already abandoned farms with broken windows, sagging roofs and fields overgrown with weeds.

About that time, when I was fifteen years old, I left the valley and I did not see it again for twenty-five years.

When I came back to that country I found it terribly changed and when I went to fish the familiar creek, I found it perhaps had changed the most. The mill dams had been carried away by floods and millponds had vanished, silted up with mud, and gone were the big holes that had provided both swimming and big fish. There wasn't a pool anywhere with more than two or three feet of water. The vegetation had gone out of the creek bed and virtually the only fish were minnows and carp and bullheads—tough, coarse, inferior fish which could survive flood and silt and drought, and in the woods and hillsides and bottoms the game had begun to move out as they will do when a countryside grows poor.

What had happened in these twenty-five years of absence was simple enough. First the soil, being farmed out, grew less and less hay per acre per year and then the automobile came along and replaced the horse, and the market for timothy hay, so easy to grow, so easy to harvest long ago on the once rich land, had shrunk along with the price and demand. Some of the farmers gave up and moved out, leaving the farms either to a locust horde of fly-by-night tenants or to solitude and desolation, producing nothing, supporting and feeding no one, often paying no taxes.

As the market for hay declined other farmers had looked west and had seen on the flat lands of the prairie country that the farmers there were growing rich by raising corn and hogs and they said, without thought or knowledge, or wisdom, "If they can do it, we can." And so they ploughed up the grass and meadow land and even the pastures of that rolling, hilly country and planted corn. They planted the corn in rows, running more often than not up and down slopes and hills, and every time it rained each furrow between the standing corn became a miniature gully, carrying off the precious rainfall as rapidly as possible and bearing with it the good topsoil that remained and the fertilizer the farmer had bought out of his diminishing hard-earned income.

In winter after the corn was harvested the fields were left bare for the freezing and thawing and heavy rains of winter to disintegrate the soil and sweep it away. And rapidly the corn ate up the residue of organic material left in the soil by long years of hay and pasture growing, and as the organic material went out and ceased to soak up the rainfall, the soil became more and more like cement, turning off the water instead of soaking it up and the little gullies became big gullies until sometimes whole fields had be to abandoned. As more and more land was turned into corn and the pasture and meadows produced less and less, the farmers took to turning livestock into the woods and wood-lots to graze. The cattle destroyed the new forest seedlings and came in at the end of the season with ribs showing because ferns and forest seedlings will not fatten cattle or even make them grow. And where too few big trees remained, even the woodlots began to develop gullies that channeled the water quickly off, leaving the bigger trees to die slowly from the top down.

Each year the fields produced a little less per acre, and presently more farms went out of circulation or fell to the pos-session of the banks which didn't want them. The banks wanted the deposits, the loans, the interest of prosperous, productive farms; they did not want the worn out, weedy fields which pro-duced nothing. Many a farm had become unsalable, even for ten dollars on the courthouse steps at sheriff's sale.

What happened to Kemper's Run, which had once been a clear flowing stream with its millponds, its deep holes, its game fish? It became a monstrosity and a menace, flooding badly af-ter each thunderstorm, filled with silt and devoid of vegetation, inhabited only by minnows and mud fish. As the land grew less productive the farmers crowded in on the marshland to turn it to some use and they began to ditch and drain it and they told the local authorities that they could never accomplish their pur-pose unless the floods from the bare, higher land were con-trolled and the stream bed deepened and straightened so that there would be "fall" for their ditches and drainage tiles.

So Kemper's Run was straightened and deepened. They brought in machinery which cut brutally through the marsh-lands in a straight line down the center of the valley. They cut down the protecting willows along the banks and destroyed the deep holes and what remained of the silt-filled millponds. They created a deep ditch through bare gravel which channeled the floodwater from the bare fields as rapidly as possible down-stream to damage fields and cities and farms all the way across the United States to the mouth of the Mississippi. And all of it did no good; it did only damage; and Kemper's Run with its willows, its swimming holes, its game fishing had been murdered.

The big ditch did no good because within a year or two it was silted up again with the millions of tons of topsoil that came off the bare eroding cornfields, and within a short time the "fall" for drainage ditches and tiles was gone again and the mouths of the tiles buried beneath layers of topsoil, fertilizer, and mud from the sloping fields that bordered Kemper's Run. The farmers didn't ask to have the stream dredged again for they had discovered the hard way after paying thousands of dollars in special assessments that you couldn't use these marshy lands even after they were ditched and tiled. The water in the water-logged soil was seepage water from the hill country all around and no amount of drainage would make it possible to get into it early enough in the spring to plant corn that would ripen. If you planted wheat, it was drowned out in winter despite all the tiles and ditches.

So a community had murdered a beautiful stream only to fill it again in a year or two with the silt off its own fields. All the thousands of dollars of taxpayers' money and special assessments had been spent only to create more damage not only in the valley and to the stream itself but to people living hundreds of miles away along the great rivers which were fed by Kemper's Run and a thousand other small flooding streams like it. And everywhere in the nation taxpayers were paying more and more taxes for levees and dams to check at the mouth of the Mississippi the floods of Kemper's Run and streams like it which man himself had turned from valuable assets into terrible liabilities. And all the time the farms that bordered Kemper's Run were producing less and less real wealth for the nation, borrowing and depositing less money, paying less and less taxes. It was the spectacle of a country devouring itself. The final chapter of the story of Kemper's Run is more cheerful than the rest of it.

I have lived near Kemper's Run for close to ten years, and I have seen it slowly return to its old state, the way I knew it as a small boy. It has been slowly finding its old level again, curving and winding through bottom pastures and marshland. The deep holes where the big bass used to lie beneath the tree roots are coming back. The cress is beginning to grow again in water which is once again clear and free of silt. There are deep holes with bass and bluegills and crappies and sunfish and the mud-loving fish have almost disappeared. The willows are growing again in spots along the banks and for two years there have been no floods at all, save during the disastrous spring of 1947. Bottom pastures which only a few years ago were flooded a dozen times a year to a depth of two or three feet have not been flooded once in the last two years. The springs that feed the creek have begun to flow again as they used to flow long ago, all the year round, regardless of drought. Old dried-up, half-forgotten springs are coming back to life and beginning to flow.

How did this come about? It came about because the farmers in the valley learned the hard way. They had to give up and get out like the farmers who once lived on the abandoned farms that lay high on the shoulders of the valley, or they had to mend their ways. The abandoned farms have been, ironically, friends of Kemper's Run for their fields are no longer left bare to erosion in the process of being farmed out. Their fields are covered with weeds and poverty grass, and forest seedlings are moving across them to reclaim them less than six generations after the forest was cut down by the first settlers. No water runs off those abandoned fields. Most of the good precious topsoil has long since disappeared from them down Kemper's Run into the distant Gulf of Mexico, but Nature has begun to build it back, now that man has left her in peace. When the rain falls it stays where it falls, sinking into the ground to feed wells and springs in the valley below. Even near the abandoned hilltops springs have begun to flow again for the first time in a hundred years.

And today as you drive up the valley you see few fields of corn with furrows running up and down hill and virtually no fields left bare all through the terrible, destructive winter rains. They are covered with a kind protective blanket of wheat or rye. And where corn is grown it is mostly on the contour, *around* the hill rather than up and down it. Along the hillside lie wide green strips of meadow sod that catch and hold all the rain and any topsoil that shifts. And instead of the old timothy hay that helped to ruin the valley there grows alfalfa and red clover and ladino and everywhere piles of lime dot the hillsides waiting for the spreader. Each year one sees rich fields of healing meadow and pasture spreading along the hillsides.

It isn't only Kemper's Run which has changed but the look of the whole countryside itself. Houses and barns and fences are painted and prosperous again, and skinny cattle no longer pasture on the young green seedlings in the woods and woodlots. Millions of young trees are growing up into good sound timber that the nation needs so badly.

But here and there in the valley there remains a farmer who still believes that "what was good enough for grandpappy is good enough for me." He leaves his fields bare and cheats on fertilizer and pastures his skinny cattle in the woods and plants his corn up and down the slopes. And each year he raises less and less per acre. Each year it costs him more and more to produce a bushel of grain because he produces less and less per acre. High prices can't help him because he produces so little per acre that the first major decline in prices will wipe him out, one more victim of the school of agriculture which *fights* Nature. In less than another generation there will be no more of his kind remaining. They are the last representatives of the army which carried on a furious rape and assault upon our good land. They are defeated because no man ever yet won a victory by *fighting* Nature and the laws of Nature.

Most of them in the valley learned the hard way, the greatest of all lessons—that by working *with* Nature man can be prosperous and even rich and happy and healthy. Fighting or cheating her, man is always defeated, poverty-stricken, bitter and miserable, and eventually is destroyed himself. I have lived long enough to have seen three phases in the history of the valley and I have lived long enough to have seen Kemper's Run murdered and come back to life again to what it once had been, a clear, bright stream with fishing and swimming and cress and mint-bordered pools with clear, cold water all the year round for the cattle in the bottom pastures. I have seen the game fish return and the game birds and animals come back to a valley which they had almost deserted during the evil days. And on the hillsides the farmers are raising better crops and better livestock than have been raised on those slopes for the past fifty years. It all goes together. It's simply a question of working *with* Nature. Work with her and she gives back health and abundance and prosperity.

The story of Kemper's Run is the story of a single creek, but it is the story, too, of land, of prosperity, of good hunting and fishing, of health throughout all the nation. The story of its rebirth for farmer, for sportsman, for the city dweller in search of peace and recreation, for the country banks and the nation which need its prosperity and its wealth is a simple one. Through the knowledge which man has developed, the farmers of the valley are restoring the conditions that existed when the whole valley was a paradise for the Indian hunter and fisherman. Game fish, quail, mink, rabbit, muskrat, and raccoon are coming back in abundance, and so are the yields of hay, wheat, corn, and the health, the prosperity of the farmer, of his fields and his livestock. It is an easy business and a profitable one. It takes a little time but it has made the difference between life and death in the little valley drained by Kemper's Run.

The Business of "Plowman's Folly"

One visitor to the Big House at Malabar was Edward H. Faulkner, who was to start a revolution in farming, though neither he nor Louis Bromfield would live to see it. Faulkner wanted Bromfield to help him publish a book entitled Plowman's Folly. *Bromfield was taken with Faulkner's ideas but, since he had his own literary projects to attend to, put his visitor onto someone who could help find a publisher—Paul Sears, author of the acclaimed* Deserts on the March.

Faulkner maintained that the cause of erosion and loss of fertility of the soil was the moldboard plow, which, in turning the soil, destroyed its ability to be "self-sustaining." If crop residues—the "trash" remaining after harvesting a crop—were left at or near the surface of the soil rather than being turned under, nutrients would be restored, erosion lessened, and soil moisture retained.

The publishing history of Faulkner's book is a fascinating one. Ultimately, it sold hundreds of thousands of copies; but the book never made a dent on the world of agriculture, dominated as it was by agricultural bureaucrats and university professors who simply did not believe in what was called "the Faulkner method." Edward Faulkner was, they said, a nut.

Today, with the advent of modern herbicides, various versions of the Faulkner method are practiced, under the rubric "conservation tillage," on roughly a third of all U.S. cropland. It has been a farmer's movement, and as the farmers have developed and tuned their techniques they have found that less and less herbicide is needed—in fact, less than is required by conventional tillage. In the process, Faulkner's historic contribution (he maintained that "weedless farming" was possible without chemicals) is beginning to be recognized. This outcome might well have been a different one had Louis Bromfield been unwilling to hear out

this "smallish, graying man, with very bright blue eyes" who was
to show the world that the basic assumption of agriculture, the
turning of the soil, was all wrong.

O ne morning not long after the farm was started there
came to the farm office a smallish, graying man with
very bright blue eyes. He said his name was Faulkner
and that he wanted to talk to me about a new theory of cultivation which did away altogether with the conventional, long accepted moldboard plow. Because I am articulate and because I
frequently write on subjects other than fiction, a great many
messiahs have come my way, so many that there are times when
I am inclined to believe there are more unbalanced people and
more cranks in the United States than in any other country in
the world. No nation has ever produced so many economic pan-
aceas, so many plans for doing away with work and getting
something for nothing. During the long course of the New Deal
more than one reformer associated with it has brought forward
fantasies of thought and planning no more related to reality or
fact than the ideas of the Townsendites, the Dowieites, the
House of David or any of the other countless economic and religious groups which have found the answer to everything.
These messiahs call upon me and write me long and occasionally abusive letters and so, slowly over a period of years, I have
developed a kind of phobia about them. In their presence, fixed
by the half-mad look in their glittering eyes, I feel my heartbeat
slow down. My face turns gray and presently I am seized with
indigestion. All of this, no doubt, is no more than hysteria born
of boredom because for me nothing is so boring as a crank with a
single-track mind, especially when his plan is to take the human race by the scruff of the neck and force it to follow out his
own half-mad ideas.

And so when the man who said his name was Faulkner and
that he was for abolishing the plow, came into my office, the old
symptoms began to make themselves evident. I listened with
only half my mind and said "yes" and "very interesting, I'm
sure" and at last bade him good-by and got back to my own
work, thinking I should never see him again.

But Ed Faulkner was a persistent fellow and rightly so, for he had discovered, for himself and entirely by himself, some important and fundamental truths and he was not prepared to have them overlooked. In short, Ed Faulkner came back, and when he came back I began to listen and as I listened, I began to be interested and to understand why it was that he had had a hard time getting a hearing.

His ideas were in one sense revolutionary; in another sense they were as old as time and as old as Nature herself. The revolutionary ones were not likely to be welcomed by either bureau men or by the academic world of agriculture. They were upsetting because they ran counter to much that farmers had been taught by bureau men and professors over a long period of time. Someday, if there is ever time, I should like to compile a whole book of the wrong and destructive things which have been taught in American agriculture, with a second volume dedicated to the things which have been taught more for the benefit of manufacturers of farm machinery, of chemical fertilizers and of prepared and expensive feeds than for the good of the earth or the welfare of the farmer. Not all the false things were taught deliberately by men who knew they were false; some were mistaken, others merely stupid, a few were prejudiced cranks and a good many spent their academic years simply in looking for the short cuts which exist neither in agriculture nor in Nature. Not all bureau men and professors are bigots—to many of them our civilization owes great debts; but the mere fact of sitting long behind desks lecturing young people or of passing years on a swivel chair far from the earth out of which all agricultural knowledge must come, does tend to produce an inflexible and sometimes a closed and prejudiced mind.

So when a man proposed to abolish the plow, it was not likely that he would meet with a sympathetic reception from circles which had acclaimed the plow for at least one hundred and fifty years as a great instrument of civilization and of man's welfare.

As Faulkner talked, my interest grew because what he proposed seemed so reasonable and because I knew out of my own experience, both in gardening on a small intensive scale and in farming on a large scale, that much of what he was saying was true, with that truth which lies in the very processes of Nature.

He had been a county agent and had resigned because of differences with the Extension Service authorities over his unorthodox ideas. From then on he had worked at various jobs, mostly at the insurance business, which he found not too profitable. In his own town of Elyria, Ohio, forty miles from Malabar, he was regarded by those who knew him as a man with an obsession. He was the son of a Kentucky farmer, whose own farm had remained green and fertile while the neighboring farms slipped farther and farther down the scale of production until many of them were abandoned. In a way, Faulkner had given all his life to the earth and what it could teach him. When I first saw him he was conducting his experiments with soil in his own back yard and on two acres of poor land which he rented by the year, a testing ground that was obviously inadequate in terms of commercial farming. Nevertheless, on that little piece of land he had arrived at proving many things with which I found myself in agreement, not the least of which was that, given reasonably good subsoil, topsoil could be rapidly rebuilt, not by short-cutting Nature but by adopting her own methods and by speeding up and intensifying them. And Faulkner, like myself, was a great believer in the virtues of mulch as a means of growing crops and doing away with much labor and cultivation.

And so I listened and presently I too began to talk. I, at least, was learning something. I had never thought of the evil the moldboard plow might do until I listened to Ed Faulkner.

And then one day he brought me a thick manuscript in which he had set down all his ideas and the results of his experiments. It was a very long book and not too well organized, not nearly so well expressed as when Faulkner talked and the light came into his blue eyes. He wanted help and advice with it and I had to tell him that I should only be deceiving him if I told him that I could find the time to do a conscientious job on it. And so he left me; and Ollie Fink, who is in charge of conservation education in Ohio, and Paul Sears, head of the botany department at Oberlin College and author of *Deserts on the March,* gave him the needed professional help and advice. The manuscript was rejected by four or five of the largest publishing houses, all on what I must say were reasonable grounds, commercially speaking—that few people, even farmers, would be interested in a book on plowing. I heard no more of the book or of Faulkner until one day I received a thinnish, nicely printed book called *Plowman's Folly,* by Edward H. Faulkner. The Oklahoma University Press and its active manager, Savoie Lottinville, prompted by Paul Sears, had had the courage to publish it. I stayed up that night until I had finished the book. I knew that Faulkner had something important to say but still doubted that it would receive attention.

I was wrong. Within a few weeks, half the publications of the country had published editorials concerning it, even such unlikely ones as the *New Yorker* magazine and the New York *Daily News,* which devoted a full column editorial to the subject. Everywhere you went you heard people talking about it, from practical, solid farmers to two Hollywood actresses who, in a Chicago hotel, asked me, "What is all this business about *Plowman's Folly?*" I myself did a piece about Faulkner for a national magazine and was forced to set up a special post-card department to answer queries as to where the book could be purchased. The queries came from every part of the country, from servicemen abroad and from farmers in South Africa, in England, in Persia, in Canada, Australia, South America and Palestine. The press could not turn out copies fast enough for the demand and the war restriction on paper presently made it impossible for the Oklahoma University Press to meet the demand. Another publishing house then took over the book and the latest edition scheduled is for 250,000 copies, far more than the sale of most best-selling novels. Mr. Faulkner was engaged as agricultural consultant by one of the great radio corporations and today receives more invitations to lecture than he is able to fulfill. In a recent letter I received from him, he wrote, "I have been forced to increase my lecture fee in order to control the demand."

The story of Ed Faulkner is the story of a man with an idea, who stuck to it. It is essentially a success story, almost a fairy tale in its happy ending. The reasons for the success of the book are many. It came out at a time when there was more interest in agriculture than ever before in the history of the nation. It came also at the moment when the agricultural revolution, which has been going on slowly and imperceptibly in America for more than a quarter of a century, was beginning to take form as a fact. It came at a moment when there was an immense and rising wave of popular concern over the conservation of our natural resources, and at a moment when many intelligent farmers were looking for something that they were not getting, either out of the Department of Agriculture or the agricultural colleges, something which had to do with what is perhaps the fundamental fact of our national existence, the soil. I think that is also the reason why there has been so great and widespread a demand for Faulkner to talk to farmer groups.

Not all his readers have been practical dirt farmers; many of them have come from women's garden clubs, and it would be foolish to underestimate the knowledge of garden club members regarding the soil and even agriculture in general. Many of them know far more about soil than most second-rate farmers. And many of Faulkner's readers have come from among the so-called city farmers, whose knowledge and initiative and brains it would also be unwise to underestimate. Most of them are successful in their own fields because they are men of brains, ideas and initiative, and many of them at middle age or later have transferred their brains, energy and initiative from business and professions to the realm of stockbreeding and agriculture.

The city farmer is not content with farming as his grandfather farmed. He does not consider it good enough. City farmers are looking for new and sound ideas in agriculture. They are making experiments of great value which the average dirt farmer is unwilling to make either because the experiments represent financial risks which they dare not take or because they lack the initiative or the energy to make them. It was only natural that *Plowman's Folly* should find many readers in their ranks.

At Malabar we do not agree with all of Faulkner's original theories and since the publication of *Plowman's Folly* he has himself modified some of them. I do believe that he is fundamentally right, that the moldboard plow has wreaked great damage and that it is still doing so. More than that, the type of agriculture and cultivation it induces is largely an unnatural and faulty one. In one sense, the moldboard plow is a short-cut implement. It was designed to do too quickly and too neatly what cannot be done too quickly and too neatly without grave damage in the long run.

Speaking broadly, Mr. Faulkner's case against the plow is that it turns over and buries all protective mulch on the surface of the earth and leaves the soil exposed and bare to the burning sun and invites destructive erosion both by wind and water. More than that he contends that by turning over the surface trash, whether it be weeds, sod, green or animal manure, the moldboard plow packs the surface trash into a narrow layer subject to great pressure both from the weight of the soil above and the weight of the tractor and machinery passing over it. This pressure produces heat and fermentation rather than decay (which is the natural and beneficial process), creates harmful acids and reduces the production and availability of beneficial nitrogen. Still further, the compacted layer of trash serves to create a barrier which prevents moisture from rising from the subsoil below to the roots of the plants growing above and prevents the roots of the plants from seeking the moisture that lies below. At the same time the earth above the compacted layer is left bare to all the drying process by wind and sun, the erosive processes of wind and water, thus creating a condition of artificial drought between the surface of the soil and the compacted layer of organic material below.

With all of that, I think any thinking farmer, indeed anyone familiar with the mysteries of the soil, will agree. I do not believe, however, that the plow can be done away with entirely. On our own farm, where in the garden and the fields we have largely practiced *tillage* as well as plowing, there are cases where the old-fashioned plow is the only implement which can do the job. On our poorer fields on the Bailey Place where bad farming reduced some of the fields to a kind of cement, only an old-fashioned plow can break up the soil and permit the mixing of organic material to improve it. And there are cases where sod is so heavy and tough that it is not possible in terms of labor and time to dispense with the plow. It would require too many days of disking to fit the field for planting. And there are many conditions of soil and of climate which render tillage rather than plowing impractical in commercial farming, at least with any tillage implements now in existence. Nevertheless Mr. Faulkner is right. The plow has done great damage. While we at Malabar are not implacable enemies of the plow, we are enemies of "good plowing," the old-fashioned kind which buries everything and leaves the earth bare as a bone.

The single-crop wheat country was the first to discover that the use of the moldboard plow was rapidly destroying productivity and the soil itself. In the first fortunate years when the soil of the wheat country was deep and virgin and apparently inexhaustible, it was the habit to burn the straw to get it out of the way and then plow the fields, fit them and plant. This process was the perfect example of taking everything from the soil in a single-crop agriculture and returning nothing to it. Nowhere in history, save perhaps in the single-crop cotton and tobacco areas, has mankind made such a record for the destruction of soil as during the first forty or fifty years of wheat farming in this country. Largely speaking, the great wheat area is one of little rainfall, and after a number of years this process of mining the soil brought about a rapid loss of humus, with a consequent rapid decline of production. More than that, with little or no humus, the soil dried out and blew away and the desert storms began in the wheat area just as they had come to China for similar reasons two thousand years earlier. In the thirties, billions of tons of soil from the wheat country were blown eastward to be deposited over cities and farms as far east as the Atlantic Ocean. Obviously, unless something was done, the whole of the great wheat-producing belt was destined to become a desert like the Gobi and large areas of China. And the first step was to do away with the moldboard plow which turned over all protective straw, weeds and trash, and left the soil bare to wind and sun.

Today the soil of nearly all the wheat country is prepared not by plowing but by the use of heavy disks or disk plows which do not turn over the earth and bury the trash but rather chop it up into the soil, leaving a mulch on the surface or chopped *into* the surface which not only prevents the evaporation of the precious rainfall of the wheat country but checks or prevents the blowing or washing away of the soil. Soil Conservation Department experts estimate that the velocity of a fifty-mile wind can be reduced to something under ten miles per hour at the surface of the earth by the presence in the soil of thin, chopped-up mulch. And in the wheat country good farmers no longer burn the straw either in the fields or in the stacks but chop it back into the soil.

The efficiency of this non-plowing surface trash method of preparing the soil in relation to erosion by water has been proved in our own fields many times. In our valley all land is rolling or hilly country and some of our fields cannot be properly contoured or farmed in strips because the hills and slopes are neither wide nor long. They slant in many directions. Nevertheless these fields must produce crops if we are to farm at all and that is where trash-farming has proved a salvation. Our roughest, steepest terrain is kept in permanent bluegrass, white clover pastures. The next steepest fields—the ones *possible* for cultivation—are utilized to grow rotations of alfalfa hay and small grains, in our case, wheat and oats. Only on land which can be strip-farmed or contoured do we grow row crops or soybeans. The middle category of land is protected by hay crops from all erosion but periodically we find it necessary to put in a crop of wheat or oats in order to get a new seeding of hay. In theory the small grains, wheat or oats or barley or rye, protect the soil from erosion in winter or during heavy rains, but we have found that the theory by no means proves itself absolutely, especially during the long winters or before the small grains have grown sufficiently to *cover* the soil and break up the impact of heavy raindrops. I am, of course, speaking of fields which have been *plowed* before seeding to small grains, leaving them bare and without any protection by mulch or chopped-in trash. Always on such fields we have had losses of both rainfall and soil and the formation of small gullies.

Only when we ceased plowing these fields did we find the absolute check to loss of the rainfall and topsoil. The preparation of a field that has been in hay sod by disking is a long and tedious process, sometimes not economically possible from the point of view of time and cost in labor and gasoline and tires. A disk plow, well managed, will do the job of fitting the field without leaving the soil bare, but not so efficiently as we wished. The solution came with the use of a tiller, a kind of cultivator similar to those used in orchard cultivation. It enabled us to rip up the soil without turning it over and without burying the sod, roots and trash. Once or twice over with the disk after the field had been roughly torn up permitted time for the sod to die and left the field with a surface mulch of rotting roots and stems which acted all through the winter as a kind of sponge. *No* water runs off those steeply sloping fields. *No* topsoil is lost and no small gullies form. As a means of checking erosion either by wind or water, the method has, with us, proved absolute.

But there were other advantages, profitable especially upon a farm like ours which consumes large quantities of good hay. The seedings of clover and alfalfa on these fields showed a germination of very nearly 100 per cent as against the 50 per cent or 60 per cent which we were able to obtain on fields plowed and left bare save for the slowly growing winter wheat or even the more rapidly growing oats. This enabled us to cut the expense of clover or alfalfa seedlings by 40 per cent and still we had a thicker and more even stand of seedlings than we were able to obtain on fields that had been plowed. The results were the same whether the seeding was drilled or broadcast. The results have been very nearly the same whether there was plenty of rain or a dry season.

An examination of the surface of the field told its own story. On the fields which had been trash-farmed the whole surface was covered by a mat of decaying vegetation mixed *with* the soil and this served to prevent evaporation and conserve moisture not only in the soil beneath but actually in the mulch itself. Wherever a tiny seed fell, there was moisture enough in the mulch to bring about germination. No seed fell on hard, bare ground dried out by the first day of sun and wind, for there was no hard, bare ground. No seeds were buried too deep or choked by clods of earth. No seeds were washed across the surface of the soil to collect all in one place in a low spot or between the little ridges left by the drilling of the wheat the autumn before. It was evenly distributed, it stayed where it fell, and the mulch always provided *natural* conditions for the germination of alfalfa and clover seed, and Nature in response rewarded us richly.

It is true that in wet seasons or when we made a late and hurried fitting of the soil, not all the sod chopped and ripped into the earth died. We sometimes found timothy or brome grass or even clover and alfalfa growing up with the ripening wheat, making it difficult or impossible to combine the following season. We are not in wheat country and do not raise wheat as a crop save as a means of getting in a moderately profitable extra crop while reseeding a field to hay, and so this fact did not disturb us, especially since the mixture of grass and wheat, cut when the wheat was in the milk, gave us a crop of excellent protein silage far more valuable to a dairy, sheep and beef cattle farm like ours than the wheat itself.

One charge made against trash-farming in the Faulkner way is that it produces an abnormal crop of weeds, and the charge is not without foundation although ground infested with weeds will be *weedy* whether plowed or trash-framed. Seeds of the commonest weeds will lie dormant if buried deep enough by the plow and germinate a year later when the plowing process brings them again to the surface. After combining the wheat or oats on trash-farmed ground there is occasionally a thick crop of weeds which in a wet season threaten at times to choke out clover, timothy, brome grass and alfalfa seedlings. But we have managed to turn this crop of weeds from a menace into a benefit by the use of the mowing machine. One clipping, or at most two, cuts down the weeds before they have reached the seeding stage; and left on the field the clipped weeds provide a mulch for the seedlings, shading the earth from hot wind and sun, keeping it loose and moist to promote the growth of the seedlings before the arrival of winter. The same mulch by insulating the earth tends to keep the ground *frozen* throughout the winter and prevent the alternate freezing and thawing process so disastrous to clover and alfalfa seedlings in the more northern regions. As the clipping process continues year after year the fields actually become almost clear of weeds, a condition I am not altogether certain is good for them.

One discovery in agriculture often leads to another and very often men or women unknown to each other are engaged in making observations and experiments moving in the same general direction, and so we found that while we were making our own experiments with trash-farming and methods which did not employ the conventional plow, others were working in the same direction—Mr. Faulkner in his back yard and his leased two acres; Dr. H. L. Borst in the fields of the United States Soil Conservation Service at Zanesville, Ohio; Christopher Gallup on a small Connecticut farm; men at agricultural colleges in the great wheat factory of the far Middle West; and Mack

Gowdy and a few intelligent "live" farmers in the South.

The experiments in trash-farming led us into discoveries regarding the best way to grow alfalfa in our part of America. In the past we had been taught that in order to grow alfalfa it was necessary to make a careful preparation of the ground, adding lime and phosphate gradually sometimes over a period as long as three or four years before seeding. Next we were taught that the way to plant it was to prepare a powder-fine seedbed and make the seeding in late August or September on ground that had been plowed and left bare.

We never had any success with this method, perhaps because the light soil of our glacial hills dried out too much during the hot months of late summer. I have rarely seen a really good crop of alfalfa grown by this method in rolling or hilly country, but only in bottom land where there is enough moisture to insure germination, but on such ground, the alfalfa, which insists on good drainage, often suffered later on by being drowned out when the rains of spring and winter came along. Also, having made only a feeble growth by the time our winter came along, the young plants were decimated by the process of freezing, thawing and "heaving" out of the ground.

This method of alfalfa culture was the traditional one in the dry and irrigated lands of the West where alfalfa first became a profitable commercial crop, where drainage was good and moisture could be controlled and where there was, in most regions, little or no winter and the problem of "heaving" was nonexistent. Apparently, it had never occurred to the men to whom it should have occurred that the culture of alfalfa might be a quite different problem in Ohio and in California. In any case, the farmers of Ohio went on struggling to grow alfalfa in the "California way," sometimes, when all the conditions of moisture and weather were right, with success—more often without, until many of them came to abandon alfalfa altogether although, intelligently, they recognized its great value as the finest of protein hay with the possible exception of the virtually unknown Ladino.

At Malabar we found the whole business disturbing. In the first place the whole approved process seemed artificial in a country where the rainfall was well distributed and other legumes, notably the clovers, flourished naturally along the roadside. I had a personal theory with which Max, with his agricultural college education, did not agree. It was a revolutionary one to be sure—simply that alfalfa, being virtually the nearest relative to the common sweet clover which flourished on the clay of any open roadside cut in our country, was a natural in Ohio if treated properly, and that it was really a "poor land" crop and a soil improver. I did not believe that all the fuss and bother was necessary to grow good crops of alfalfa. More than that, I suspected that all the pampering was unnatural and actually harmful.

At the same time Dr. Borst at Zanesville was working along the same lines, quietly, without announcing his results until he became sure of them. Without any direct scientific experimentation, but only by observation we on our side began to arrive at the same results he was achieving. We did it by watching the fields, the fence rows and roadsides, where alfalfa grew as easily as our native sweet clover if it was simply *let alone*.

We discovered that a spring seeding, rather than one made in late summer or autumn, done simply as we made seedings of clover, but on trash-farmed fields rather than on the bare, plowed soil, achieved results. We knew that lime and phosphorus were considered essential and helped, but presently we made another startling discovery—that alfalfa would thrive on poor soil in *our* county even *without* applications of lime and phosphorus; in other words that in our county it was definitely a poor soil crop. Poor soil to be sure is relative and the subsoil of our glacial hills all the way through is potentially good soil as compared to many subsoils elsewhere. Nevertheless, the field we chose for the "accidental experiment" was the worst field on the four farms. Owned impersonally through a defaulted mortgage by a bank in a distant town, it had been rented out to the first comer for nearly twenty years, with everything taken off it and nothing put back until even the neighbors no longer found the fifty acres worth farming at a rental price of five dollars a year.

Our discovery came about as an accident as so many discoveries in agriculture have come about. We set out merely to put the weed-grown field in order by plowing under in the spring the accumulated mess of goldenrod, wild carrot, other weeds and even sumac which had taken over. It was impossible to do a good job of plowing because of the accumulated trash, and the weedy sod stood on edge behind the plow rather than falling over to bury the trash. This troubled Kenneth who did the job because he was ashamed of not doing what in our neighborhood was accepted as "good plowing," which meant that *everything* was buried and the earth left free and bare of all trash. As it turned out, the "bad plowing" which troubled Kenneth was a very "fortunate accident" and in connection with other accidents and experiments finally convinced us that the traditional clean "good plowing" of our neighborhood was, so far as we were concerned, the worst kind of plowing.

In order to whip the rough, weedy field into shape we disked it roughly with the spring tooth following the disk. The results were not good so far as "fitting" went. The seedbed was rough and trashy but we only wanted to get the field in order and as it was already late in the season we hastily drilled in a seeding of oats. Immediately afterward we broadcast a seeding of the legumes we had left in the seed bin. We hoped, not too optimistically, to get a cover crop of legumes which we could plow under as the first stage in the rehabilitation of the field. Fortunately the contents of the seed bin was mostly alfalfa with a little red clover and a little mammoth clover, a little alsike and a little brome grass. In order to get the seeding the best opportunity the seed was inoculated with nitrogen-fixing bacteria. The oats were given in drilling the average amount of fertilizer, nitrogen, potassium, phosphorus in the hope that we should get a crop that would be worth combining.

All the conditions were as far apart as possible from the traditional instructions on seeding and growing alfalfa. One natural element was in our favor—that we had plenty of rainfall after the seeding and the percentage of germination was high, especially since the seeding was made while the ground was still open and the seeds worked their way into the soil with first rain. But germination did not necessarily mean success; seed will germinate in damp cotton or in pure, moist sand. The real problem was whether the tiny seedlings could find in that poor soil the elements necessary to grow into sturdy, hay-producing, soil-improving plants.

The moisture helped them to a good start. The soil was so poor that the oats were not worth combining and we left them in the field, to ripen or die, eventually leaving a residue of broken and rotting oats straw above and among the alfalfa and clover seedlings.

As the summer progressed, the seedlings, especially the red clover, made an astonishing growth, wholly inexplicable in view of the poorness of the soil and the lack of lime. No doubt the excellent moisture contributed to the growth and the trash left on the field by the "poor plowing" job conserved moisture and, in decaying, provided nitrogen until the seedlings had established their own nitrogen-fixing nodules. In any case, by autumn there was a rich growth of legumes over the whole field to the height of eight or nine inches. Mixed with it there was a large amount of ragweed which led us again to suspect some sort of affinity between ragweed and clover which benefited the clover, some beneficial influence beyond the mere fact that the ragweed provided a certain amount of shade and protection to the young seedlings during the hot weeks of August and early September.

Despite the agreeable outlook, we knew our problem of alfalfa as a poor land crop had not yet been solved. There was still the winter to be passed, with its perpetual freezing and thawing, which could cut our prospective crop in half by heaving the plants out of the ground.

The winter of 1940 was one of the hardest I have ever known. Freezing and thawing alternated during most of the weeks of the whole season and by spring some of our best fields of clover or mixed hay were white with the roots which had been forced out of the ground by the variations of temperature. Oddly, the poor field, where our unconventional operations took place, suffered not at all. There was *no* heaving and our seeding came through as thick as it had been at the beginning of the winter.

Looking for the answer in the field itself, we arrived at a theory which during the three years since has proven infallible. It was this—that the decaying oat straw left in the field, the residue of ragweed stalks and the dead vegetation of the clover and alfalfa plants which were not clipped had provided a mat of mulch over the whole field, covering the roots of the plants and acting as an insulator to check the freeze-thaw process which had been so disastrous in other *well plowed* bare fields with much better soil. In other words, the earth itself had become frozen early in December and it *remained* frozen throughout the bad winter because the mulch of dead and decaying vegetation prevented any warm spell or burst of sunlight from reaching the soil and thawing it.

The field by hay-cutting time revealed a thick, vigorous stand of red and mammoth clover and alfalfa and we cut some of our finest hay from it, although we were a little disappointed that there appeared to be much more clover than alfalfa. There was no ragweed whatever. At the second cutting, however, the alfalfa showed up. There was a little clover and about the right amount of brome grass, and a thick stand of alfalfa, not 100 per cent, but an extraordinary stand considering the fact that we had violated all the rules. The thick growth we did not cut for hay but pastured lightly, permitting the beef cattle to cover the field fairly thoroughly with droppings and urine. The field went into the winter with the decaying mat of vegetation still in evidence between the alfalfa plants.

The following winter was less difficult than the preceding one and again the field came through with no loss from heaving. In the second year the alfalfa plants had increased in size sending out ten or twelve stems of new growth where in the field year there had been only six or seven stems. The red clover was nearly choked out. The brome grass remained and here again there appeared to be some affinity between the brome grass and the alfalfa. Apparently they liked living together and each contributed something to the health and vigor of the other. Despite the loss of the clover from the field, the yield from the thickening brome grass and alfalfa gave us more hay than in the preceding year.

Then came a remarkable discovery. In walking over the field in late May of the following year Bob and I discovered something neither of us had ever seen before in a field of mixed hay. On the by now virtually decayed surface mulch between the alfalfa plants there had appeared millions of tiny seedlings of red clover and alfalfa. As the summer progressed, they continued to grow and we made our first cutting of hay early in order to let in the sun and encourage the growth of the volunteer seedlings. Wherever the alfalfa had developed into a 100 per cent stand the seedlings were choked out but where the stand was thinnish the seedlings developed into sturdy plants and actually *thickened* the stand of mixed hay in the third year by the production of young new plants.

Whence these new seedlings in an established stand of alfalfa came from I do not know. I only know that they appeared, that some grew into mature plants and increased the stand. Either they were seeds from the original sowing which remained dormant for a period of time or they were seeds from the alfalfa plants already established which seems unlikely in view of the history of the field with two hay cuttings and a light pasturing in the late summer season. Also any theory that they were distributed by birds is unlikely in view of the perfectly even distribution of the new seedlings over the entire field. I do know that I have never observed the appearance of seedlings in such extraordinary numbers in fields of alfalfa where the ground was prepared in the conventional fashion and left bare to the elements. It seems true beyond much doubt that the mulch of oat straw, dead ragweed and unclipped clover growth, provided a damp layer of decaying vegetation which encouraged germination and growth, by keeping the soil below moist and cool in summer and immune to the evil results of freezing and thawing in winter.

The observations led to other speculations for which we have been unable to find definitive answers. Had the poor land ragweed, for example, any effect upon the vigorous growth of the original seeding and ultimate germination of dormant seeds? Could it be that ragweed in itself possessed soil-restoring qualities or some special affinity for legumes? During the first seedling season, it served to shade and protect the seedlings and vanished utterly during the second season. Does ragweed, which flourishes in poor soil and on bare fields, have a place in the natural scheme of things for the improvement and restoration of run-down land? Does the ragweed produce any vitamin, hormone or acid which stimulates germination? Did the distribution of animal manure and urine over the whole field during a period of pasturing provide hormones, vitamins or other organic animal gland secretions, which stimulated not only growth of the adult plants but the germination of dormant and reluctant seeds?

Certain things we know—that the experiment had the

benefit of good rain distribution and that the *apparent* absence of lime and phosphorus from the thin leached-out topsoil did not prevent the establishment of a fine stand of alfalfa on poor land. It is highly probable that the favorable growing season and the thinness or absence of any real topsoil permitted the roots to thrust their way quickly into the subsoil of our glacial hills where the plants found, in the great mountains of glacial soil scraped across half the American continent, not only lime and phosphorus but all the other elements, down to trace minerals, which they needed for growth and health. This speculation is both interesting and important in view of the fact that the stand of alfalfa has always been remarkably healthy and free of any of the diseases which can attack alfalfa subject to malnutrition or lack of a balanced soil diet. The fact remains that a wretched field produced for us an excellent stand of alfalfa and brome grass, from which we have made three cuttings a year of excellent hay for three years, without any sign of weakening the stand.

All of these speculations are largely, of course, in the realm of things not yet discovered or determined by scientists and may well lead to new and important ideas concerning agriculture. A few men are already working on them, confronted by an opposition based upon complacency, conservatism and in some cases, ignorance.

So far as we at Malabar were concerned, the rather carelessly initiated "accident" proved two things—that so far as our Ohio land was concerned the whole traditional culture of alfalfa was wrong and wrong fundamentally because the whole process—the powder-thin seedbed, the late summer sowing, the exposure of the immature seedlings to the damage of freezing and thawing through the long Ohio winters, the growing of alfalfa as a single crop (without the ragweed, the brome grass and even the red clover) was unnatural and in actual contradiction to the natural habits of alfalfa. What struck us as important was that the whole of the process we used was a natural one— the seeding, the ragweed, the rough plowing and careless fitting, the natural protective mulch, even the pasturing part of the process. Save that we have substituted tiller and disk for plow in fitting the fields, we have used the same process since then in establishing alfalfa and the results have been uniformly excellent. The only changes have been that we have added lime and occasionally phosphorus although I am not yet convinced that with the quantity and quality of the glacial subsoil peculiar to our region this was absolutely necessary. It has very likely hastened the growth and stimulated the health of the alfalfa.

It was a part of this field which by necessity became incorporated in wheatland when new strips and contours were laid out. The wheat sown in the ground which had been a part of this field grew rich and dark green and yielded three times as much wheat as the ground adjoining it. The line between the good wheat on the plowed-up alfalfa ground and the sickly wheat on the ground of the poor field adjoining was as straight and clean as if drawn by a surveyor. The alfalfa had undoubtedly added much nitrogen to the soil, but there were other questions involved. How much and what had been contributed by the ragweed, the decaying, natural mulch left on the field and the manure and urine of the herd of beef cattle? Was it possible too that the roots of the alfalfa thrusting deep into the minerally rich subsoils brought up from below valuable elements and trace minerals which, fixed in its roots, stems and leaves, refertilized and revitalized the worn-out soil above when the field was cultivated again and the roots and stems left to decay? There remains also the question of the bacteria closely associated with all legumes and especially with the deep-thrusting roots of alfalfa and sweet clover. Beyond fixing nitrogen could they not have had some other revitalizing effect on the worn-out soil? In any case, the fertility of the poorest field on the farm had been increased almost beyond belief within the short span of two years.

The experiment and subsequent variations of it have proven that in our part of the world alfalfa is both a poor land crop and an impressive soil-restoring crop. For us the discovery has been of great economic importance for it permitted us to utilize our steep poor land to grow one of the most valuable of crops for a livestock farm and at the same time to refresh and revitalize our land with a minimum of expenditure of cash for fertilizers. On the roadside and fence rows of Malabar there is ample evidence that the natural way of growing alfalfa in our country was the right way. Wherever seeds of alfalfa have dropped accidentally, alfalfa has sprung up and has grown as lustily as its cousin the sweet clover, without fuss or interference. Some of the plants are already five years old. The earth in which they grow was never plowed but each year it is mulched by the death and decay of the natural vegetation around it.

In the meanwhile, Dr. Borst of Zanesville announced, after seven years of tests, the results of his own experiments, conducted far more conclusively and scientifically than our own fumbling efforts. Dr. Borst, as a scientist, knew what he was driving at; we only observed results and drew our own conclusions from them. Dr. Borst proved beyond a doubt that, in our climate and in soil reasonably related in character to our own, alfalfa was a poor land crop and as much at home on poor soil that had been given lime and phosphorus as its cousin, the sweet clover. He has succeeded beyond any doubt in raising fine crops of alfalfa on miserably poor, hilly land merely by disking weeds, wire grass, poverty grass, broom sedge and other rubbish and sowing alfalfa on the trash mulch after application of lime and phosphate. His discovery is of immense value not only to the farmers of Ohio but of much larger sections of the country where for twenty-five years or more farmers have been persistently instructed in exactly the wrong way to grow alfalfa.

The benefits of a mulch on any field of clover or alfalfa or mixed hay have been proved on our previously established hay seedings where the straw, falling behind the grain combine, was left on the fields. This action was taken originally to leave the straw on the fields to decay and to be plowed under eventually in order to increase the humus content of our worn-out fields. That result was achieved but we soon found that the straw mulch benefited the hay crop as well by keeping the soil moist and cool during the hot months and by acting as an insulating layer to keep the ground frozen all through the winter and thus prevent the destructive heaving process. Not only were our seedings more successful on fields where the straw was left, but the hay yield was greater and the length of life of the existing crop as productive hay was greatly increased.

Leaving straw on the fields meant of course that we should be short of bedding for the livestock, but that shortage we managed to overcome by doing custom work among our neighbors with our pickup baler. By baling straw on shares we brought

straw onto the fields rather than selling it off them as had been done in the past. Nor did we feel that in the process we were robbing our neighbors for in almost every case straw piles after threshing were either burned or allowed to rot, although good farming practice could have put it back on the fields or worked it out through the barns in large quantities in the form of manure. This, however, was not the traditional practice and all but a few of our neighbors regarded the redistribution of straw over the fields after harvest as a waste of time and a foolish practice. That tradition accounts for the waning humus content and fertility of many farms in our country and elsewhere in America. By baling the straw we made it more convenient to handle and actually induced neighboring farmers to use more bedding and work more straw by way of stables and manure spreaders onto the fields.

The value of mulch in gardens has long been recognized by good gardeners both of flowers and of vegetables. It is valuable not only as a means of producing better and healthier blooms or vegetables, but is actually a great saver of labor since it does away largely with cultivation by hoe or cultivator and if used thickly enough actually smothers out weeds. Growing tomatoes under mulch is an easy and profitable practice known to most amateur gardeners. Straw mulch on strawberries serves not only to keep the fruit clean; it has perhaps a more important purpose, until lately overlooked or regarded merely as incidental—that of keeping the soil about the roots of the berries cool and moist and loose, thus producing more berries and berries of better quality. The natural habitat of the wild strawberry is on partly shaded banks heavily mulched by natural accumulation of leaves, and its cultivated and highly developed cousin, the commercial strawberry, has not yet come to like or to tolerate hot, dry, bare earth about its roots.

Since we have available large quantities of manure in many forms and very often hay or straw left over at the end of the feeding season, we gradually extended mulch culture in the communal garden at Malabar to crops such as lettuce, broccoli, celery, peas, carrots, cantaloupe, sweet potatoes and other common vegetables. The results were the same in every case—that productivity, quality and flavor were all improved.

The answer lay beneath our own eyes and feet. On lifting

the mulch on a day during the hot, dry weeks of August, the soil beneath was found to be cool, moist and loose from the surface all the way down into the subsoil—far looser and more open to the thrust of roots than any soil worked by hoe or cultivator. More than that, the moisture made available to the plants chemicals and elements which are not available to them in hot, dry soils, and encouraged the natural processes of decay and the growth and increase of the bacteria which promotes that process. Also beneath the mulch there was always a notable population of earthworms, where in dry, hot, cultivated soil there were none. It is probable that the earthworms, moving upward and downward between the subsoil and the topsoil in which the vegetables thrust their roots, brought with them, in gizzard and body, minerals and trace elements from the almost inexhaustible supply in the glacial subsoil into the topsoil where they are constantly being consumed or leached out, especially by the action of heavy rainfall on bare, exposed, *cultivated* soils. Naturally, on the mulched portions of the garden there is no runoff water and no erosion whatever. As a supplementary benefit, all the organic material used as mulch is left on the soil to be plowed under or chopped into the soil in the following season, thus increasing greatly the humus as well as the nitrogen and mineral content. The process of mulching is not only beneficial in an immediate sense but for its great cumulative value season after season.

The virtues of mulch were evident to us not only in the natural process we used in growing alfalfa and in the vegetable gardens but in many other instances of farming and horticulture. In the very first year of the operations at Malabar, a plantation of red raspberries was established as part of the self-sufficiency program. They were put out in rows and clean-cultivated according to the traditional method in a part of the vegetable garden. The soil was free of weeds, of mulch, of surface humus, and from the first the raspberries were sickly and unproductive and subject to attack from insects.

We were on the point of giving up the cultivation of red raspberries altogether as not worth the labor of cultivation, spraying and dusting, when the idea occurred to me that the whole method of intensely *cultivating* raspberries was idiotic. In our country the wild black raspberry abounds but it grows never in a bare cultivated field but only in shaded fence rows and on the borders of the woods where the canes are partly shaded and the earth covered by a thick mulch of decaying leaf mold beneath which the soil is always loose, moist, cool and rich in humus.

Taking the habits of native wild raspberries as a model we made a new plantation in the semi-shade of the old orchard behind the Big House, less than five hundred yards from the old cultivated sickly plantation. When we came to the farm the old orchard had been cultivated in row crops and was badly eroded. The soil itself had been in much worse condition than that in the old garden where the original sickly plantation was made. During the first year of operation, we managed to get a good grass cover by sowing the eroded orchard with Ladino clover and orchard grass. Those then were the conditions of soil when we made the new raspberry plantation in the old orchard.

No preparation of the soil whatever was made. Holes were dug in the orchard grass sod and the canes planted in them and the whole plantation mulched heavily with barnyard manure. Most of the canes were fresh from the nursery but a few from the sickly plantation were used to fill out the last rows. We knew the risk of mixing the sickly canes from the old plantation with the healthy, uninfected new ones from the nursery but, in a way, that was a part of the experiment. We wanted to see what would happen.

The case history has been startlingly successful. No hoe or cultivator has ever touched the new plantation in the orchard. Once a year it has been mulched heavily with barnyard manure. Beyond that and the slight task of cutting away old canes there has been no labor expended on the plantation, not even any dusting or spraying.

From the first the plantation flourished. It is now in the fourth year of bearing and it is impossible to produce more raspberries on the same amount of ground. There are no weeds, for the mulch and the rank growth of the berry canes has choked them out. The new uninfected canes from the nursery have never become diseased from the canes brought in from the sickly plantation. What is perhaps even more remarkable, the new shoots springing from the roots of the sickly canes have thrown off all disease and are as healthy as their neighbors.

The two plantations, the sickly and the healthy one, are visited by the same birds and the same bees from the thirty hives near by.

The old sickly plantation we have kept on merely as a check patch and contrast to the mulched but uncultivated and healthy plantation in the half-shady orchard. Because the old plantation had no value save as an exhibit of how *not* to grow raspberries, we ceased to cultivate it and in three years it grew weedy and accumulated a mulch of its own from dying and decaying vegetation. But the remarkable thing about the old plantation is that with its abandonment to the *natural* process of growth, its health has improved and each year in its half-wild uncultivated state it displays a little more vigor and produces a few more berries and new canes.

I am not, of course, suggesting that it would be profitable to grow weeds along with raspberries. I am only suggesting out of a rather startling experience that man, by following the *natural* process and perhaps accentuating it (by heavy mulch and the fertility values of barnyard manure) can save himself labor and produce bumper crops of raspberries. For the second plantation we did nothing but reproduce the natural conditions under which the native wild black raspberry flourished, with the added stimulus of the nitrogen, potassium and phosphorus contained in the manure. Beyond that, of course, we came into the realm of more or less undiscovered values of the bacteria, the hormones and the vitamins contributed by the barnyard animals themselves out of their own physiological processes. There is also to be considered the cool temperature and the loose, moist condition of the soil surrounding the roots of the raspberries in the healthy plantation. And there is the question of earthworms which exist in large quantities in the same loose, cool soil. They are in some part attracted and their growth stimulated by a considerable amount of lost or undigested grain in the manure which in the natural process of fermentation turns to sugar and provides for the worms a rich diet.

A neighbor of ours, Cosmos Bluebaugh, one of the best farmers in America and famous throughout our state, who has large commercial plantations of black raspberries, now grows them in the same fashion with infinitely less work and much greater health and production. He discovered the virtues of the mulch system because he is a "live" farmer and noticed that where shoots from his cultivated berries found their way into a fence row and "went wild," the canes were healthier and more productive and that with them spraying or dusting for insects or disease was unnecessary. After a few experiments he went over to the "natural" method of growing raspberries once and for all. He no longer cultivates his berries. Twice a season the weeds and grass between the rows are clipped and left on the ground as a mulch. This has kept the earth cool and moist and has checked absolutely all loss of soil or water by runoff. But as in the case of alfalfa both our neighbor and ourselves had been taught to grow raspberries in exactly the wrong way and at a cost of much labor, of insecticides and pocketbook. Nature's way was much more simple and effective.

And then there is the case of the two plum trees which were planted about fifty feet from the house and not more than twenty feet apart where in season one could pick off a green-gage to eat in passing by. Both trees came from the same nursery; both were greengages and both were planted in the same soil at the top edge of a steep well-drained bank. In the second year one of the trees (No. 1) showed a remarkable growth of two or three inches more at the tip of all its branches than the other tree (No. 2). The same record of No. 1 continued in the third year. It far surpassed the other (No. 2) in growth and vigor. In the third year I stumbled upon what appeared to be the answer.

I was putting in jonquil bulbs in the heavy grass sod of the bank one evening in September. It was hard work for the sod was heavy and the ground dry and hard. Each thrust put a strain on the wrist. Unconsciously and without observing my progress as I planted I worked my way toward plum tree No. 1. Suddenly when I was about a yard from the tree the trowel entered the earth with the greatest ease, burying itself up to the handle from the force I had been using elsewhere on the hard hillside to make an impression. It was only then that I discovered how close I was to the flourishing tree. The discovery I made next was a simple one.

At some time when we were making improvements in the garden, someone had heaped clumps of unwanted sod lazily about the roots of the newly planted tree (No. 1). As the sod at the bottom of the heap decayed, fresh grass grew on the top so

that the accumulation about the roots of the tree passed un-
noticed, save for the evidence of its presence in the accentuated
and vigorous growth of the tree above. It was only now, two
years later, on that hot, dry August day that I discovered the
accidentally accumulated layer of mulch. Beneath it the soil
was loose and very moist. The finest of roots could push their
way through and the moisture made available whatever elements of growth were present. An investigation of the earth beneath the slow-growing tree (No. 2) where there was no mulch,
revealed earth as hard and as dry as the rest of the sun-beaten
bank.

In this case the fertility elements of barnyard manure were
wholly lacking. The mulch was pure sod yet its effect was strik-
ingly noticeable. Here in the small area scarcely a dozen feet
away beneath tree No. 1 the earth revealed earthworms. A foot
away in the dry, hard un-mulched soil there were none.

Of course the value of mulch to orchardists has long been
recognized. Our friend Bluebaugh who has one of the finest orchards of peaches and apples I know anywhere, does not use either orchard cultivator or ordinary mulch of straw and old hay;
he uses his best alfalfa and feels that he makes money by doing
so, not only from the ordinary beneficial effects of mulch in
looseness and moisture of the soil, but from the contribution of
the added nitrogen from the highly nitrogenous alfalfa. Only
last summer we used some of a weather-spoiled hay cutting
from a field of mixed alfalfa and Ladino as a mulch on our small
commercial orchard. Bob took time out during the busy hay-
making season to distribute a couple of bales about the roots of
one tree. He did this only in July but the effect even two months
later was striking. The single tree mulched with alfalfa and
Ladino stood out dark green and vigorous from among the others on the hillside. The difference was noticeable at a distance
of five hundred yards or more.

We are able today to carry about three times the number of
cattle we were able to carry on the same fields when we first
came to Malabar. A large part of this is due to the application of
lime and phosphorus, but again one of the important elements
is mulch and humus. Both bluegrass and white clover, which
are the basic plants of our pastures, like most plants flourish
best in cool, moist soil. The is especially true of bluegrass which

has acquired the bad reputation of going into a dormant state, sulking and refusing to grow at all during the hot weeks of mid- and late summer. It is a reputation which I believe is not altogether deserved. It has been imposed upon the bluegrass largely because of careless and unintelligent treatment.

In the past and even today the average farmer chooses for his permanent pasture the land which he finds the least valuable on his farm. Mistakenly, he does not regard pasture as a crop but usually as wasteland where he can turn his cattle in summer and let them feed themselves. In some parts of the country there are permanent pastures more than one hundred or one hundred and fifty years old which have been neglected and overgrazed every year of their existence with the result that they become dormant and unproductive during the hot months and gradually are overrun by ironweed, thistles, sumac and wild thorn.

Gradually, through years of draining calcium and phosphorus from the soil (for animals do not return to the soil as manure and urine *all* the minerals they consume but carry off quantities as bone and flesh), both the quantity and quality of the pasture declines. But another element equally important in the decline of productive pasture is often overlooked and that is the gradual destructive loss of humus and mulch. Through overgrazing no grass is left to wither and decay and add its contribution of humus and mulch to the cycle which produced our deep prairie soils and our best virgin pastures. With the natural cycle destroyed, the roots of bluegrass and other grasses gradually become bare or at best remain covered thinly by bare, hard, dry soil. Under such conditions the bluegrass goes into a dormant stage until the cool weather and rains of the autumn season start it to growing once more. This means a loss of good and valuable pasture to the farmer for a period of from six to eight weeks during the summer months, a loss represented in dollars and cents, in lessened milk production for the dairy and the beef breeding cows with calves, and a loss rather than a gain in the weight of beef stock.

The bluegrass and other grasses cease to grow not because it is their habit to do so during the hot months but largely because an artificial and uncongenial condition is produced by bad farming practices.

One of the worst of traditional farming practices, now happily dying out except in the most benighted and poverty-stricken areas of the South, was the burning over of pastures in the winter or spring of each year. This was done in the short-sighted and ignorant belief that the burning made clean and earlier pasture. The illusion was created by the almost unhealthy greenness of the first grass on burned-over land. It was unnaturally green because the potassium through the ashes of the burnt-over dead grass was released all at once instead of gradually through the natural process of decay. After only a year or two of the burning process all humus and mulch was destroyed and the tender roots left bare to wind and snow and sun. The grass went dormant at the season when it was most needed and eventually died and was replaced by poverty grass or the coarse and unwanted Johnson grass. In the West and Southwest millions of acres of the richest natural legume and grass-grazing areas in the world have been destroyed by over-grazing and burning over and the destruction of all natural humus and mulch.

Since our livestock is in the fields for more than six months of the year we have always regarded our pasture as one of the most important crops in the farm economy. In relation to the production of milk, beef, wool and mutton, our pasture land to-day represents as a crop a greater value per acre than any corresponding acre of corn, wheat, soybeans or other cultivated crops, save perhaps alfalfa alone.

It was not so when we came to the farm. Save in the bottom lands the pasture was thin and in places there was no bluegrass or white clover at all but only wire grass and poverty grass. All the bluegrass went dormant for a period of from six to eight weeks. Even in the bottom pasture where the amount of underground moisture was much higher, the bluegrass stopped growing during the hot weeks.

Almost at once we started treatment of the worn-out pastures by the application of ground limestone and phosphates. Where the pasture was poorest and we wanted quick action the more expensive hydrated lime was used. The bald spots covered with poverty and wire grass were given light coatings of precious animal manure as well and Dutch clover and Ladino clover were seeded. Slowly, as the calcium and the phosphorus began to be available, the clover began to grow and as it restored the nitrogen to the soil the bluegrass moved in. The manure not only added fertility but the decaying, leached-out straw provided mulch for the young seedlings. After two or three years the effects of the treatment became evident everywhere in increased and thickened growth of both bluegrass and white clover.

But another practice contributed enormously to the restoration of our pastures; that was the practice of mowing the pastures twice a summer, once in late July and once in early September. In theory the practice killed weeds and brambles and promoted a new growth of young and succulent grass. Actually the greatest benefit of the mowing process was the gradual building up of a layer of mulch and humus through the accumulation of the decaying clippings. Each year as the layer increases we have more pasture all through the weeks when once the bluegrass ceased growing altogether. It was not the clipping process in itself which produced the new growth; it was the steadily increasing layer of mulch-humus which insulated the soil from wind and hot sun and kept the ground cool and moist and loose. As with the alfalfa and clovers it insulated the earth from varying changes of temperature in winter and prevented "freezing out." We had done no more than to restore the natural cycle in the life of the bluegrass.

Today we are able to carry three times as many cattle and sheep on the same ground as when we first began the treatments and during the hot, dry months there is always a supply of fresh and succulent grass, not so much as in the growing seasons of spring and autumn but a considerable growth where we had none before. Our cattle grow and put on weight steadily throughout the summer and the milk production has been kept up even during the fly season. The beef cattle come off pasture looking as if they had been fed on grain and the finishing-off process is shortened by many weeks of feeding and labor and countless bushels of corn.

Treating pasture as a valuable crop has paid big dividends in all directions. In the future we shall have even better returns, for not all the pasture has yet reached that peak which we hope to maintain simply by restoring the natural processes in the growth of grass. The struggle to find adequate labor in wartime has held back the whole process of restoration.

The greatest lack we found in the run-down farms which went into the making of Malabar was the lack of humus or organic material, and the same condition holds true for most of the worn-out agricultural land in America. Even in an agricultural area so fabulously rich as the delta region of Mississippi crop yields have been declining through the steady decrease of humus. I had a letter not long ago from one of the biggest planters of the area saying that he observed that his soil was slowly becoming hard and impervious. The reason, he was certain, lay in the fact that for a hundred years or more, the only organic material returned to the soil had been the hard woody stalks of the eternal cotton. Our problem was to return to the soil as rapidly as possible and in the largest quantity possible this missing humus. Without it, the most expensive and concentrated commercial fertilizer would have been of little value. We were eager to bring up the productivity of the land, both pasture and cultivated land as rapidly as possible, but we were also determined to accomplish this by a system which recognized the fact that the average farmer was forced to grow a crop from his land *while* he was restoring it since there were always interest, taxes, seed and fertilizer costs to be paid. So the problem resolved itself into how to restore land while producing one crop a year off it which would as far as possible pay the expenses of the upkeep and the process itself.

We found a formula by which we are able to build approximately one inch or more of good topsoil a year *while* producing crops from the land. To this system Mr. Faulkner's theories made an important contribution. It is a system in which *both* trash-farming and the use of the moldboard plow play their parts. There is in it nothing unusual and nothing which is not known to any good *"live"* farmer. We have simply put the elements together in a special pattern by which the maximum results are obtainable. It is a concentrated, high-pressure system, which is in no sense a short cut that would in the long run be profitless. It employs the methods by which Nature originally built our topsoil, simply speeding up the process about a hundred thousand times. I set it forth here because we have tried it and succeeded in building six to seven inches of good topsoil in five years while growing crops on the same land.

For the sake of simplicity I shall take one field, or rather one contoured strip 150 feet wide and about an eighth of a mile in length.

This strip was a part of the farm. The whole of the field represented a problem for it consisted of low hills or mounds with the slopes running in all directions. Nowhere save in the low hollows where the topsoil from the higher parts of the field had been deposited was the topsoil more than two or three inches deep. In spots there was none at all. Below this lay the glacial moraine, a mixture of clay, sand and gravel which in itself was good potential subsoil but which was completely devoid of humus or organic material of any kind. It was what we at Malabar call "dead soil" without earthworms, bacteria or life of any sort of the kind which flourishes in the presence of humus.

When we took over the farm the whole of the rolling field was being treated as a *square* field so that there were always parts of it plowed up and down hill and when planted in row crops, the furrows between the rows each became small gullies carrying off water and topsoil from the crests and slopes into the hollows or off the fields and carrying flooding rains into the creek near by. The fall before we took over, the field had been seeded to wheat by a predecessor and the wheat drilled up and down hill. Even with wheat as a cover crop, the roots did not hold the melting snow and the runoff water from rains since the check rows ran up and down hill. Wherever the slope was steep the surface of the earth was covered with small gullies, none more than two or three inches deep, but each one carrying off water and topsoil. Save in the hollows and low spots the wheat was thin and poor.

In the spring we seeded the whole of the field with a mixture of legumes—mammoth and alsike and Ladino clover. During the winter we limed as much of it as we were able. Part of the wheat was not worth combining but where there was wheat worth harvesting we combined it and left the straw on the ground. The legume seeding was spotty. Where we had limed, the mammoth clover made a good growth and in the damper hollows where the good topsoil had accumulated the alsike did well, but the Ladino seemed to adapt itself to all conditions. It grew in the damp, low, rich ground, on the bare crests and slopes, on the ground which was limed or not limed. Over the whole of the field there was a fair cover of legumes but not worth too much as hay.

In the autumn of that year, Hecker, our friend from the Soil Conservation Service, helped us to strip and contour the rolling field as effectively as possible. It was clear that our first job was to stop runoff water and erosion. Thus strip No. 1 came into being. It ran the whole length of the long field, most of it across a fairly steep slope. At the time it was laid out the worn-out ground was covered by a thin seeding of mammoth and sweet clover, alsike and Ladino, with part of it covered with the thin straw left behind the combine and part with the whole wheat which was too poor to combine still standing. There were a good many weeds of all kinds.

That autumn or rather early in September we plowed the whole of the strip. The season was dry and the ground, devoid of any humus, was hard and the plowing was again, fortunately, a "poor job," for the slope and the hardness of the soil prevented the plow from turning over and *burying* the rubbish and the legume seedlings. After it was disked the result was a rough field with rubbish, legume seedlings and wheat straw chopped up together. Into this we drilled wheat simply to get strip No. 1 in shape for further restoration work. Although the season was dry, the wheat came along beautifully and many, perhaps as many as 60 per cent, of the legume seedlings of the new seeding survived and grew. During the winter the whole of the strip was limed and given a thin coat of barnyard manure.

Several things were noticeable during the winter. (1) With the wheat drilled on contour instead of up and down hill, there was no tendency on the slope for the water to create small gullies, and none appeared. (2) The field, having been *roughly* prepared, was filled with hollows and ridges and covered with lumps of earth the size of a hen's egg or larger which disintegrated to powder-fine earth under the freezing and thawing action of the winter. All this served to collect and hold the water and prevent runoff or erosion. (3) Because the plowing job had been a "poor" one the soil was not bare. Chopped up into it were the weeds, old straw and legumes, some still alive and growing. This condition, too, served to hold the rain water and check erosion. But the most notable effect was the feel of the soil itself. When you walked over it, it was *springy* under the feet from the presence in the soil of decaying straw and rubbish which had been mixed *into* soil instead of being buried. When one walked over the field the year before it was like walking over a cement pavement from which all the water ran off. During this second winter the surface of the whole field was like blotting paper. It held *all* the rain and checked *all* erosion.

The effects showed on the wheat yield. From the very beginning of spring it was evident that despite the fact that we used no more fertilizer than the farmer had used the preceding year, we would have a pretty fair crop of wheat on land which the year before had produced a crop not worth combining. The season was an average one and the wheat averaged over twenty bushels to the acre, a poor yield but approximately 300 per cent more than the preceding years. Certainly we owed a large part of the increase to keeping the water where it fell instead of permitting it to run off. But the looseness of the soil with the chopped-up organic material in it also permitted better root growth and the added moisture made the fertilizer used available to the plants and about twice as effective. The barnyard manure, although much of it had been left in the barnyard by our predecessor and was badly leached, contributed its good effects in terms of all the valuable known and unknown elements which animal manure contains. And there was the nitrogen being given off slowly by all the decaying weeds, straw, etc., mixed into the soil. The legumes which had survived the "poor plowing" and disking continued to grow with the wheat, supplying nitrogen to the soil. These, particularly the sweet clover, grew high and caused some trouble in combining, but not enough to outweigh their great value.

The straw was left in the field together with the legumes, principally the tall sweet clover, which had been clipped in the process of combining. In the autumn of that year (again, early September) strip No. 1 was put into cultivation. This time it was not plowed but ripped up with a tiller and disked once. The tiller was equipped with alfalfa "knives" which tear through the soil but do little damage to alfalfa or sweet clover roots. Despite the disking which followed, most of the original legume seeding still survived and grew. This time there was chopped into the earth, but not plowed under and buried, a second year of straw, the remains of the clipped legumes left behind the combine and what was left of the application of barnyard manure. The surface of the field still remained rough, which was what we desired. This time all the material was chopped into a depth of three to four inches and for the first time there appeared the elements of topsoil.

Into this was drilled rye and vetch seed which, in the stored moisture of the blotting-paper surface, germinated almost at once and made a quick growth. By the time winter came there was a thick green mat of rye and vetch over the whole of strip No. 1.

In the spring the strip was ripped up again with a tiller and disked again and this time sown to oats. We did not sow the oats early as is the proper rule if one is to catch the cool weather and early rains of spring. There were two reasons for the delay— one, that there was more important work to be done and as we did not expect a great yield of oats from strip No. 1 we let it go until last, and second, we wanted the rye and vetch to make as much growth as possible before disking it in, in order to get as much organic material as possible.

We rough-disked the field and sowed the oats nearly a month late when the rye and vetch was about two feet high. Because it was thick, it took a good deal of fitting but when we were finished, the soil for a depth of five to six inches was a mixture of earth and chopped and decaying rye and vetch stalks and roots. Into this the oats were drilled with no nitrogen fertilizer and the usual amount of potassium and phosphorus. We were right in holding back on the nitrogen; the legumes, the decaying rye and the vetch supplied all the nitrogen and more than was needed. The oats grew rankly, too rankly in spots where the original legume seeding had been thick. They showed no bad effects from the late planting because the heavy mulch of decaying rubbish kept the ground both cool and moist. Before the oats appeared above ground we seeded the strip to sweet clover and, owing to moisture and mulch, we secured a fine even stand of this tricky but valuable legume which is sometimes difficult to get started.

The oats yield was startling, from four to five bushels per acre above the average yield in our county which is not the best oats country. The straw again was left on the strip and the sweet clover seedlings came through it easily and grew far ranker than any sweet clover seedings we had ever made, no doubt because the whole of the soil, filled with decaying vegetation, beneath the mulch of oats straw, remained loose and moist throughout the summer.

That winter the stems of the sweet clover seedlings froze back and fell to the earth to add their nitrogen to the already thick layer of mulch, and the following spring we were ready for the third stage. By now without plowing we had from three to four inches of pretty good topsoil and at least another inch or two of oats straw and sweet clover mulch lying on the surface. In late May of the third year when the sweet clover had reached a height of about two feet, we put the plow to work and turned the whole layer of new topsoil, decaying mulch and the heavy growth of sweet clover completely over or upside down, plowing deep to bring up from two to four inches of the buried soil and topsoil. This was disked heavily to mix it as much as possible with the newly created topsoil we had buried. The strip was planted to corn with soybeans sown in the rows with the corn, the whole to be cut for silage. We did not, of course, measure the crop yield in ears. We planted hybrid De Kalb No. 604 and the results were remarkable, thick deep green corn with two big ears on two out of three stalks, with succulent soybeans growing three to four feet high. The strip filled our biggest silo and part of another.

The best comment came from our neighbor, Charlie Schrack, who said, "I've lived next to that field for fifty-four years, since I was born, and I never saw on it as fine a crop of corn."

Once we had turned the soil upside down, the same process of small grain rotation with intensive planting of legumes was followed. Next spring we shall turn the top layer upside down in turn, plowing deep to bring up subsoil if possible. At the end of five years we had built six inches of good topsoil, as good— indeed I am not certain that it is not better topsoil than Nature had spent several thousand years in creating. For the mineral balance is better than that of most topsoil produced by Nature, especially in areas once covered by forest. We shall husband it carefully in the future and see to it that we do not take off more than we put back.

The system we used was an intensive but not unreasonable

one, and after the first year we succeeded in raising a profitable crop each year. Both nitrogen and organic material were restored to the soil in large quantities, as well as the minerals brought up from the subsoil through the roots, stalks and leaves of the deep-rooted legumes. To all this, lime, potassium and phosphorus and trace minerals were added artificially to restore them to the leached-out soil.

I do not believe that the rebuilding of topsoil could have been accomplished so speedily if we had plowed instead of using the trash-farming methods advocated by Mr. Faulkner. There are many reasons for this belief, principally that by plowing and burying manures, stubble and straw, much of their value, both in nitrogen and humus, is destroyed. The surface rubbish of all kinds, when *plowed* under by a good job of plowing is compacted into a narrow tight layer pressed down by the weight of the earth as well as that of the implements passing over the ground during the process of fitting. During the heat of summer, the compacted mass does not decay, but ferments, creating acids which actually eat away into nothingness the organic material which should be converted by the slower process of decay into humus. The process also locks up nitrogen instead of releasing it and by the acid fermentation and the absence of air destroys the bacteria so valuable to plant growth or checks their action in the *natural* process of decay.

When the same amount of manure and trash is chopped into the soil, there is no heating or fermentation. The organic material is converted into a maximum of humus, slowly, through the natural process of decay. The soil remains loose and open, springy as you walk over it, open to the action of bacteria, of air and of the water which it entraps. In other words, plowing is the unnatural process and trash-farming the natural one.

Long before the experiment was made I had seen in the state of Indore in India the results of experiments made by Sir Albert Howard during his long stay there. The basis of Sir Albert's process of rebuilding and revitalizing soil was that of composting not only animal and green manures but all available rubbish and refuse. It was a process which began actually in the stables themselves where an effort was made to preserve *all* animal secretions and to keep alive and promote the increase of bacteria. Toward this end Sir Albert had six inches of absorbent clay laid down in the stables to absorb all liquids. This clay was removed periodically and placed in the compost heaps along with the manure, straw and disintegrating rubbish. During the process of decay the compost heaps were turned by coolie hand labor from time to time to prevent heating and fermentation. When the composting process was completed, the residue was removed to the fields where it was mixed with the worn-out Indian soil and produced prodigious results in health, vigor and the productiveness of plant life.

The Indore process of Sir Albert Howard produces perhaps the ideal fertilizer, containing not only chemical elements necessary to plant growth but also the residue of *all* animal secretions and billions of active and stimulating bacteria. Beyond that, it is in itself *living* humus and as such absorbs and preserves moisture and helps to achieve the *maximum* result from any chemical fertilizer used in the field.

Such a process and a result would have been invaluable to us at Malabar as it would be to any farmer, but the expense of time and labor made it impractical and indeed impossible. The coolies employed in Sir Albert's process received approximately twenty cents a day—a wage that is nonexistent in America or even in Europe. The lowest wage in our Middle Western country for unskilled farm labor is approximately ten times as great. Throughout much of the period during which our own experiments were carried on, farm labor at any price was very nearly unavailable. We had, therefore, to find some adaptation or variation of the Indore process.

So far as the stables and feeding barns were concerned, we simply substituted ordinary sawdust for the absorbent clay employed by Sir Albert. This we used as bedding twice a week in layers between the straw. The sawdust absorbed all urine and glandular secretions and the urine began almost at once a process of breaking down the tough cellulose structure of the sawdust, thus hastening the natural process of decay into humus and available plant food. The stables were cleaned periodically and the manure spread over the fields, without the loss of any essential elements. During the period it remained in the stables no leaching by weather occured at all and the liquid content prevented heating or fermentation.

Once in the field, the manure was not plowed under to ferment and form destructive acids. It was stirred into the soil along with whatever rubbish, weeds or green manure lay on the surface. During the processes of cultivation, or even without cultivation, the mixed soil, rubbish and manure was left loose and open, available to air, water and even light so that the essential processes of decay which took place in Sir Albert's compost heap also took place in our impoverished topsoil. Actually we did no more than transfer the composting process from the compost heap into the topsoil of our fields. Actually we were growing crops in a living compost heap, with *no* additional costs either in time or labor.

I have not made tests as to the different amounts of nitrogen released respectively under the two methods. I have not counted the abundance or lack of bacteria at work. I only know by the evidence of the plants growing in the trash-farmed soil. They *like* it and are healthy and productive. I have seen the topsoil grow under my eyes and beneath the tread of my feet. I have had good farmers and scientists comment on the springiness of the soil which five years earlier was little more than cement devoid of humus. I have heard neighbors comment on the darkened *color* of the soil. I have seen the earthworms increase from none at all save in the damp topsoil-filled hollows of the field to a very busy population distributed evenly over the whole of strip No. 1. I have seen the population of bumble bees increase from virtually none at all to numbers so great that their humming could be heard at a distance of fifty yards from the field. I have seen pheasants and rabbits and quail return to land they had deserted because it was dead. In short I have seen the stripped, worn-out soil come back to life and productivity.

The system used on strip No. 1 has been used with some variations on other fields and always with similar results. The increase of humus proved another fact of great importance— that once the content of organic material is sufficiently increased, erosion, even on steep slopes, is checked for the soil acts like blotting paper and absorbs all the water which falls on it. In other words, once we restore the natural humus content of the soil in the whole field crossed by strip No. 1 it will no longer be necessary to either strip or contour it. So long as that humus content is kept high there will be no runoff water and no loss of topsoil.

The processes which we came to use in the restoration of organic material and the building of topsoil were no more or less than the processes used by Nature herself or in the conduct of any well-managed compost heap. The natural process was hastened by the added concentration of organic material in the form of green and animal manures and by the fact that all this bulk was not plowed under, buried and compressed but mixed loosely into the soil where the crops were growing. The compost heap, in other words, was transferred from the pit or shed to the topsoil itself. We had built upon the natural formula of life and vigor growing out of death and decay. All we did was to speed it up several thousand times. Thus we achieved a kind of resurrection by which dead soil rose from the dead and became alive once more.

The Cycle of a Farm Pond

Although Louis Bromfield was not a trained scientist or agriculturist (he attended Cornell Agricultural College for less than a year and his only other university experience was part of a year at Columbia School of Journalism), he had an instinctive understanding of the science of ecology, at a time when its importance was only beginning to acquire the recognition it has today.

In this essay, Bromfield shows how ecology works and how it can be put to practical use. For those owning a farm without a pond, this chapter should surely inspire them to follow Bromfield's advice: work with nature, which can, in short order, turn a raw, bulldozed hole in the ground into an "old pond, fertile and teeming with life."

According to David D. Anderson's 1964 literary biography of Bromfield, "The Cycle of a Farm Pond" ranks with "the very best nature writing of our time." That anthologists have overlooked this essay is a pity, for it is central to Bromfield's intellectual contribution to an understanding of the rural environment, and it is still very much up-to-date.

O f the three ponds at Malabar, the low, shallow one at the Fleming Place is the most productive of big fish. This is so because it is the oldest and the richest in vegetation. It was made out of an old ox-bow left when Switzer's Run was foolishly straightened by the County Commissioners before we came here. We raised the banks about two feet by a day's work with hand shovels and thus raised the water level by the same depth. It is fed by a big spring in the bottom which has increased its flow by at least 100 per cent since we began keeping the rainfall where it fell on our land, and by the flow of an abandoned gas well which has turned into a first-rate artesian well flowing hundreds of gallons a minute of ice-cold water. Drainage from the neighboring barnyard during heavy rain occasionally reaches the pond and fertilizes the heavy vegetation in it. It is a comparatively shallow pond with a gravel bottom long since stopped tight by layers of decaying water vegetation.

The natural balance and cycle of this pond is very nearly perfect. The population is made up of bass, bluegills, sunfish and innumerable hybrid variations of the sunfish family which occur in fish ponds. There is also a single large carp caught by the children in Switzer's Run as a small fish and dumped into the pond along with a miscellaneous assortment of minnows, shiners, suckers, etc. All but the carp have long since disappeared, devoured by the big bass. On the richness of the table set for him by Nature beneath the surface of the water, the carp has grown to nearly three feet in length and must weigh in the neighborhood of thirty pounds. He is occasionally accompanied by a gigantic goldfish which seems to have for him a romantic attachment—a situation not unusual, since carp and goldfish belong to the same family, and found in Lake Erie where huge goldfish, descended from a few which escaped from a pond in Cleveland years ago during flood times, are not uncommon and frequently breed with the big carp to create new crossbred strains puzzling of identification to the amateur and sometimes to the commercial fishermen who find them in their nets.

The goldfish also came into the Fleming pond through no design but through the zeal of the children who, six years ago, dumped into the pond a dozen fingerling-size goldfish bought at Woolworth's. On the rich diet of the pond they have grown to eighteen inches and more in length and to a weight of two or three pounds. They are very fat and lumbering and awkward beside the swift-moving streamlined bass and bluegills and have the appearance of red-gold galleons wallowing through the deep green-blue water moss and weeds. Some have the appearance of large luminous streamlined carp and others have long flowing tails and fins which trail behind them in the clear blue water like the veils of brides. Some have their red-gold scales variegated with silver. It is easy to see why the Japanese and Chinese long ago regarded goldfish as works of art, of high artistic value in their shallow ornamented pools, and made a science and an art of breeding them into fantastic almost artifi-

cial shapes and colors. A glimpse of these big, brilliantly color-
ful fish seen moving through the gently undulating weeds in
the blue, clear water from the high bank of the Fleming pond
gives the beholder the sudden delight that comes from the con-
templation of an old Chinese painting or from the luminous
beauty of Redon's flower pictures.

Neither the goldfish nor the great carp belongs in a properly managed Ohio fish pond but all efforts to remove them
have failed. The goldfish, fat and contented, will sometimes
nose about a worm-baited hook but never take the worm. The
great carp has refused all baits persistently and has even managed to escape the marksmanship of the boys who regularly attempt to shoot him with a twenty-two calibre rifle.

However, beyond consuming some of the food supply of the
pond, neither goldfish nor carp does any serious harm. I am not
at all sure that they are not an asset in the cycle of the pond and
to the food supply of the big, smallmouthed bass. They have
never succeeded in producing a single surviving descendant
and there is consequently no way of knowing whether the ro-
mance of the great carp and his love-lorn accompanying goldfish has ever been fruitful. Each year the goldfish gather, after
the fashion of carp, in a herd in the shallowest water and there
thrash about in the ecstasy of reproduction for several days at a
time. But apparently the big bass immediately devour the roe
or any young goldfish which by chance have hatched out. Thus
they continue—the great carp and his fleet of goldfish cousins—to lead, if not a sterile existence, a fruitless one, taking
their place in the cycle of pond life and producing a perpetual
supply of caviar for the bass.

I have seen literally acres of great carp spawning in the
shallow waters of the big Pleasant Hill lake at the end of the
farm in late May or June. In the late spring they gather from
the deep holes of the Clear Fork and the deeper waters of the
lake itself by some common and terrific urge and then move
into the shallow waters where they indulge in a wild orgy of
reproduction continuing for several days. At such times it is
possible to walk in water up to one's knees among hundreds of
thrashing, wallowing carp, which in their ecstasy pay little attention to one's presence—so little indeed that it is possible to
knock them over with blows of a club. In Lake Erie at spawning

time, the big carp put on a similar performance in the shallow waters along the beaches and boys amuse themselves by shooting at them with rifles.

The fresh-water shad which exist in great numbers in the waters of the lake and the Clear Fork have another way of spawning. They will gather in schools on the surface of fairly deep water and swarm and flash, jumping in and out of the water in the brilliant sunlight of June. They are prodigiously fecund and reproduce themselves by the hundred thousands and their offspring are devoured in great quantities by the big bass which fit into the cycle of life in the streams, ponds, and lakes of most of the Mississippi basin. So intent do the shad become during the season of breeding that you can swim among them while they continue their gyrations and silvery leaps above the surface of the clear, blue water.

There are no shad in our ponds but their place is taken in the pond cycle by the bluegills and sunfish which also reproduce themselves in prodigious numbers. Tom Langlois of the Ohio Fish Laboratories, one of the great authorities on mid-American fresh-water fish, tells me that not only are there many distinct and identifiable members of the sunfish family, but that they have an indiscriminate way of crossbreeding an infinite number of variations. Many of these are sterile, like the mule, and each year go through the fiercely compulsive process of breeding and laying eggs without producing anything. It appears also that the urge to breed overtakes them earlier in the season than it does the accepted and recognized members of the sunfish family. Very often they will pre-empt the available nesting grounds on shallow gravel beds in their fruitless and sterile efforts and fiercely fight off the fertile members of their tribe when these attempt a little later to find nesting places, a fact that can upset the regular cycle of pond life and food supply within the pond.

The mating habits of many fish and of most of the sunfish family in particular are fascinating to observe. In our ponds, they begin to nest about the end of May, and all along the edges of the ponds in shallow waters you will find them in great numbers beginning to clear away the mud or the decayed vegetation that cover the clean gravel which they like for nesting purposes.

The bass, the bluegills and the other members of the sunfish family all follow a similar urge and procedure. Each one will select, not without considerable fighting, a chosen site and then begin to clear off the silt or decayed vegetation that has settled over the gravel during the year. Each one will take a place above his selected site and without moving either backward or forward will set up a fluttering motion with his fins which in turn creates a current in the water that washes the gravel clean. This procedure sometimes requires a day or two of work. When the gravel has been washed clean and a slight depression of from one to two inches deep has been created (similar in appearance beneath the water to the nest of the killdeer plover which lays its eggs and hatches its young on a nest of gravel on the adjoining dry ground), the female will deposit her eggs in the nest and the male will swim over them and fertilize them. From then on the duty of guarding the nest becomes that of the male and until the young are hatched he will remain over the nest, moving his fins very gently, unless another fish of any species comes within an eighteen-inch radius of the center of the nest. Then he will attack furiously until the molesting fish is driven off. The bluegills and some varieties of sunfish build their nests in clusters side by side, each with a male fish fiercely guarding his own nest and darting angrily at his nearest neighbors if they attempt to cross the invisible line which guards his nursery from that of his neighbors.

When the tiny fish hatch, overnight the whole pond will become infested with millions of tiny fish no bigger than a pin which move about in schools of thousands and promptly seek refuge in very shallow water or among the algae which by the time they have hatched covers large areas of the pond. There would seem to be some purpose in the presence of the algae as a protection for the tiny fish not only because its fabric makes it impossible for the big bass to swallow the young fish in a single sweeping gulp but because the larger fish find the algae itself distasteful and unpalatable. I have observed that even the smallest filament of algae attached by accident to a baited hook or fly will prevent the bigger fish from swallowing or striking at the bait.

I doubt that the male fish is aware of the moment when the young fry hatch out and flee the nest for the safety of the very shallow waters or of the webbed, clinging algae. I suspect that very often, driven by an urge which covers a comparatively fixed period well overlapping the period of gestation, the male fish remains on guard long after the roe have hatched and fled the nest.

In certain parts of the pond which the fish have chosen as nesting and spawning beds, the whole character of the pond bottom has changed over a period of years. On bottoms which once were clay and mud, the clay-mud element has been entirely washed away by the motions of countless small fins season after season until they have become clean, gravel shelves, bars and beaches. If, as sometimes happens during the spawning season, which usually coincides with a season of rains and thundershowers, floodwaters cover the nests with a thin layer of silt, the male fish will immediately and frantically go to work washing away the deposit of silt to make the nests clean once more.

During the spawning season, the male becomes fierce and even the little male bluegill will stand by his particular nest and give battle to a stick or a finger thrust into the water near him. I have had my finger "bitten" by big male bass when I thrust my hand into the water above his nest. At other times when the fish are not nesting my mere presence on the bank or shadow cast over the water will suffice to send them in a darting brilliant course into deeper water.

All of these elements play their part in the "balance" of a good fish pond. The algae and vegetation shelters and produces vast quantities of minute animal life upon which the fiercely fecund and reproductive small-mouthed, purse-lipped bluegills and sunfish largely feed along with the flies and insects which fall on the surface of the ponds during the long, hot, insect-breeding months on a fertile middle-western farm. In turn the small-mouthed sunfish produce millions of small fish which provide food for the big, predatory bass and trout and some of the larger-mouthed and predatory green sunfish.

Weather and flood conditions occasionally alter the nesting habits not only of fish but of marsh-nesting birds. During the disastrously wet spring and summer of 1947 the red-winged blackbirds provided a remarkable example of the effect of weather upon nesting habits. These lovely birds which normally nest among the sedge grass and bullrushes of marshes, creek banks and ponds, abandoned their usual habits and took to nesting on the high ground in the alfalfa fields. When I began mowing alfalfa in mid-June I started up considerable numbers of fledglings just old enough to fly and found several old abandoned nests set into clumps of alfalfa exactly as the birds normally set their nests in a clump of sedge or marsh grass. The fact raises again the old question of whether birds by some instinct are aware in advance of weather or the exact time of changing seasons. The migration time of many birds varies a great deal. In this case I do not know whether the birds anticipated the floods which later inundated their usual low-ground nesting places or whether they took to the higher ground because the whole of the spring had produced continuously flooding rains and abnormally high water. In the same season of disturbed and turbulent water in the ponds, the sunfish and bass did not breed and nest until five or six weeks later than usual. Whether they attempted to do so earlier at the normal time and found their efforts thwarted or whether their later nesting and breeding period produced the usual results I do not know. In that same summer, the red-winged blackbirds developed or at least exhibited habits that in my observation were new and strange. They appeared in great numbers, indeed in flocks, following the mower and gorging themselves on the leafhoppers which infested the alfalfa. Except at migrating time the red-winged blackbirds had generally flown about in pairs or occasionally appeared in groups of five or six all of the same sex. It scarcely seems possible that the birds, through nesting on high ground, suddenly and for the first time discovered the leafhoppers as a rich source of food supply. The occurrence, however, was one more proof of the benefit to the farmer of supplying adequate cover in fence rows or isolated patches of undergrowth and marshland for the bird population.

In the same season the killdeer plovers, which also nest on low ground along creeks, made no apparent change in their nesting habits. They are among the most careless of nest-builders, taking no trouble at all beyond hollowing out a shallow nest on a bare spot of gravel or sand in a low pasture by a creek. Presumably the eggs and the young killdeer which were not yet old enough to leave the nest were destroyed by the floods. Like quail, however, the young of the killdeer are extremely precocious and leave the nest very early, running about on the sandbanks and on the short bluegrass pasture even before they are able to fly. The young of the red-winged blackbird, on the other hand, must be fully feathered and well grown before they are able to leave the nest. They live almost entirely in the air or by clinging to high bullrushes and weeds, rarely making excursions on the ground as walking birds.

The green sunfish is the broad general name in our part of the country for a group of fish with varying characteristics. Although they rarely attain a length of more than six inches, there is no fish which fights more gamely. Indeed, if their size is taken into consideration, I know of no fresh- or salt-water fish which puts up so valiant a fight. They are, so far as I have been able to discover, the only group of the minor sunfish which feed upon the young of other fish. I have observed them greedily pursuing young bass, which is a little like the fox turning upon the hounds. Naturally they are equipped with much bigger mouths than the other minor sunfish and some of them actually closely resemble small bass in appearance. When they get out of balance in a pond or lake they may become a menace even to the predatory bass population. The green sunfish is altogether a very aggressive little fish and a gallant fighter which will provide good sport on a light flyrod.

All will take a worm from a hook and, of course, artificial flies, but at times it is difficult to take the bluegills or some of the varieties of sunfish because of the extreme smallness of their mouths. The bass, even the smallmouth, which is the variety which inhabits our ponds, has an immense mouth and gullet, sometimes making up very nearly half his length. The great mouth and gullet permits him to swallow a good-sized sunfish at a single gulp. In the case of the Fleming pond, the bass provide an absolute check or block upon the increase of carp or goldfish by devouring their roe or their young very soon after they are hatched.

This process and control and the operation of a natural cycle and balance of life is observable not only in ponds but in the free, open, fresh-water streams. In almost any clear running stream with abundant vegetation throughout most of the Mississippi basin, the balance and life cycle will include some carp and catfish as well as bass, crappies and other members of the sunfish, game fish family. If the stream becomes polluted either by sewage or siltation or is swept clean of vegetation by periodic floods, the balance is upset and the game fish will gradually disappear and the mud-loving fish will presently dominate in overwhelming numbers until gradually and finally only coarse mud-loving fish—carp, catfish, et al.—alone exist.

This has been the history of many once-fine fishing streams and lakes in the Mississippi basin where either sewage pollution from cities or steadily increasing siltation coming from ignorantly and poorly managed farm lands gradually produces conditions which exterminate all the game fish and leave only the coarse fish and finally exterminate all stream life save turtles and frogs.

That is what happened to countless streams in the South which were once famous for good sport fishing. Increasing erosion has turned many of them at certain times of the year into what is little more than a mass of viscous, thin, slow-flowing mud in which all fish life becomes impossible.

For the sportsmen this gives the problem of soil and water conservation and reckless deforestation an important place in the scheme of things. In the past, stream after stream, pond after pond, and bay after bay in the bigger lakes which were once famous fishing grounds for sportsmen have been reduced, by incessant floods and siltation coming from bare, poorly farmed fields, to the category of coarse, mud-fish territory or of no fish at all. In Lake Erie even the commercial fishing business, representing millions of dollars a year, is being threatened by the pollution of the big industrial cities and the siltation of spawning beds in its shallower waters. On the other hand, in a few streams in limited areas where good soil, water, and forestry practices have come into existence, clean water and vegetation have come back into the streams, ponds, and lakes, and periodic floods have been largely eliminated with the result that in streams which only a few years ago had been reduced to the level of coarse-fish carp and catfish waters, the proper balance and cycle is being restored and the waters are becoming known again as fine places for game fishing.

In our own farm ponds every effort has been made to prevent siltation. The practice of proper forestry and soil conservation and a program of grass farming has reduced siltation virtually to zero, and after and even during the heaviest rainfall the excess water reaching at least two of the ponds is as clear as the rainwater itself. In one pond the water becomes discolored from the run-off of a neighboring gravel lane which cannot be controlled, but the siltation amounts to little more than discoloration and is mostly very fine sand which settles quickly leaving the water clear and blue after a short time. Under these conditions the balance of aquatic life quickly establishes itself and the ponds rapidly become filled with too many fish, so that fishing becomes not only a pleasure but a duty, for unfished ponds existing under proper conditions need no stocking; on the contrary it is necessary to fish them constantly in order to keep down the population. Otherwise the population exceeds the food supply and the pond becomes filled with innumerable fish which are too small either for good sport or for food.

The pond on the Fleming Place has long since reached the point of ideal balance and cycle. If fished steadily it goes on producing quantities of big game fish providing both unlimited sport and "fish for supper" for every family on the farm as often as they want it. Because the pond is a fertile one filled with vegetation, it produces a constant supply of food for small fish and the small-mouthed sunfish which in turn provide food for the bass and the bigger fish. The cycle of production for sport and food is constant and prodigious despite the fact that the pond is little over an acre in size. Constant fishing is in itself a part of the cycle of abundance since the pond is land-locked and would quickly become overpopulated and the fish small and bony if a considerable poundage of fish were not removed from it annually.

The Fleming pond is an old pond. Those on the Anson and the Bailey Places are newer. The one on the Anson Place was constructed only seven years ago and the one on the Bailey Place only two years ago. In the Anson pond the perfect balance and cycle has not yet established itself. It is a deep pond with a comparatively small amount of shallow water. In the beginning no stocking was done, save the fish caught in other ponds or in neighboring streams and dumped into it. Two years ago about 500 fingerling rainbow trout were put in. The fish from local ponds and streams were largely bluegills and varieties of sunfish with a few suckers and minnows. Among them were a score and more of big smallmouth bass weighing from one to two pounds upward. These were taken out of the older Fleming pond which at the end of each summer is cleaned systematically by worm and hook fishing to eliminate the biggest fish which turn cannibal and devour not only the "food fish" within the pond cycle but also the young and half-grown bass.

Of all the fish put into the six-year-old pond on the Anson Place, the minnows and suckers very quickly were eliminated, either by being eaten or by going out of the outlet into the flowing streams which were much more their natural habitat than the still ponds. A heavy winter following the transplantation of the big bass kept the pond frozen over solidly and the lack of oxygen and sunlight was apparently too much for the bass for when the ice thawed in the spring all of them were floating dead on its surface. They never had a chance to nest or breed.

Fish ponds and even lakes of considerable size throughout Ohio suffered similar losses of the bass and some other fish during the same severe winter. Open streams did not suffer similar losses because the movement of the water kept them open wherever there were ripples. Ponds, of course, are not the natural or ideal habitat for the smallmouthed bass which prefers streams, varied by deep pools and swift flowing water over steep gradients. The fish for which the pond is a natural habitat suffered much less from the shortage of oxygen and sunlight.

As it turned out, this worked into the plan of control on the six-year-old Anson pond. Its waters ran to a depth of twenty feet and it was spring fed both at the inlet and from springs in the bottom and even in the hottest days of August the deeper water remained cold, at a temperature of about fifty degrees. This depth and temperature made it a possibility as a trout pond. Trout could never have survived in the old shallow Fleming pond which was too warm and which already contained a flourishing population of bass. We found long ago that trout and bass cannot exist indefinitely in the same waters; the bass inevitably exterminate the trout, perhaps because they have much bigger mouths and can outswallow the trout both in number and size of fish. Therefore, the elimination of the big bass by a severe winter left the deep, cold, six-year-old Anson pond ready for stocking by trout, especially since the food supply of the smaller fecund sunfish of all varieties was already well established.

Rainbow or brown trout were chosen as the most likely to flourish in the Anson pond and eventually we put in the 500 fingerlings not more than three or four inches in length. During the first summer there was no evidence of them whatever. They were never seen at all, either alive or floating dead upon the surface, and I came to the disappointing conclusion that they had all left the pond through the open outlet. When spring came the following year there was still no evidence of the rainbows. None of them were seen either dead or alive or in the shallow waters where the sunfish could be watched nesting.

During the six years of the pond's existence, following the "amateur" stocking of native fish from neighboring ponds and streams, the fish population increased immensely until this spring it became evident that there were far too many fish and that we should have to go to "work" fishing them out. There were thousands of them, mostly too small for table use. When we went to work, we made a remarkable discovery. Among the scores of fish which we took out as rapidly as the hook struck the water, more than 99 per cent were of two varieties—either long-eared or green sunfish with some odd unidentifiable hybrids. There being no big predatory fish in the pond, we came to the conclusion that these two varieties had survived and dominated and that, because the green sunfish had the biggest mouths, they could swallow the other varieties of smaller, purse-mouthed sunfish like the bluegill, the punkinseed and even the long-eared sunfish. They had simply eaten the other fish out of existence and had had no control placed upon them since the small-mouthed fish could not swallow them once they were above a certain size, even if they had been inclined to include other fish as legitimate articles of diet which, as a rule, the small-mouthed fish do not do.

In any case, we were made sharply aware of the vast population of green sunfish, which I suspect in our case may have been a crossbred variety in that particular pond, for their mouths and gullets appeared to be much larger than the ordinary green sunfish described and pictured in all books dealing with the fish of the Mississippi basin.

These voracious green sunfish, although they never attain much size even under favorable conditions and I have seen only a few that approached a pound in weight, make excellent sport with a flyrod. They take the fly with a rush and ounce for ounce put up a fiercer and longer fight than any trout or bass. That summer we did not look for sport in the Anson pond so much as to reduce the population of fish, so we used cane poles and worms to fish. Even with this steady tackle, I have seen the little fellows take a worm on the rush and bend the bamboo pole half way to double.

"Cleaning" a pond to reduce the fish population is a pleasurable procedure. Armed with cane pole and worms and with a big milk can at one's side we take fish after fish off the hook at half-minute intervals and throw them into the milk-can for transference to a new pond or to the neighboring streams, but there is not much real excitement in it. At times eight or ten of us will spend an evening simply "cleaning" a pond.

I began the "cleaning" process on the six-year-old Anson pond to cut down the population of green sunfish and I got my excitement, even with a bamboo pole and worm-baited hook, when after I had half-filled the milk can with fish, the bait was taken by a fish which behaved differently from the ones I had been catching. I brought him to the surface and the sight of his silvery speckled body gave me one of the thrills of a long fishing career. He was no sunfish. He was a rainbow trout, ten inches in length, one of the 500 I had put in a year earlier and bemoaned as lost. He was not only still in the pond but he had grown in the span of a year from three inches to ten. I raised him reverently from the water. I had hooked him through the cartilage around the mouth and he was unhurt. Reverently I threw him back into the pond to go on growing into a two or three pound big fellow who later on will make wonderful sport and wonderful eating.

And about every tenth fish we took out in the process of "cleaning" was a handsome, silvery, speckled fellow, one of the rainbow fingerlings we had put in a year earlier. Most of them were uninjured and were put back to grow some more.

It is clear what happened. The trout fingerlings stayed in the clear, cold, deep water and never appeared in the warm shallow water where the sunfish nested, frolicked and ate. They are still staying most of the time in the deep, cold water but now the fingerlings are big enough to go foraging into the shallow haunts of the sunfish, clearly in search of food which meant that they were after the young sunfish. The latter are now having competition from predatory fish with as big or bigger mouths than their own and it is probable that a balance and cycle like that between bass and sunfish in the older Fleming pond will establish itself between trout and sunfish in the six-year-old Anson pond. In the evenings we see the trout foraging on the surface for insects.

The vegetation and life growing in the algae of the pond are clearly already sufficient to support a considerable population of food sunfish, enough to give the rainbow trout as fat a diet as the bass already have in the older Fleming pond. Whether the trout, whose breeding habits are different from those of the bass-sunfish family, will manage to reproduce themselves as rapidly as the bass have done in the Fleming pond or even at all, remains to be seen. I am hopeful. If they do, the productivity and balance of the newer pond will be established and we shall, in order to maintain it at the maximum level of food and sport, have to fish it regularly, a hardship any fisherman is willing to suffer when it means that he is getting fish from a pound to four or five pounds, all fighters whether they are big bluegills and sunfish or bass or rainbow trout.

The life cycle of fish is a subject of some dispute among scientists and, to be sure, varies greatly with the species. Legend has it that there are carp in the moats and ponds of Fontainebleau and Chantilly which were there at the time of François Premier and guides point to the rings set in the snouts of the huge, mangy old carp with the statement that they were thus ringed two hundred years ago. All this may be true for certainly the carp are immensely old and very large. Recently a female sturgeon weighing 175 pounds was taken in Lake Erie and the press attributed to it an age of over a hundred years. This particular fish was a female and yielded many pounds of caviar at the time of the catch. It is a sad fact that the sturgeon population of the Great Lakes, like that of many other fish, has been steadily decreasing as siltation, sewage, and industrial pollution has increased.

Growth and size of fish and perhaps their age is determined largely by food supply. A green sunfish in the controlled Fleming pond will reach what is apparently maximum size much more rapidly than in the six-year-old Anson pond where the population of its own kind, feeding upon its own diet, is much too great at present. In the Fleming pond, where its food is abundant, a bass will reach a weight of three or four pounds in approximately the same number of years. The largest bass taken from the pond weighed a little over five pounds. I do not know its exact age. But because the Fleming pond is comparatively small and shallow it is possible to observe and check with a considerable degree of accuracy the age and growth of the fish. There appear always to be a least four sizes: (1) The newly hatched pin-sized fry. Those which survive apparently reach a length of three to four inches in one season. (2) The two-year-olds which at the end of the second season have grown from the four-inch length to a length of eight or more inches. (3) The three-year-old crop which runs a foot to eighteen inches. (4) Those fish of all sizes above eighteen inches which are the biggest ones and whose cannibalistic habits with regard to the five to eight inch bass lead us to clear them out of the pond at the end of each summer.

The newest of theories among fish experts is that if a pond or stream provides the proper conditions, and is not subject to violent periodic flooding, siltation or pollution, and the food supply is adequate, there is no need for stocking; that, on the contrary, there is a need to fish the stream or pond constantly in order to control the population and secure bigger fish and better sport.

The Ohio State Conservation Commission, of which the author is a member, has opened several lakes and some streams, where the food and control conditions are right and pollution is virtually non-existent, to unrestricted fishing without season, size or bag limit, and the results tend to show over a short period of time that such wholesale fishing improves both the size and quality of the fish without diminishing the amount of the catch. Other states are making similar experiments and if the final results are in line with the early indication of the experiment it is likely that stocking fish in polluted or heavily silted streams where they cannot live or reproduce will be abandoned, together with bag and season restrictions and that the emphasis and expenditure of taxpayers' money will be diverted from expensive fish hatcheries and stocking programs to the cleaning up of streams and lakes and the establishment of conditions which permit and encourage almost unlimited fish populations, which actually *demand* unrestricted fishing to keep their populations in control.

Among the great and beautiful artificial lakes created in the Tennessee Valley Authority area all restrictions as to season, bag and size limit have been removed. The result has been to create a veritable fisherman's paradise. The creation of proper conditions, clean water, vegetation, etc., has proven that legal rules on take, season, etc., are unnecessary and that actually the more fish taken the better the fishing becomes. This is both reasonable and scientific procedure since a single female bass will produce as many as a hundred thousand and upward of eggs which when fertilized become small fry. Sunfish, crappies and coarse fish reproduce themselves at an even more prodigious rate. Not long ago I happened along the shore of Pleasant Hill lake at the end of the farm when a Conservation Commission employee was dumping five thousand fingerling smallmouth bass into the lake. As he poured the bass into the lake he remarked cynically, "Each one of these fish cost a lot of money to produce and all this stocking is a lot of hooey. Maybe it makes some ignorant sportsmen feel they're getting something, but a couple of pairs of good bass could do the same job without any expense at all." The man was not a scientist. He was an unskilled laborer but he had learned a great deal of wisdom through observation. I am told that in Colorado where hatchery-raised trout are introduced into streams, the cost of each trout is about $4.75. This, of course, is paid out of the sportsman license fees which could be expended far more profitably in providing clean streams and proper habitat where the fish could reproduce themselves successfully by the million. The new belief that money expended upon clean streams and habitat is better spent than on hatcheries and stocking is growing among state fish and game commissions and sportsmen generally. The same theory is spreading to the realm of hatchery bred and stocked quail, pheasant, partridge, to raccoon "farms" and all fields of game conservation and propagation.

This is a revolutionary idea, but it is also a wise development in reason, science and common sense. If the streams and lakes of the country were cleaned of pollution and siltation and floods checked by proper agricultural and forestry methods, there would be fine fishing in unlimited quantity for the whole of the population which enjoys fishing. Certainly our own experience with both ponds and streams has proven that this is true and that fishing becomes not only a sport but at times a duty and occasionally a real job.

One of the most fascinating spectacles in the world is the fashion in which Nature herself will take over a naked, newly constructed pond and set to work to make it into an old fertile pond in which natural controls are set up throughout the whole cycle of its life.

We have had an opportunity during the past years to observe the process in the case of the new ponds constructed and particularly the one on the Bailey Place. The site chosen for this pond was the corner of a field which even in midsummer was too wet for use as cultivated ground. Nearby was a very fine, big spring and several smaller ones as a source of water. In two days' work with a big bull-dozer and scoop a pond was constructed of about three acres in size varying from under a foot to fourteen feet in depth. The shallow area is large and makes an ideal feeding and breeding ground for fish once aquatic life is fully established. The barrier was made by excavating the soil from the bottom of the pond and piling it up as a dam which also serves as a roadway to and from adjoining fields.

Nearly seven weeks were required to fill the pond to its full depth for some of the water evaporated and much of it seeped through the bare, newly created bottom.

Watching the pond carefully, I observed a number of things. The first life to appear was the native killdeer, accompanied now and then by a dozen or more of their cousins, the rare golden plover. They waded about, crying and fluttering apparently in delight over the shallow rising water. They did not appear to feed but simply to wade about screaming and flapping their wings. Then a few frogs appeared from the damp spots in the neighboring fields and numbers of water skaters and water beetles. In the water warmed by the sun a few thin strands of algae, possibly carried in on the feet of the killdeer and plovers, appeared and began to grow in long strands, like the green hair of mermaids; and presently as the frogs increased in number the smaller herons appeared; and at last the pair of great blue herons, which has been with us winter and summer for six years and ranges the ponds and the shallows of the big lake at the end of the farm, acknowledged the existence of the new pond by visits to do a little frog hunting. What new life they brought to the pond clinging to their feet or in their excreta I do not know, but they too undoubtedly made their contribution to the growing, expanding life of the pond.

On the naked sides and on the newly constructed dam we put a layer of barnyard manure and sowed rye to bind the soil with its deep, wide-spreading fibrous roots and stop all erosion. In the manure there must have been millions of undigested seeds of ladino clover and other plants for there quickly grew up a carpet of vegetation which included ryegrass and bluegrass, white, sweet, red alsike and ladino clovers, and within a few weeks all danger of erosion or siltation from the naked soil surrounding the pond was eliminated. Even after a heavy rain the water remained clear. The apparent high rate of germination in the manure-sewn clover seeds could doubtless be traced back a season or two to the activities of thirty hives of bees which we keep on the farm to provide honey and pollenize the legumes. During all that first summer the level of the pond continued to rise and fall, varying according to the seepage in the pond bottom as it settled itself. By autumn there was a thick growth of algae over a considerable part of the surface. The winter came, the vegetation froze hard, the frogs and beetles disappeared, the killdeer and plover went south and the great blue herons abandoned visiting the pond for the richer, shallower, unfrozen waters of the big lake. Then the pond froze over and went dormant.

With the coming of spring, the ice melted and presently the crying of frogs and spring peepers was heard from along the shallow edges. The vegetation came back with a rush. Then in the shallows occurred the mating orgies of the hundreds of toads which appeared out of nowhere—accompanied by struggling and crying which put to rout the excesses of the Babylonians, and presently great strands of frog and toad spawn appeared in the shallow waters. In the same shallow waters the coarse, hardy dock plants, submerged the summer before where they grew, thrust their tough heads up through the water and presently began to turn yellow and drown to slow death to be supplanted by the new growth of seedlings and water grasses brought in as seeds clinging to the feet of water birds. And the seepage problem seemed to have solved itself. The pond had settled, the weight of the water closing up the open places in the bottom. And the algae had done its part, for with the coming of winter it had sunk to the bottom and laid a network of fine webbing over the whole of the pond bottom. The clay which had been squashy the season before so that when you waded into the pond you sank very nearly to your knees, became firm and hard under the weight of tons of water and remained only a little sticky on the top surface. What had once been a naked excavation walled in by a naked earthen dam had become within a year a watertight reservoir, its banks covered with protective vegetation, its shallow waters alive with vegetable and animal life.

The beetles and water skaters and water flies reappeared in vastly greater numbers and presently the shallow water was filled by millions of animated exclamation points that were tadpoles. And along the banks one came upon various kinds of water snakes which had discovered the new pond and taken up residence there to feed upon the young frogs and fish which their instinct told them would soon provide a rich source of food. But most curious of all, there appeared presently, in a pond completely shut off from outside waters, among the myriad tadpoles, a few pin-sized fish. Where they came from I do not know unless the eggs became attached somehow to the feet of the plovers and herons as they waded over the nests of fish in the other ponds or in Switzer's Creek. They were, at the time, still too small to be identified as to species save through the use of a magnifying glass or microscope. The eggs may have remained wet, the germ still living during the flight of the birds from one pond to another or from the creek or the shallows of the big lake at Pleasant Hill dam. Those who live near to water know that in the business of carrying on life, Nature can be incredibly tough and resistant and overwhelming. As the summer progressed all of these small fry turned into varieties of sunfish indicating that their origin probably lay in neighboring ponds.

In the case of the frogs and tadpoles which appeared early during the second year of life in the pond, we were indeed overwhelmed. The tadpoles appeared by the thousands in the shallow waters and presently were turned into myriads of small frogs, mostly of the handsome green and black spotted leopard varieties, none of them too big to sit comfortably on a silver half dollar. As we walked along the banks they went into a panic and leaped into the water like flights of grasshoppers in a grasshopper year. One could understand easily the Old Testament plague of frogs brought upon Egypt in Moses' time. One could understand too why Nature produced tiny frogs in such vast quantities for their behavior during panic was idiotic and made them an easy victim of any predator, snake, fish, or raccoon. As one approached, they went into a panic-stricken hysterical flight, some jumping into the water, some away from the water. The truth was that the new pond, still partly undeveloped by Nature and with no natural balance established, contained not yet enough enemies and predators to cope with the prodigious fecundity of the frogs which produced in the scheme of things thousands of frogs in order that a few score might survive. There were in the waters of the pond no bass or trout or pike which would have made short work of the hysterical young frogs which leaped into the open water, and not yet enough snakes, raccoons and herons to devour the more foolish of their numbers on land or in the very shallow waters.

It is easy to see how the frogs of the world, unhampered by natural checks and predators, could soon increase to such numbers that they would overrun everything, fill the whole of the land, and leave no room for the rest of us.

The muskrats were certain to be the next settlers at the new pond. Always in the second year they make their appearance, coming up the narrow silver thread of overflow water in the moonlight from the marshes in the Jungle, a wild piece of wet land in the middle of the farm, and from the marshes about the big lake where they exist by the thousand. One rarely sees them save sometimes in the moonlight when the nose of a muskrat moves across the ponds leaving a long V-shaped wake behind it in the still, silvery waters. One rarely sees them but the evidence of their presence is all around the edges of the pond, in the holes they dig for dens in the banks, in the nibbled foliage of certain plants and in the runways they make along the edges of the streams that feed the ponds. Usually they migrate during the second winter of the life of a pond and once they are established they like the easy living and remain there. When their numbers exceed the food supply, the younger ones go back to the marshes about the big lakes which are a muskrat's paradise.

The ones which remain are an endless source of trouble. They devour the succulent roots of the water lilies and the bull-rushes and the tender underwater shoots of the arrowleaf which we try to establish in a new pond, and they attack even the tubers of the irises in the flower garden only fifty feet from the house. Two years ago during a hard winter when the ponds were frozen over for three months they burrowed beneath a tree wistaria and ate off all its roots so that in the spring, it simply fell over, rootless and dead. They burrowed into the dams and threatened to destroy them until we discovered that twenty-four-inch chicken wire laid along the dam at the surface of the water, where they like to dig, prevented further burrowing. They are tough and shrewd and sly and prolific and no amount of trapping by the boys on the farm, who pick up a good many extra dollars that way during the winter, either intimidates or discourages them. Now and then one of the dogs catches a foolish young muskrat offside and ends his career, but the dogs do not serve as a sufficient check upon the fecundity of the water rodents. There are no more wolves in our country but there are an abundance of foxes which at night bark from the wooded ridge back and forth in the moonlight. Save for the dogs they are the only check upon the woodchucks and the muskrat and they get only the young and foolish ones. A big muskrat is too shrewd for a fox and a big, old woodchuck can outfight him. Without the dogs, the woodchuck would, like the frogs, eventually take us over.

It must be said, however, that one of the last things we should desire at Malabar is the total extermination of wood-chucks. The holes they dig and their generous hospitality in sharing them with other animals make them a great asset in building game and wildlife populations. Their holes serve at all times, but particularly during the winter months, as shelter and refuge for rabbit, quail, possum, skunks, partridges and other animals and birds. Female raccoon, when natural tree dens are scarce or non-existent, will house their litters in wood-chuck holes. So valuable does the Ohio Conservation Commission consider the place of the woodchuck and the hole he digs in the whole cyclical balance of wildlife that in 1947 it established a closed season from March, when the woodchuck wakens to emerge from his hole, to August, by which time the young are able to take care of themselves. The ruling does not prevent a farmer from reducing the woodchuck population which gets out of control but it does put an end to the idiotic and unsportsman-like habits of some city dwellers who go into the country-side merely to use the woodchuck for target practice. Among emigrant Southerners, both white and colored, woodchuck is considered a delicacy.

Rarely have I seen a muskrat by daylight and then only when, lying very still among the sedge grass and weeds, I have been so well hidden that he was unaware of my presence. His habit is to travel in the shallow water of a creek close to the bank and even though the water is clear he is difficult to notice or to see. The concealment arises less from his fantastically protective coloring than from the undulations of his wet shining body which are like the movements of the flowing water itself. He moves, half-swimming, half-walking with a flowing motion and only a sharp eye can detect his presence where there is any current at all.

Perhaps the most beautiful newcomers to the pond during the second summer were the dragonflies. They appeared in prodigious numbers, looking like gaudily painted miniature planes. At least three varieties were noticeable. One variety, the largest, was about three to four inches long, with purple-black body and with bars of black on the widespread transparent wings. Another smaller dragonfly came in various shades of green with deep emerald green wings. The third, smallest and most beautiful, was a fragile dragonfly all of one color, an iridescent turquoise blue with a body which appeared to be almost transparent as they hovered over the surface of the water. All three varieties spend the whole of their brief lives in frantically eating and breeding. They dart and hover over the shallow water, the floating algae and the water weeds, devouring hosts of tiny gnats, mosquitoes and other insects which deposit their eggs in the water where they hatch into larvae to feed the sunfish as well. The prodigious number of dragonflies over the new pond probably arose from the fact that the fish population has not yet become established to devour the larvae and act as a check upon the almost unlimited increase of insects.

The great numbers of hatching insects brought not only hordes of the delicate dragonflies, but wild, soaring flights of deep, iridescent blue and red swifts and barn swallows which each year build their neat mud nests on the beams of the big Bailey barn beside the pond. In the evenings they circle, hover and dive-bomb the newly hatched insects, dipping their tiny, swift wings into the water, sending up tiny jets of spray in the evening light.

Of course, within the depths of the new pond there came quickly into existence trillions of amoebae, rotifers and tiny plants and animals invisible to the naked eye which flourish in the warm shallow waters of ponds and in the form of fresh water plankton which makes up a large part of the food supply of the fish from the smallest pin-sized fry up through the larger sunfish. These animals and plants, seen under a microscope, reveal complicated and brilliantly beautiful patterns of life. Although invisible they comprise a vital part of the natural lifecycle of a pond. Doubtless they are carried there upon the feet of birds and muskrats or the damp skin of frogs and on the bellies of slithering water snakes from adjoining ponds and streams. Many already existed in the wet ground of the pond site. The Natural History Museum in New York City contains a truly wonderful exhibit of these organisms executed brilliantly in colored glass many thousands of times larger than life.

Nature has a million subtle ways of quickly converting a raw, new pond into an old pond, fertile and teeming with life, but in all our ponds we have helped her as much as possible to speed the rate of conversion. One thing which a good farmer quickly learns is that in fighting Nature he will always be defeated but that in working with her, he can make remarkable and immensely profitable progress. Beside the barnyard manure and the seeding of the banks we have thrust young willow butts here and there along the banks and every three or four feet along the crest of the dam. Within two or three years the fast growing willows, the particularly beautiful and hardy, semi-weeping variety known as *Babylonica,* will grow twelve to fifteen feet and along the dam their roots create a solid mat which binds the earth together and makes it resistant to the waters of the most devastating cloudbursts. Along the edge they provide the shade which the big bass love and a resting place for insects which drop into the water and feed the hungry fish waiting below.

The Conservation Commissions of many states send out free to all farmers of the state bundles of shrubs and trees for planting around farm ponds. These hasten the efforts of Nature to convert a new pond into an old one and provide food and shelter for small game. The bundles include native flowering wild crabapple, standing honeysuckle, fruit-bearing viburnums, hazelnuts, pines and many other shrubs and trees. These are now planted in the areas about the ponds and help to build up that balance and cycle in the pond and the area about it which is a part of any successful fish pond. The new ponds are treated with fertilizer along the edges in the shallow water to encourage the growing of vegetation which plays so large a part in the cycle of pond fertility and life. A little fertilizer—particularly phosphate—will increase the number and size of the fish enormously.

During the first summer of the Bailey pond's existence we transplanted to its borders a few roots of arrowleaf and some of the water plants already growing in the older ponds. It was a simple enough process, simply that of thrusting the roots into the soil in the shallow water. These took hold immediately and increased prodigiously during the summer, as much as many hundreds of times, joining the water and marsh vegetation already seeded there through visits of muskrats and water birds in providing shelter for all sorts of minute animal life as well as for the small fry which appeared mysteriously and those hatched out after the stocking of the new pond in the early spring with mature bass, bluegills and sunfish from the older ponds.

By the end of the second summer the first evidence of balance had become apparent. The plague of small frogs and toads had leveled off to a normal population, the number of dragonflies diminished and the whole cycle of birth, life, death, and rebirth had begun to operate.

At the end of the third year the new pond on the Bailey Place already took on the aspect of the older ponds. The shallow water had been invaded by thick growths of arrowhead, bulrush, water lilies and a great variety of water grasses and subaqueous vegetation. Within the refuge they provide against the attacks of the bigger fish, the water snakes and birds, there appeared in due course of time literally thousands of young bluegills, sunfish and young bass up to three or four inches in length, the fingerlings of the pound-size bluegills and the big bass which will make the sport of tomorrow.

A week ago we began seriously the annual "cleaning" of the older ponds with bamboo poles, worms, and a couple of big milk cans, transferring fish wholesale from the fertile older ponds into the newer ones. The task becomes a sport in which all the farm takes part. The boys, the older men and even some of the women join in, and in the crowded ponds every cast means a strike, and one never knows what one will get—a bluegill, a bass or any one of the varieties of sunfish, and sometimes in the Anson pond a nice-sized trout. Only the trout are thrown back because we want to establish in the Anson pond that cycle of trout and sunfish based upon the bass and sunfish cycle which has proven itself so productive in the old Fleming pond.

Fish after fish, the catch is tossed into the milk cans, kept aerated by changing the water and pouring in fresh bucketfuls constantly from the pond. There is a wide range of beauty in the catch from the lovely deep sea-green of the bass and the silvery-spotted beauty of the trout, through the whole range of sunfish up to the iridescent, fantastic beauty of the long-eared type with his brilliant yellow belly, his stripes and changeable colors and the jet-black spot behind his gills.

Last night we sat among the willows along the old Fleming pond, fishing, nine of us, as the sun went down and a virgin crescent moon appeared as the sky changed from scarlet and gold to pale mauve to deep blue. The women sat in the grass shelling the glut of peas from the garden for canning and the quick freeze and the small children yelled with excitement each time they managed to hook and bring in a fish. We fished until it was too dark to see the bobber and then set out with a flashlight to transfer the fish to the new ponds. There was at least thirty pounds of fish ranging in size from a few baby sunfish to a fine big bass of about four pounds which somehow had eluded us in "cleaning" the pond of big fellows the preceding autumn. And everyone had fresh fish for breakfast the next morning.

The farm pond is becoming rapidly not only a pleasure but

a necessity. State Conservation Commissions are encouraging them. Ohio aids the individual farm without cost in their construction. Missouri plans to construct 200 thousand farm ponds during the next few years. They tend to catch and hold the precious rainfall on thousands of farms, to supply water for the livestock, swimming holes, and fish for the table. On our farm whenever a family wants fish for supper one has only to take a pole and a line and in a half hour or more get all the fish he wants.

But there are other advantages to farm ponds which are not wholly utilitarian. Our ponds are each one a spot of beauty, a small universe teeming with life. The big herons visit them and the lovely red-winged blackbirds build their nests in the rushes along the borders. They are the delight of the big fierce Toulouse geese and the tame mallards. They are the source of much music in the night from the peeping of new young frogs to the booming bass of the big Louisiana bullfrogs which we put in as tadpoles years ago and which now measure as much as eighteen or twenty inches when stretched out. In April their borders turn green and gold with the lush foliage and flowers of the marsh marigold, and later they are bordered with the blue of Siberian iris and the purple and gold of the native wild flags. At night the muskrats move across the surface in the moonlight and the raccoons and foxes and possum come down out of the thick woods to drink and catch unwary frogs, leaving the imprint of their small paws in the wet mud along the banks. And there are the scavenging mud-turtles and a few big destructive snapping-turtles which the mallards avoid by shrewdly never taking their young onto the ponds until they are well grown. And there are countless birds, the swifts and barn swallows which skim low over the ponds in the blue evenings, to catch the insects hatching from their depths, and the flocks of goldfinches which finally mate off and build their nests from the down of the purple thistles growing in the damp ground. And in spring and autumn there are the visits of the wild ducks which join our mallards and feast off the richness of the farm ponds and the neighboring fields for three or four weeks at a time. For a lonely farm a pond provides life and fascination.

Each year, spring and autumn, we have been accustomed to visits of wild ducks. Usually these were mallards and so-called shallow-water ducks, but with the establishment of the Bailey pond we began to receive visits from flocks of bluebills and other deep-water ducks. We discovered presently that they were attracted by the tender shoots of the fast spreading arrowleaf, spending hours diving and burrowing for the young growth. Wherever they burrowed, their bills left tiny holes in the mud bottom of the pond. Dessie and Al often sit on the veranda of the big, old Bailey house in the evening watching the life on the pond until darkness comes down, the swallows take to the barn and the muskrat and raccoons come out to haunt the reeds and the shallow water.

In a way, a farm pond is a symbol of life itself. It is a bright spot on any farm, a whole universe in which the laws of Nature operate under the close and intimate gaze of the interested. One can find in farm ponds and along their borders almost everything. They change with the season, awakening from the frozen, silent sleep of winter, going into the beginning of spring and the fierce breeding life of early summer. They provide skating in winter and swimming in summer and good fishing for three seasons of the year. For the children they are a source of inexhaustible delight. And like the fishponds of the abbeys and castles of medieval Europe and the Dark Ages, when all the world fell apart in anarchy and disorder, they provide not only food for the table but peace for the soul and an understanding of man's relationship to the universe.

Gardens and Landscapes

An essential purpose of farming, Louis Bromfield believed, was not just to operate a commercial enterprise to grow crops and raise livestock but to create a "whole farm." This included the agricultural landscape, with its own aesthetic imperatives and potentials. Bromfield soon learned that having a garden around the house, in the fashion of the French, was not enough. He wanted his landscape to be of a piece, after the manner of an English country house. This essay describes how he achieved this and displays his firm grasp of the aesthetic principles necessary for its accomplishment, although it took an expert British horticulturist to show the way.

O ne does not simply plan, lay out and establish full-blown a garden or a landscape. If it is to be properly your own garden or your own landscape viewed from your bedroom window, you cannot hire it done. By doing so you may create a spectacular show of flowers and shrubs or a handsome somewhat artificial landscape but it will not be your own. Both may attract visitors who admire gardens and landscapes and who find both very fine examples, but they are likely to go away with a sense of something missing or a hidden sense of deadly familiarity on which they cannot quite place their fingers. Magnificent but they have a sense of having seen it all before. Perhaps because frequently it resembles those artificial, flower-stuffed gardens moved in wholesale to flower shows from the estates of Long Island millionaires.

A garden, a landscape or even a whole farm, if it is to be successful by any standard, is essentially a creation and an expression of an individual or at least of two or three individuals who feel alike toward it, who share the same aims and traditions; for tradition has much to do with the beautiful garden, landscape or farm. There should be a *rightness* in relation to the whole landscape, to the climate, to the country, to the regional architecture, to the type of soils, even perhaps to the existence of the natural birds and wildlife. It should have a relation to the past of the region, to history itself.

When we first set out to work on the gardens and the landscape of Malabar Farm, we inherited little but the natural wild beauty of the valley, the forest and the little stream that fed the marshes which later were to become known as the the Jungle. It was a frame and foundation but little else, for the areas around the various houses and farm buildings, save only at the Anson Place where old Mrs. Anson had constructed with infinite pains and labor a handsome rockery, were neglected and abandoned, shaggy and unkempt. A great many of the buildings were simply falling into ruin, and leaned at crazy angles waiting only for someone to give them a push or set a match to them. Here and there were piles of discarded rubbish and worn-out, rusting machinery, truckload after truckload of it. The only effort at order or planning was the annual cutting down of every bit of wild growth surrounding one or two small ponds and along the roadside, an action caused, I think, simply by some atavistic fear inherited by many in our countryside of a devouring forest which took over every small clearing unless one maintained a constant vigilance.

Our Ohio forest, which, if left alone, becomes thick and tropical and impenetrable during the summer, quite naturally takes over even today any field which is abandoned for a few years. The early settlers, who wrested their farms with so much labor and hardship out of this thick virgin forest, were forced perpetually to fight against the encroachment of the forest, and out of this ancient fear there still remains on many an Ohio farm a mania for cutting down every tree or shrub and all the vegetation along the roadsides and fencerows. It is very fortunate that the destroyers fight a perpetually losing battle in this rich country. One of the finest of American novels, written by Conrad Richter, is *The Trees* which is concerned largely with the struggle of one family of pioneers in the Ohio country to clear the luxuriant forest and the battle to prevent the forest from constantly moving in upon their little island of cleared land.*

Even large areas of the forest at Malabar had suffered before we came there for they had been pastured heavily by cattle and sheep which found little there to eat and so devoured the very wild flowers and forest seedlings in order to fill their hungry stomachs.

Except for the Anson Place and a little wild bottom pastureland and the impenetrable Jungle, the whole landscape had the look of a devastated area. But the natural frame was there, waiting. Perhaps it took some imagination to see what might be created there, but money, thought, imagination and hard work were necessary. I think I saw quite clearly the picture that might eventually fill the frame, but it has taken nearly fifteen years to arrive at something approaching the realization of that picture. Today the whole valley is unrecognizable as the same valley to which I returned one snowy day sixteen years ago after being away from home for nearly thirty years.

I have seen and known landscapes in many parts of the world, marvelously beautiful landscapes created out of the climate, soils and traditions of given areas. I am not a lover of arid desert countries or landscapes. While it is possible to recognize the spectacular beauty of rock and sky which sometimes occurs in such countries, I have always found myself miserable and unhappy in them after a short time, perhaps because I belong by nature, inclination, and perhaps even through atavistic forces, to rich green country with rainfall and four marked and distinct seasons. I am happiest in the landscapes and the countrysides of England, France, Austria and in general the temperate zones of Europe and North America. There is where I belong—a feeling which most readers, and especially gardeners and farmers, will recognize at once, whatever their pref-

---

*There never was any pine forest in the State of Ohio. Because of the ample and well-distributed rainfall and the natural mineral richness of the soil, the forest was all hardwood save for remnants on north slopes here and there of the beautiful preglacial hemlock. Even today where pine plantations have been used to reforest abandoned hill farms, the hardwoods frequently seed themselves in and eventually crowd out the pines.

erence. There are of course individuals who are insensible to these things and are perhaps happy anywhere so long as they are prosperous.

Again, while I can recognize the wild grandeur and beauty of the Alps or the Rocky Mountains, I do not want to live among them. I like mountains as a tourist and for skiing and fishing purposes, but I would certainly be miserably unhappy either on a summit with an immense and overpowering view or in the bottom of a narrow dark valley where the sun rises two hours later and sets two hours earlier than in the world outside. High wild mountains can be a prison to some people as they are to me.

I think the mountains I have loved best were the biggest, most overpowering mountains in the world, the Himalayas, and this was not because I ever visited them or really knew them, ever attempted to scale their immense heights or even to approach them, but because I saw them always from a great distance, a whole white and glistening world rising against the horizon as the background to the lush, green jungly country— the rice paddies and ponds, the leopards and the wild elephants of Cooch Behar in the north of Bengal. On the hottest, muggiest day the sight of this immense and distant frozen world filled one with a sense of coolness. Fortunately I was far removed from their ice and snow, their storms and wind, their barren rocks.

And so at Malabar in those first struggling days, I saw in my imagination a countryside that was soft and verdant with a little river running through it, where the fields were neat and green and rich and the forest and marshes as wild as it was possible to make them. I did not see a landscape with harsh wire fences and clean fencerows and straight rows of corn, good or bad. I saw the kind of landscape that one finds in well-managed and well-farmed areas of Northern Europe and this country— the kind of landscape one finds most naturally in those areas where the great glaciers have deposited whole mountains of gravel and silt that have an eternal and indestructible fertility. In such areas—one finds them in Northern Europe, in upper New York State, northeastern Ohio, Wisconsin and Illinois— the hills are not eroded mountains; they are more often simply great heaps of fertility, where side by side there are rich valleys and slopes, well cultivated and fertile, together with forests and marshes that are completely wild. It is a kind of country in which there are always birds and abundant wildlife, streams and lakes and ponds and, above all, countless springs of clear, cool water. That is the kind of country in which we set up Malabar Farm and went to work to repair the damage and devastation created by generations of bad and careless agriculture.

But one does not repair a whole landscape, heal the wounds and restore the natural beauty and fertility, overnight. It takes work and thought, imagination and, I think, above all else, time, patience and love. It is essentially a creative job, one of the most difficult and fascinating in the world. One can neither hurry nor short-cut Nature.

I think it is imagination and a kind of vision which drives the good farmer and the good gardener to work all hours of the day in every kind of weather, often enough beyond his strength. Arthritic old ladies forget the agonies of their rheumatism in order to tend some tender plant or shrub; the old and tired farmer will work into the darkness far beyond his strength to keep his fields neat, productive and in order. This urge and drive has made of me, as it has made of many a gardener, a kind of contortionist, this drive which forces one to stretch muscles and sinews into impossible positions merely for the sake of a seedling or the pruning of a plant surrounded by other plants which must not be trampled or injured. Certainly it has done much to keep a figure which should have become large and heavy and rotund by nature in ordinary city life, and maintained muscles and a suppleness which are quite as good as they were at eighteen.

In his imagination every good gardener and farmer sees the harvest with the planting of the first seed. As the earth covers it he sees the flowers, the rich grain, the beautiful grass that will soon be born from the seed. With each hoeing, with each weeding, with each cultivation he is driven by the vision. And the true gardener and farmer suffers with his plants and crops; if it is too hot and dry, he becomes ill and really suffers himself; if the plants are ill, he feels their illness in his bones. It is this vision and drive which keep the good farmer forever planting, forever hoping, persistent and undefeated in the face of flood, of drought, of every disaster.

And so for fifteen years I have worked and suffered and

sometimes spent money which I should not have spent, not merely upon restoring land and achieving rich crops, but in the creation of something more than that—a whole farm, a whole landscape, in which I could live in peace and with pride and which I could share with others to whom it would bring pleasure. The most satisfactory things about such a vision and such a goal are that one must work perpetually with Nature and that the task is never really finished nor the vision ever really achieved. There is always something more to be done; and so I shall be well occupied until I die at last, I hope in the midst of that very landscape and garden I have helped to create. It is not a task or a vision with which one can grow bored, for one is living with the whole of the universe which, as all will agree, is fairly inexhaustible during the short span of our lives.

Because I have lived long in France and loved it just as much and in some ways perhaps even more than my own Pleasant Valley, the first vision I had was a very French one—a landscape with tall poplars and many willows, a misty, feathery landscape with great trees like those in the pictures of Claude Lorrain. I didn't think this all out clearly in any definite terms; it was just there in the back of my mind.

After fifteen years, the landscape is at least partly achieved. The fields are green and well ordered. In place of bare wire fences there are the hedges of multiflora rose, impenetrable alike to hunter and to old sows. The willows are everywhere along the streams and around the ponds. Even the white barns and silos with their green roofs fit into the picture now, for the areas around them have been cleaned and tended and the trees planted long ago have grown to great heights in our rich soil and now the half-hidden houses seem surrounded and protected by them against the hot sun of August and the cold blasts of the winter blizzards which sweep from the north down the valley. Indeed, the houses, instead of appearing simply stuck into a bare landscape, appear to have grown there like the trees themselves.

It is a landscape which has grown more rapidly than I ever expected, partly because of the richness of our soils and partly because of small things done here and there—a mulch of stones or manures around a tree or a shrub, the thrusting into the wet spring earth of willow cuttings carried under the arm during long Sunday walks along the streams and ponds, the good manure coming from the big cattle barns, the legumes and the green manures grown in the field, the operations of modern machinery and deep tillage, together with the love and care and imagination of children and grown-ups. All of these things have helped Nature herself on the way; no force on earth will give such a response and such a reward as Nature when you understand her and work with her.

Mount Jeez, which for two generations had been overgrown with brambles and poverty grass and was known throughout the township as Poverty Knob, is a green hill today where the cattle in summer, as if by arrangement, come out of the shade as the hot sun begins to descend and move across the green pastures in the fading blue light. Mount Jeez is more than a mile away across the valley from the Big House and you can watch the cattle in the evening from the terrace or the verandas, a sight which warms you and makes you feel good. And the forest land is no longer pastured and scraggly and gullied but grows wild and thick with its carpets of wild flowers and wild ferns, where in early spring the delicious morels grow here and there in clumps amid the wild geranium, the trilliums, the dogtooth violets.

There are also those areas near the houses which have become in time gardens that have been built partly by care and love and partly by the response of a kindly, benevolent Nature. Somehow, it seems that Nature understands at times what it is you want to do and helps you along the way. With us she has certainly done so with the hundreds of thousands of jonquils and daffodils which now grow wild in the bluegrass pastures and along the edges of marsh and forest. A few bulbs placed in the ground, and presently there comes in spring a whole drift of blossoms where before there was nothing. In the forests of Chantilly and Ermenonville and Compiègne, the whole earth between the great oaks and beeches is carpeted in spring with wild daffodils, bluebells and lilies of the valley, the *muguet* which brings luck and when it appears on the flower stands of Paris means that summer is at hand. All my life I have wanted so many jonquils and narcissus growing wild that one could pick baskets of them and never notice the loss. We can do that now at Malabar in the orchards and green pastures. They are everywhere on all sides with the cows and calves moving among them, feeding on the young spring grass without ever touching the blossoms.

The first gardens we laid out around the big houses were, consciously or unconsciously, conceived in imitation of the gardens on the small place where we lived so long in France. The house there, described in detail in *Pleasant Valley* was an old *presbytère,* built in the seventeenth century and inhabited by the priest who tended the old twelfth-century chapel until it became half-ruined and disaffected. Like the fields of Malabar, the place had been half-abandoned and neglected for years before we came to Senlis. As the gardens went, there was nothing but a semicircle of ancient shaggy lilacs; the rest was weeds. But again the natural frame was a beautiful one. An ancient gray wall separated the *presbytère* from the ancient chapel and the graveyard that lay beyond—a graveyard dating from the Middle Ages which some thrifty Frenchman had changed into a vegetable garden perhaps a century or two earlier. Beside the chapel and the house ran a small clear canal with the charming name of La Nonette or The Little Nun. On the opposite side of the small canal lay an old orchard actually below the level of the running water, so that one descended steps from the canal down into the lower garden. Save for a few ancient apple and pear trees there was no vegetation worth consideration. But the important thing was that we had a kind of vision of how the whole place should look and after ten years it looked much as we saw it in the creator's vision and it became known as a famous small garden which was visited year by year by gardeners and architects from all Europe and America. Being small, not more than two or three acres in all, it became literally crowded with flowers, with roses spilling over the walls down to the water of the little canal, lilies which grew magnificently, pinks, seven-foot delphinium, really giant foxgloves, and the fuchsias, the geraniums, the ageratum that grew in the pots on the terrace.

It was essentially an English garden and its exuberance frequently astonished the French who, with their logical and civilized point of view, regarded most gardens not as a part of Nature but as merely geometric designs which were an extension of the ordered terrace and the classical façade of the house. Yet it was at the same time a kind of international garden for the ideas came from everywhere. The pots of flowers on the hot stone-flagged terrace were in imitation of the beautiful potted gardens I had seen in Mysore in Southern India where everything was grown in pots and flowers were brought in during their period of blooming and replaced by other plants in bloom when they began to fade. It was a small, intimate, lush, well-kept garden—a garden which I soon discovered could *not* be reproduced at Malabar.

There were many reasons why this was so. The landscape itself was much larger and wilder than the surrounding landscape in France. There were no ancient gray walls against which the clematis and roses could display their deep, rich and delicate colors. I myself, now the proprietor of a hard-working big farm that desperately needed restoration and with far greater responsibilities to community and state than I had ever known in France, simply had not the time to tend it carefully and meticulously, to keep an eye on every plant. Labor was scarce and expensive and badly trained. But most of all, I think, the thing which proved defeating was the exuberance of growth and the wildness that was characteristic of our Ohio country and which in my long absence I had nearly forgotten.

Plants which took naturally to our Ohio soils grew and increased with an abundance and exuberance which was almost nightmarish. The day lilies which I had tended so carefully in the French garden to keep alive and in modest health became in Ohio real monsters of reproduction and vigor. It was necessary to separate them at least every three years. If they were the type which grew by underground shoots, they quickly overtook and smothered everything that grew near them. On the roadside, the common red variety grew everywhere like the most vigorous weeds. Actually the perennial asters, varieties which I had seen tended carefully in the gardens of my English friends, grew wild everywhere along the roads, in the marshes and on the borders of the forest. And, of course, the goldenrod, so carefully cultivated in Europe under the name of *solidago,* was our worst weed on the poorer land, where in October it produced literally seas of gold. And the dogwood and wild crab-apples, regarded in Europe as rare ornamental trees difficult to force into bloom, invaded constantly our orchards and pastures wherever birds and other wild creatures dropped the seeds.

And here in this larger, wilder country with no walls to protect the gardens, weed seeds blew in from everywhere and invaded everything. Some even grew vigorously beneath the snows all through the winter. Even in the beginning it became apparent that despite any desire on our part or any amount of nostalgia, Nature simply did not want the kind of carefully tended and ordered garden that one had in Europe. This was no ancient ordered countryside with centuries behind it of care and work and tending; this Ohio country was still wild country, exuberant, vigorous, primitive and only a few generations away from the forest wilderness.

In virtually the only time at Malabar when we attempted to force Nature, she simply refused to co-operate and turned hostile. For in the end we could not reproduce there the particular kind of garden and beauty we had created in France. Standard roses presently curled up and died but the half-wild bramble roses, the wichurianas, the rugosas, the China roses overtook and overran everything or turned into small trees of their own accord without the least help. The wonderful large-flowered climbing roses which had covered walls, houses and bridges in the garden in France could not take the violence of the American winter but the floribundas turned into giant flower-covered shrubs. Because of the highly available lime content of our glacial subsoils, rhododendrons and even some forms of azaleas were impossible; once their roots penetrated deeply they turned sickly and presently they died. But since I never believe in trying to force plants and shrubs to grow under conditions in which they are unhappy, we presently abandoned all efforts to raise them and instead expended our knowledge and efforts upon the whole range of plants and shrubs, an enormous one, which flourished in our native soils. Every kind of weed invaded the gravel paths which in France had been so easy to keep neat and clean. Even elm trees and maples and black walnuts seeded themselves behind our backs and threatened to turn the whole garden back into forest once more.

Then came the war and all thought of continuing the struggle was abandoned and Nature was permitted to have her way. For nearly five years the garden went wild and in doing so produced what Nature wanted. Once we yielded to her, she rewarded us handsomely.

This was really forest country and wild country. It was a wild and natural garden that Nature meant us to have and by the Good Lord that is what we ended up with; and I know now when all the trees and shrubs and bulbs burst into flower everywhere around the Big House each spring that Nature was quite right. There is for weeks a kind of glorious blaze of color visible nearly a mile away from the Pleasant Valley Road, and in the gardens themselves there is a kind of misty, even mystical, beauty created partly by the delicate spring colors and partly by the misty green of the weeping willows and the tall upward thrust of the Lombardy poplars, partly by the pale drooping Chinese splendor of the wistaria which would never bloom so long as it was carefully tended in an ordered garden but which, when neglected and turned wild, filled the hundred-foot height of the Balm of Gilead trees with a misty cloud of white and purple flowers hanging low on the reflecting water of the ponds.

In our country, trees grow quickly into giants and shrubs into trees. Forsythia and Cydonia grow fifteen to twenty feet high and layer and spread themselves in all directions. Flowering Japanese crabs and cherries quickly attain the height and the size of the great gnarled apple trees in the ancient orchard behind the house where the land rises upward toward the clifflike outcrops of pink sandstone, covered with ferns and wild columbine and tilted as if by design of Nature to make a background for the drifts of crocus and grape hyacinths, jonquils and narcissus in the bluegass beneath the blossoming apple trees. Once we turned Nature loose, and let survive what belonged there and pleased itself there, she presented us with one of the loveliest of gardens, especially during the exuberant Ohio spring.

Many people contributed to the change and increasing beauty of the valley landscape: Orrie Zody, a neighboring farmer, who helped during the first summer with the cleaning up of the rubbish which had first to be got out of the way; Dan Quinn, who with his lusty crew of young helpers moved to Florida in winter and back to Ohio in summer, who built walls and did the grading of the rough ground around the house and made the first plantings of flowering shrubs and trees; and Charlie Martin, who, single-handed during the war, kept the farm in vegetables and battled against the encroaching weeds and forest. And there were countless friends, come for a week-end visit or to spend a week or two, who set to work with good heart, to weed, to hoe, to prune.

During all the war, it was a scattered fight, intermittent and fought with guerrilla troops, volunteers and drummer boys, of an intensity which only an Ohioan can perhaps appreciate and understand; but the significant fact was that we never gave in and when the war was over we had no victory but only a breathing spell. War returned once more and everything on the farm and in the garden began to slump back into a tangle.

There is such a thing as a wild and natural garden becoming *too* wild and *too* undisciplined, and with the coming of the Korean mess and of a second war that was what began to happen to the gardens surrounding the Big House. Again the young men were all drafted for the ugly, uncivilized, meaningless business of war and the older ones were drawn back into an industry to which war, carried on with the blood and suffering of the younger men, brought new prosperity and new high wages.

It was about this time that two young Englishmen stepped in and took over. Daviad Rimmer, trained at the North Wales College of Horticulture, came first. He came not primarily as a gardener but to take over and carry on the work of experimentation and research in the soil plots, a position for which he was well trained. But he came from Cheshire and was therefore English of the English. He had grown up in the ordered beauties of English countryside and farms. Their beauty was actually in his blood and he saw, almost at once, that while Nature at Malabar had helped us out by co-operation, she had begun, with the ever increasing fertility and preservation of rainfall, to overdo the job. He had what I had never really acquired as a gardener, the sense of a garden being a part of the whole landscape, of seeing a garden or landscape as a whole and not in small restricted bits and pieces, concentrated, lush and isolated—a conception with which I had perhaps become corrupted during years of life in France where everything is ordered, pruned, staked and grown against walls.

It is out of the broad conception which David brought with him from Cheshire that the magnificent beauty of the English garden, farm and landscape has been created throughout centuries of thought, taste, practical good sense and even genius.

The French look upon a garden as an ornate extension of the architecture of the house or as a neat and ordered, practical, utilitarian affair which fills the larder or makes a living; but with the Englishman, from the owner of the semidetached villa along the tracks of the Midland Railway to the owner of the great English country house where once was practiced the most civilized living ever known to mankind, the garden must be a thing of romantic beauty as well as part of the landscape. Indeed, in some great English country houses in the past the whole of the landscape for miles has been treated as a single vast garden. It was David who brought this conception to Malabar.

Even as a resident for years of Europe, I still remained an American when it came to gardening and even, perhaps, to farming; I was and am impatient for quick results. I planted shrubs and even flowers too closely together in the hope that in a few weeks or a few years, the whole place would be lush and overgrown and have a look of age. It is this impatience, this overplanting, this passion for speed, even in Nature, which makes many a new householder the victim of a swindling commercial landscape gardener.

From the very beginning I had definitely overplanted everywhere and when the war came and the gardens and shrubbery had to be neglected because there was no help, they became a veritable jungle through which it was difficult to fight one's way. It was David who ruthlessly saw the picture not in parts but as a whole, as a garden, or a farm or a valley or landscape should be seen. He had a fearful struggle to realize his conception for each clump of lilies, each shrub, each tree was precious to me. But David, like myself, is a Capricorn, of a tribe characterized by stubbornness, persistence and undefeatability, and he kept persisting, pruning a shrub or tree here and there when I had my back turned, refencing the shaggy ill-kept orchard so that the cattle were admitted to keep it all clean and well grassed and to wander across the scene just outside the windows of the Big House. Each discovery of his perfidy was at first an anguish, and it might have taken years for him to accomplish by persistence and guile the fullness of his purpose. Essentially he was an artist creating a picture on the grand style. I was a miniature painter and pretty messy about it at the same time. As a practitioner of the Green Thumb category I would yield to no one; but in laying out the gardens I was fussy. In general I practiced the very antithesis of the excellent maxim given me a generation ago by an old French gardener who said, "Never make a small and narrow path in a *small* garden or, in fact, in any garden."

The triumph and the achievement of David's purpose came when I acquired a big farm in Brazil and went there for part of each winter. On my return at a time when in the North the winter was still with us and the branches of the trees were still bare, I was appalled, for the landscape all about the house seemed stripped and almost bare. It was only when the shrubs and trees began to burgeon that I began to see what he had seen and I had not seen. The overplanting, the crowding was gone. I even discovered trees and shrubs whose existence I had forgotten and which now began to show their full glory. Part of the gardens was turned into a calf lot planted with fruit trees, and here drifts and clouds of crocus, grape hyacinths, jonquils and narcissus began to appear as they did in the orchards and in the bluegrass pastures. The cows did them no injury but seemed to walk almost daintily in order to avoid crushing them.

Around the ponds, where the trees and shrubs had become a tangled jungle, trees and flowering shrubs emerged in a singleness of form and color which was reflected in the water; and I understood what David was doing and had already done, perhaps without even knowing it. He was creating not a pinched garden or a crowded garden or a tangled, ragged, untidy field or farm, but a kind of Constable landscape in which the flowers and shrubs and ornamental trees merged and blended into the native landscape of our part of Ohio with its magnificent oaks, beeches and maples. The hedges of multiflora rose, so practical and useful, became a part of the whole picture. The farm was no longer crowding the overgrown gardens. The whole of the farm was itself becoming a garden, planned skillfully and with the taste and understanding of an artist . . . an artist who could perhaps only be an Englishman with the misty dreaminess and perfection of the English landscape in his very blood. One could not really discern where the gardens ended and the farm began. The very pastures and orchards gradually became gardens.

In the exuberance and fertility of our country, the trees, the hedges, the wild flowers, even the lilies tend to get out of hand. Each hot damp summer they make a prodigious growth, and each winter season they must be subdued and brought back again to the discipline and order without destroying romantic naturalness. There is a common assumption that the formal garden with its ordered rows and beds is difficult to create and maintain and that a romantic informal garden takes care of itself. No assumption could be less true. The formal garden requires merely architecture and some transplanting, hoeing and weeding; the romantic, natural garden is an unending burden and requires a discipline and a concentration which no formal gardener ever attains or understands. A twig or branch must be snipped here and there, a shrub removed or transplanted. The drifts of daffodils and the apparently spontaneous beauty along the borders of a pond must be watched, guarded and disciplined constantly. The burgeoning clumps of lilies must be separated and transplanted. A tree or shrub must be given air and space to emphasize its beauty. Like a painter one must study the very landscape, regarding it with squinted eye; one must consider it in differing lights. But most of all one must never leave a landscape or any part of it to itself unless it is the thick forest or marsh, and even here there is work to be done with the planting of marsh marigolds or carpets of the wild violets, which grow so easily in our country, or with the apparently careless growth of dogwood and wild crabapple.

The work is never ended, and if one neglects it for a single season the picture becomes altered and changed and a certain ragged, untidy effect to carelessness creeps in. Just as agriculture is the most difficult and complex of all professions, so is the creation and maintenance of a beautiful landscape one of the greatest and most difficult of arts. I am not speaking now of the vast and lurid "views" of monotonous forests or craggy snow-capped mountains which only emphasize the puny insignificance of man but of the beautiful landscape which provides evidence of his civilization and his sense of industry, intelligence, taste and art. Without these things, the insignificance of man and his unimportance become simply overwhelming.

A little later Patrick Nutt, who had his training in the greatest of all schools, Kew Gardens, came over to join David. Patrick's primary job was that of hybridizing, propagation and greenhouse work but during the summer months he too is occupied with the experimental and research plots and the vegetable gardens where much of the experimentation is done. He too came to contribute his share of the genius which English gardeners, both amateur and professional, possess and he too has left the imprint of his knowledge and taste across the face of the Malabar landscape. No one, I think, understands better what it is that a growing plant likes and needs. Whatever he grows is essentially a specimen plant and out of a very small greenhouse and a few hotbeds he produces quantites of flowers through the winter, apparently with little effort and time. He is like a good dairyman with his cows; the plants seem to like him and he seems to like the plants and out of the mutual affection, miracles are born. I doubt that any two young men now working in this country are contributing more to the knowledge and science of soils and production than these two young Englishmen. Fortunately, they have come to the States to stay and David is already a citizen of this country for which I think American agriculture and horticulture may well be grateful.

Once I gave David and Patrick a free hand, I began to realize that if I still wanted my lush small perfect garden it would have to be *not* among the ravines and hills and rocks which surrounded the Big House but on the low flat land below the pond at the Bailey Place, and so there came into being there a garden where, as in the French *potager,* flowers and vegetables and fruits are grown all together under the most concentrated and intensified conditions. And it is there that I find myself most of the time, where the delphinium brushes leaves with the rhubarb and the lilies and roses flourish side by side with the asparagus and the strawberries. And in this flat rich garden where much of the experimentation is carried on, there is always a wealth of magnificent, even specimen, flowers, for cutting, for the roadside stand and for the pleasure of the thousands who visit Malabar each year. With the passing of each season this garden becomes richer and more beautiful with that special beauty that is found in the French *potager* where the flowers and vegetables all are of specimen quality, where the great leaves of the rhubarb or the ornate foliage of the eggplant or the Corinthian leaves and purple blossoms of the artichoke are quite as beautiful as any of the flowers.

I think now we are on our way with the gardens and the landscape of Pleasant Valley. We have found the things which belong there (as I myself belong). We understand the climates and the soils and each year new mysteries are unveiled and wonderful things take place in the depth of the good earth from which all of us come and to which all of us must return. It is a happy life and one in which there is an immense variety and to which there is no end, for even after death someone else will carry it along. Now when I step out of the door the whole of the valley seems to be a beautiful landscape by Constable or Claude Lorrain. It is as beautiful in winter as in full summer, as lovely in the pastel colors of spring as it is in the flaming colors of October. It didn't just happen. It took a lot of thought and a lot of work. But it has been worth it. And the task is never finished. It goes on and on.

The Roadside Market
to End All Roadside Markets

*These days, the direct marketing of specialty vegetables and fruits
is the wave of the future in an agricultural economy suffering
from a surfeit of commodity crops. Those commercial farmers as
well as part-timers who have lately gone into this business should
know that Louis Bromfield beat them to it by a country mile and
forty years. For those who are intrigued by the possibilities of this
enterprise, as seller or buyer, here is the definitive essay on the
topic.*

T here was never any plan at Malabar to go into the business of vegetables and fruits or to raise them for sale in the city. It just happened; in a way we were forced into the business by the increasing number of people who stopped at Malabar to buy the vegetables grown in the plots which supplied the people of the farm and where the research and experimentation was carried on. Many of these unsolicited customers were in the beginning casual visitors to the farm or came down through Pleasant Valley for the evening drive. Many of them stopped at Malabar to look at the vegetables and flowers, for the garden area is always open to any visitors who are interested.

It is an inviting spot, for the main plots lie in a flat area just below the pond and from the lane that runs along the top of the high dam the whole of the garden plots, with their lush and neat rows of vegetables, is visible. The beauty and quality of the vegetables raised by David Rimmer and Patrick Nutt spoke for themselves and year after year the number of those who wanted the vegetables increased.

There were two reasons for this: the obvious quality of nearly everything grown there and the fact that we had been working for years to eliminate as far as possible all dusts and sprays. When the visitors asked questions they found that no inorganic dusts and sprays and no arsenical ones were ever used and that the amount of vegetable poisons used, when necessary, had declined to less than 5 per cent of the dusts and sprays that had been needed twelve years earlier.

For years we had simply given away or fed to the pigs or plowed in the surplus vegetables, but the increasing numbers of people who wanted to buy them not only interrupted our work (for we did not want to be disagreeable) but gave us the idea of perhaps organizing the whole thing and making it simpler not only for the buyers but for ourselves. And so we backed into the whole business of market gardening and a market stand, which has become perhaps the most profitable undertaking per acre of all the projects at Malabar Farm.

Across the road from us throughout the summer and on week ends in winter live our friends, Bill and Sara Solomon, who some years earlier had bought three small run-down, half-abandoned farms, put them together and set out to restore them with the help and advice of all of us at Malabar. They have four children: Mary, who is almost a young woman, and two girls and a boy, Carol, Sara Lou and Bill, who are triplets. Bill had a small shed which he had moved out from a parking lot in Mansfield. With all of this, we seemed to have a setup. The shed was moved to the edge of the road, a home-made sign with the legend MALABAR FARM QUALITY PRODUCTS was set up, David and Pat brought in the surplus vegetables, the Solomon kids set about selling them and we were in business. Now when people wanted vegetables we did not have to interrupt our work to get them. We had only to send them across the road.

From the very beginning the business far exceeded all expectations. Despite the fact that the market stand was not located on a main highway but on the winding unnumbered back roads of our countryside, there were plenty of buyers and frequently we ran out of stock. Some of them lived in the summer cottages along the big lake, some came from neighboring villages and towns and some from a considerable distance. The fact that Pleasant Valley is beautiful country did not hurt our business. It had long since become an "evening drive" for hundreds of citizens from neighboring towns. And presently housewives who found the quality of the vegetables good told other housewives and our business grew.

By the end of the summer it became evident that our business had far outgrown the little shed with its home-painted sign and at the close of the season, when the last celery and squash and potatoes had been sold, the inspiration came for the roadside market that was to be a beautiful and airy pavilion with a whole brook of fresh spring water flowing through it. During the winter all of us sat around the fire in the evenings and "had ideas." Then when the frost came out of the ground Ivan Bauer and Dwight Schumacher came into the picture and went to work and by late June the new roadside stand was ready for business.

This time David and Pat thought they were well set to meet the demand. They had doubled and tripled the production of many vegetable crops and extended their activities far beyond the borders of the plots surrounded by the hedge of multiflora rose into the adjoining fields.

The grand opening which followed the party of the Turning on of the Waters, took place on the Fourth of July week end, and before the week end was over we knew that we were in for the same trouble as the year before—with all the expansion we were going to run short and fail to meet the demand. During the whole week end practically everyone on the farm was in the garden harvesting beets, carrots, radishes, rhubarb—whatever was ready or available. The market sold out its whole supply four or five times over, and at nightfall all of us fell into bed. It was evident that we were going to need a kind of storeroom and near-by warehouse where we could stock vegetables the night before and have them ready for the daytime demand.

So Dwight Schumacher, the building contractor, was called in again and within a week constructed for us, on the other side of the road from the stand, a storehouse which is ingenious and serves its purpose brilliantly by providing excellent cool storage for vegetables and fruits both in summer and in winter. The storehouse is built partly underground into the slope of the hillside below the road and is constructed of concrete block with a damp earthen floor. But the most efficient and wonderful thing about the storehouse is that we again utilized the hard-working spring. Inside, we constructed high wide troughs of concrete through which a whole stream of spring water flows winter and summer. It comes in from underground and flows out through wide shallow troughs on the outside which serve for washing and cleaning the vegetables. Over the washing trough there is an arbor which one day will be overgrown with grape vines. Trumpet vines are planted to cover the roof and ampelopsis to cover the small amount of wall that is exposed to the sun. As the vegetables come in each evening from the garden they are washed and cleaned and stored inside, many of them in the running spring water. By morning and the time of opening for business they are chilled through in live spring water, crisp and fresh and glistening. As supplies on the stand run out we have only to carry the chilled fresh vegetables across the road from the storehouse to the stand. One of the advantages is that the live spring water flowing through what is in reality a kind of underground cavern not only provides constant moisture but maintains an even temperature and prevents freezing even in the coldest weather.

In addition to the attraction offered to many a vegetable buyer and gourmet by the great reduction in the use of dusts and sprays and in the cases of many vegetables by their elimination altogether, the market stand has a strict rule that nothing but the best is put on sale at the stand. The best is not necessarily the biggest fruit or the biggest vegetable, as those who know and like to eat have long since come to understand. It is the flavor, the tenderness and, for the nutritionist, the vitamin and mineral content which in turn go with good flavor and good nutritive qualities. There is no better example of all this than the difference in quality and flavor and texture of the great, showy apples of the Pacific Coast and California and those from the Northeastern states. It is the reason why the real gourmet rarely buys a Western apple and why many a luxury shop in New York City sells only Ohio, Virginia, New York State and Michigan apples.

The prices at the Malabar market are sometimes lower but much more frequently higher than those of the city markets and the great chain stores, but we feel justified because of the care taken in raising the produce and the obvious and indisputable quality and freshness of those raised in the Malabar gardens. In a practical sense we have been able up to the present to sell everything that we have raised and frequently have run low on the supply or exhausted it. There is no point in the country roadside market attempting to compete with the chain stores on a basis of price and the chain store customer is quite frankly not the kind of customer we seek but rather those who want freshness and high quality and are willing to pay for it. One of the boys on the farm has jokingly suggested that we put up a notice, "Chain store trade not solicited."

One of the principal attractions contributed by the icy water of the big spring which runs through both market stand and storage house is that, by keeping the vegetables a few hours in or near it, they become chilled *through* not with the dead cold of refrigeration but with the damp live cold of the spring water. Once the vegetables are chilled through, it is possible to transport them on a hot day for a hundred miles or more in the trunk of a car without their losing their freshness. This factor has brought quality buyers from cities all over northern Ohio, who come once or twice a week to load up their cars. In some ways, the market stand on an obscure and unnumbered back road in Ohio has proven again, if proof were necessary, the saying of Emerson that if you build a better mousetrap the world will beat a path to your door.

Nor do we follow the deceptive and even shady practice of many a roadside market in these times where the proprietor buys his produce in the city market, hauls it out to his stand and then sells it to the casual passer-by as "home-grown." Much of the stuff sold on the roadside markets today as "home-grown" is frequently of much lower quality and freshness than that which can be bought in the city markets, even after its long passage through the heat and dust of the commission market.

We have also made a specialty, and increasingly followed the policy, of raising and marketing vegetables which cannot be found or are rare in the average city market and are varieties which are no longer planted by the big market gardeners for the general market. We have been producing Bibb lettuce for years, long before it was known outside the most expensive and excellent restaurants frequented by the *gourmet* and we experiment constantly with new varieties of vegetables which are sometimes superior to old ones. We have a whole following of customers who come to us to get okra and the tiny red and yellow

tomatoes and Italian paste tomatoes and white pearl onions, and there are customers so addicted to the happy and healthy habit of watercress that they will come from a great distance simply to get it dark green and fresh out of the icy, swift-flowing spring water. Sometimes they will consume a whole bunch on the spot while engaged in conversation.

We also raise old-fashioned varieties of cantaloupe, many of them far superior in flavor and taste to the standard one variety that is about all one can find in the markets everywhere, not because of its excellence but because it ships well and can be picked green and will ripen on the way to the market or while it stands round the backroom of a city store. Our own cantaloupe are ripened in the sun, go unpicked until they are ripened and are then chilled in spring water. The old varieties treated thus bring big premium prices and the only difficulty is to meet the demand. And we have found that by grading our potatoes into three sizes—(1) the big outsize ones for baking, (2) the standard grade A size for general cooking, (3) and the tiny size for cooking as "new potatoes"—they bring a bigger price and the smallest potatoes, the ones to be boiled with their skins on, sell best of all. Again this practice appeals to the customers who want to eat well and have the finest quality rather than the lowest price.

Celery root or celeriac for salads, soups and flavoring attracts a whole category of customers as do the winter radishes popular with the many citizens of Central European background in our part of Ohio. These grow to an immense size and the Bavarians and Czechs eat them while drinking beer. They are of three principal varieties: one a kind of crystal white, one pink and one (the Black Spanish) white with a black skin. Buried or kept in a good root cellar, they provide fresh radishes for the table throughout the winter.

The old watercress bed below the road quickly turned out to be a gold mine, for it required throughout the year little more than the labor of picking. Nothing is more difficult to find in prime condition on the city market than watercress, for once taken out of the cold spring water it loves, the cress begins to deteriorate in quality very rapidly and to lose, as it rapidly wilts and turns yellow, its qualities both of flavor and nutrition. One of the reasons for the high price of watercress in the city markets arises from this fact of rapid deterioration as the process creates a high percentage of spoilage and unmarketability. At Malabar it is cut from the pond, bunched and immediately taken across the road where it is put back again almost immediately into the same cold spring water from which it came. Good watercress or any watercress demands clean, clear, cold running water. If the plants have a gravel bed rather than muck or silt, the quality and flavor will be better. The original beds at Malabar were the native wild cress, smaller in leaf but more peppery and flavorsome than the "improved" big-leaf varieties. We now have at Malabar a crossed variety with larger leaves which seems to have retained the original peppery flavor of the wild cress. This was accomplished by the simple expedient of scattering a little of the "improved" but rather flat variety in all the spring streams. The crossed variety has come to dominate.*

One of the factors which give the vegetables at Malabar a high quality is the very rapid growth. The more quickly a vegetable grows to marketable size, the better its quality in terms of vitamins, flavor, tenderness and nutrition. As we built up the soils in the experimental plots at Malabar with quantities of barnyard and green manures and a good program of commercial fertilizers, the period of growth to maturity became increasingly smaller, but the great change came when we began experimenting with soluble fertilizers and a variety of formulas suited to given plants, all of which included some twelve minor elements. Eventually these formulas and the machinery for mixing them in the irrigation water were put on the market under the name of Fertileze by a corporation set up in New Lexington, Ohio, under the name of Nutritional Concentrates, Inc. The use of these soluble fertilizers has great advantages from every point of view. . . . Not only have they improved the general quality of market produce but the rapid growth has given us the advantage of supplying the early home-grown market when the prices are high and the profits greatest.

The whole of the business is set up largely for the benefit of the young people, David Rimmer, Patrick Nutt and the four Sol-

---

* Watercress, now one of the most popular salads and garnishes, is a native of America and was only introduced into Europe in 1840. Incidentally, nothing is more delicious than cream of watercress soup or watercress dipped in the juice of a chicken roasted and basted with quantities of butter mixed with chopped chives, parsley and dill.

omon youngsters who work for a percentage of the gross, in addition to their salaries in the case of David and Patrick. They buy their own seeds and provide their own fertilizers while the farm provides the equipment for the operation and the gasoline or the natural gas for the irrigation equipment. If it is possible to judge by enthusiasm, all of them are having a fine time while they are making money.

The prospect of further expansion lies ahead of the market for the boys have uncovered an excellent market at good hotels, restaurants and even hospitals throughout the area. Chilled fresh vegetables can be delivered fresh each morning with the minimum loss of freshness, sweetness and general flavor and we are able to provide a great variety of things which are difficult to find in the general market. The vegetables have not been shipped through a commission warehouse or knocked about a central market for hours and sometimes days, but come fresh from the garden, chilled thoroughly by cold spring water.

But all of this is only a part of the general expansion which has spontaneously grown out of the experimental gardens and the spring. The stand itself has gradually become a modest agricultural center at which books on modern agriculture are sold and supplies of specialized fertilizers which are difficult to obtain. Orders are taken for the multiflora rose hedges which have contributed so much to the beauty of Malabar and to the propagation of wildlife and the cutting of the heavy expense concerned with building and maintaining wire fences. Agricultural pamphlets and information regarding new and modern machinery, fertilizers and other industrial products are distributed without any charge and the stand is glad to co-operate with any company engaged in the manufacture of agricultural supplies. And of course there are the gardens across the road and below the pond which are open to visitors at all times. This year we are erecting a small open building which can serve as a meeting and picnic spot for the organizations and visitors who come to Malabar in large numbers on Sundays. It is a practical building which in winter will be used for the storing of machinery.

And before the young people there is a whole, almost unlimited prospect of food production. During the war, while the husband of my youngest daughter, Ellen, was in service, she began making homemade jams and jellies which, even before the establishment of the roadside market, sold rapidly. In the second year business expanded to such a degree that she engaged three wives of neighboring farmers to help her. Then the war ended and she decided that jam and jelly making and marketing had become an overwhelming job and, being only twenty and adventurous, she took off with her husband to Brazil. . . . But a neighboring corporation took over the making of the jams and jellies on agreed specifications and these are now among the products sold at the roadside market.

As the hog project at Malabar continues to grow, plans are also growing for the production of home-cured hams and bacon, both smoked and unsmoked sausage, smoked turkey and Cornish game chicken. Much of the ham and bacon produced today in the United States is not cured at all; it is merely dead meat embalmed by injection of various chemicals. It produces, among other things, the most abominable of all things, wet hams. The changing history of hams and bacons has followed the general pattern of food production and processing in the United States. While an increasing number of processes are employed to produce convenience and cheap, quickly prepared food, the element of quality has gone steadily downward and we have come to live more and more with all sorts of inorganic chemicals and to consume them in steadily increasing quantities.

We shall move into all the new activities as time permits and capital becomes available. I have always preferred to allow a business to grow spontaneously rather than to start at the top and go rapidly downward.

And it is not impossible that the same food enterprise will go into cheesemaking and utilize the facilities of an already established milk production and a whole farm program of fine pasture, silage and hay. It is possible that we shall end up with a good-sized mail-order business on our hands, but the roadside market with the big spring flowing through it will always be the showcase and the trade-mark, and the aim will always be quality for those happy people who like food and know how to eat.

While on the whole the quality of food in restaurants and hotels has been growing steadily better over the whole of the United States save for a few areas, the natural quality of foodstuffs and raw materials in terms of flavor and frequently of tenderness has been going downhill. While many of the plant breeders have made excellent contributions, commercially speaking, to the whole field of vegetable and fruit production by creating new varieties that will ship or freeze well or lie around for days without actually rotting, they have done little toward improving quality and flavor. The showiest and biggest vegetable or variety of vegetables is not always the best and most certainly the one that ships the best and keeps the longest is never going to win a prize from the Society of Gourmets.

The new varieties which have been created and are grown because of their shipping or quick-freezing qualities have done much toward giving the housewife green or frozen green vegetables the year round, but in the long run there is nothing like a vegetable that comes straight from the garden into the pot. Nothing loses its quality so rapidly as peas and sweet corn, but *old* vegetables of any kind tend to lose freshness and sweetness as well as nutritional quality. A tomato picked sun-ripened from a garden is in reality another vegetable entirely from the tomato that has been picked green and ripened in a truck or the backroom of a warehouse. And what can be sadder and more tasteless than two-day-old sweet corn which has been lying about in the heat, or string beans that are wilted and have lost that peculiar flavor and aroma belonging to string beans which marks the really fresh string bean from the sodden wilted pods that have been lying about even for a few hours. Perhaps the most fraudulent and inedible of all are the "keeping varieties" of early strawberries which sometimes come into our areas from parts of the South. They have all the flavor and quality of an old fishing cork impregnated with five-and-dime store perfume. They will keep all right—even Nature has a tough time breaking them down—but I will leave the eating to somebody else.

If I seem fanatic about these things it is only because, like countless other Americans, I like good food, and the older I get the more pleasure I get out of eating. And the foundation of all good food is the raw materials from which it is made. In no field is the old saying truer that you cannot make a silk purse from a sow's ear.

While many of the new and marvelous short cuts in food may make American life easier, and perhaps even less expensive, and provide greater variety all the year round, they are certainly not improving the quality of food in the average

American home. It may help the office wife to slap a frozen dish into the oven and warm it up in fifteen minutes, but she and her tired husband are welcome to it. The complete quick-frozen meal may permit the bad housekeeper to play an extra rubber of bridge at the country club but I do not want to share the meal with her. The supermarket may provide cheap radishes that have been lying about in a polyethylene bag for three weeks and resemble a wilted and elderly turnip in flavor, but where is that crisp tang which just burns the tongue and makes of *fresh* radishes one of the great delicacies? And it may please the lazy housewife to buy radishes in a plastic bag with no tops on them, but she overlooks the fact, or maybe does not care, that you can tell the age of radishes by their leaves which wilt and decay very rapidly. Removing them may be a convenience but it also has for the shopkeeper the material advantage of being able to palm off on you radishes which have not seen a garden for three or four weeks.

I remember my grandfather once saying that "a man who did not like children, dogs, music and good eating" had only half a soul. It has stuck firmly in mind ever since, and as a rule I have found his observation very nearly infallible. Nothing can put me off a woman more quickly than seeing her being "dainty" at the approach of a friendly dog, pushing him away as if he might infect her with leprosy. That is about all I want to know concerning her and sometimes concerning her unfortunate husband as well. Nor do I want around the kind of woman who "hates" cooking and slaps together makeshift meals. These are not flash opinions but the result of nearly forty years of experience, much of it with women, and of considerable variety and intensity. Certain qualities, pleasant or unpleasant, are frequently indications to the wise and experienced of rocks and shoals ahead.

But the Malabar market stand has not only furnished us with an increasing income and a growing pride, it has also provided us with a lot of experience and fun. For the young people and the children the experience of running the roadside market provides the kind of education for life that can never be found in a university. In dealing with the customers at close and intimate range they have already discovered the great variety of the so-called human race. They have had to deal with the ill-

tempered and the vulgar, the new rich and the rude, as well as
with the pleasant people who like to eat well and look on life
with a sunny point of view. They have had to deal with the hag-
gler-for-haggling's sake, the kind of woman who attempts to
pick over and squeeze everything, the kind who is just looking
around and the pleasant kind who sits around talking sociably.
They have come to know the woman in the big new Cadillac
who haggles over the price because she is starving the family at
home to keep up with Joneses and the family which comes up in
an old jalopy and buys ten dollars' worth of stuff without ever
asking the price, because they like to eat well. They have
learned that kindliness and good manners are more characteristic of the farmer and the industrial worker than of the
country-club middle class. And perhaps most of all they have
been touched by the warmth, the taste for quality and good food
of those who have foreign backgrounds either immediately or a
generation or two back—the Middle Europeans, the Balkan
and the Mediterranean peoples and now and then a Frenchman. Almost all of these peoples like to cook and to eat well and
are proud of their cooking—and very few of them are ever di-
vorced. I think, indeed, that the young people are getting an
education that may be more valuable to them in living than
anything they can find almost anywhere else.

By nature I am a notably poor salesman, of the "take it or
leave it" variety, and perhaps my inclinations have crept too
strongly into our market business; nevertheless I find a fascination in hanging about the stand watching and listening to customers and occasionally making a sale. Usually I am dressed in
ordinary farm clothes and go unrecognized by most of the customers who come from a distance, but unless there is a rush of
business I stand aside and when questioned about prices, simply say, "I don't know. I just work here." But it is all a fascinating business and the fascination is not confined to me alone, for
most of the visitors and guests who stay at the Big House also
succumb to it and sooner or later find themselves behind the
piles of fresh vegetables with the spring water falling in rills all
around them. Among the amateur and anonymous saleswomen
have been Russian ballerinas, actresses, the beloved wife of our
Ohio governor and a few very famous names known to most of
the nation. Occasionally they are brought up sharply for their

inefficiency by a tart customer, but the rebuke does not seem to dampen the enthusiasm, because the whole thing is fun, as is the work of any really happy man or woman.

Perhaps the greatest product of Malabar Farm over the years has been the fun and the excitement which we have gotten out of what we are doing. It is not *always* that the results were fun and not *always* have we been successful, but at least most of us have been doing what we wanted to do in life, and what better justification is there for living?

At the market stand there is a beautiful view across valley and forest and always in the ear is the loveliest of all sounds— that of cold running water. Friends come and go and neighboring farmers and the boys on the farm stop by going to and from the hayfield for a big hunk of cold watermelon that has been floating in the spring water or a bottle of spring-chilled beer or a long drink of spring water from the gushing column that floods the stand. And there are seats where customers and neighbors and friends sit and gossip, always with the singing music of the spring as an accompaniment and overhead the shade of the immense and ancient willows and maples, and just across the road the great bed of dark green, peppery, wild watercress that has turned out to be a gold mine for the market.

I am glad we went into the roadside market business. I have a feeling that the market will be there, run by the young folks, beside the "commodious mansion" built by David Schrack, long after I have gone. I am setting it up that way and maybe never again will the big house and beautiful spring of David Schrack go unloved. And always, I am sure, there will be people who like to eat well and to have the best or none at all.

The Bad Year, or
Pride Goeth before a Fall

Here is a sample of an extended personal narrative. It is included for two reasons: first, because it tells of an adventure that is likely to befall a farmer, for the weather—drought or rain or cold—can do him in; and second, because it is important not to forget that Louis Bromfield really is a superb storyteller. There is nothing inherently interesting in how a minor creek in central Ohio went over its banks in 1947, except as Bromfield makes it so. He was a writer, after all, and produced, while at Malabar, not only the farm books but two other nonfiction books, plus novels, screenplays, magazine stories, and a regular newspaper column into the bargain.

Bromfield's literary manager and secretary, George Hawkins, thought that "the Boss" should stick to novels and screenplays. Hawkins was especially scornful of the Malabar Farm writings, which he described indelicately as so much "humus, mucus, wretch, and vetch." In fact, the truth is probably just the opposite. Even his best novels now seem dated, their emotion sometimes lacking believability and often descending into melodrama. But the writing about Malabar, despite its occasional redundancies and lack of careful revision (repetition of words in a paragraph, for example), is the truly permanent part of Bromfield's oeuvre, important not only for its ideas but for its artistry. Bromfield, therefore, should be remembered not as an expatriate popular novelist of the 1920s and 1930s, the subject of the occasional English department master's thesis, but as an American essayist of the first rank.

The following essay, "The Bad Year," is representative of Bromfield's best. The "Bob" here, as in an earlier chapter, is farm manager Bob Huge, and "Kenneth" is Kenneth Cook, a farmer at Malabar and the mechanic in charge of the farm's machine shop.

> . . . For the Father of Agriculture
> Gave us a hard calling; he first decreed it an art
> To work the fields, sent worries to sharpen our mortal wits
> And would not allow his realm to grow listless with lethargy
>
> *The Georgics of Virgil*

T he rains began, cold and dreary at the beginning of the month of April and day after day they continued through April, through May and into June. Meanwhile, the fields grew wetter and wetter, until at last the hillsides themselves began to weep, the water oozing out of their sides down the slopes onto the lower ground. In the flat country to the west of us the fields became lakes of water, sometimes almost unbroken for miles across the level rich fields.

In our county oats, if one is to have a good crop, should be planted as early as possible; for winter oats, seeded in the autumn, rarely weather the rigors of the northern winter and a farmer cannot afford to gamble on them. Oats planted in March have the best chance for success. Planted after the middle of April the chances of vigor and yield are lessened. Planted after the middle of May the yield is cut in half, or if hot, dry weather comes on the results may be utter failure. In 1947, planting in March was out of the question for the fields were still frozen and covered with snow. The usual "false spring" which allows us to put in early oats did not come at all, and then the rains began, falling day after day, in showers some days, in drenching downpours on others. And always it was cold, so cold that even the wild flowers and the morels (those first delicious woodsy fungi that grow in the deep forests under ash trees or in old and dying orchards) grew confused. A sudden burst of sunlight brought some of them into flower and fruition only to meet disaster on cold frosty moonlit nights. The delicate, tiny Dutchman's-breeches all met a frosty death while in full flower and the trilliums turned up stunted, brown-fringed petals toward the gray skies instead of the usual luxuriant blossoms that sometimes covered whole acres of our deep woodlands in drifts of white. The bluegrass, water-soaked and cold, languished instead of growing and kept the restless cattle (who know better than we do when spring should be at hand) prisoners in the barns and soggy barnyards. They mooed and cried out in their restlessness, the sound of their mournful voices drifting far across the woods and hills.

And slowly, throughout all our county, the complaints of the farmers, impatient to get into their fields and worried over the cold, soggy fields, began to raise into a wail.

Charlie Schrack, standing in the doorway of the barn, watching the fields drenched by gray rains said, "I can't remember anything like it in fifty years." Lots of farmers talk that way when drought or floods by persistent rain begin to spell disaster, but this time it seemed to me that Charlie was right, for it rained when it seemed impossible. Rain seemed to fall in cold, frosty weather out of skies that were comparatively free of clouds. It was as if the heavens were a gigantic shower-bath with a small irresponsible child playing with the chain which released the water.

And Nanny said, "I'm beginning to wonder if the Atomic bomb didn't have something to do with all this rain. Maybe the scientists had better stop discovering things before they destroy us altogether. It begins to make you believe in the story of the Tower of Babel. Man can become too pretentious."

And the next morning I read in the papers that government agencies had warned planes to keep below the level of twelve thousand feet since the Atomic cloud from the Bikini tests was passing for the third time around the earth and had just reached us again. That night and for two days, it rained without ceasing.

Walter Pretzer, a prosperous hothouse grower, came down from Cleveland for a dreary, water-soaked week end. Curiously enough he is both an immensely practical man and a mystic. He said, "The rains are only balancing out. We're getting what we missed during the past four or five years." To which I replied cynically, "Yes, but it isn't raining into your greenhouses."

But he answered me, "Nor is the sun shining." Sun, or lack of sun can make all the difference to the grower of hothouse vegetables. The lack of it can delay the crop until fresh vegetables, field grown from some other part of the country, come onto the market and run the prices of hothouse vegetables below the level at which it is even worth harvesting them. Sometimes it can ruin a crop altogether.

In modern agriculture, the weather is about the only thing which a farmer cannot somehow control. Against the next most disastrous potential—a sharp disastrous fall in prices—the good farmer can protect himself and manage to survive, but when the rain comes in floods at planting time or refuses to come at all for one dreary week after another, there is not much that he can do. And flooding rains are worse than drought; a farmer can irrigate dry burning soil if he possesses the facilities; he cannot mop up heavy persistent floods.

At Malabar and among the hills of our neighbors we were better off than the flat country people, for the water did not stand in lakes on our hills of glacial gravel loam. The worst we had to face were the seepage spots and "wet weather springs" which appeared here and there, sometimes at the very top of a hill. These we could plow around, leaving them water-logged and fallow, for another and better year. Our soil was loose and open and you could work it wet without too much damage if there was enough organic material mixed with it. And we had the advantage of mechanization—that when there was a break in the weather we could get into the fields and with tractor lights burning, work on shifts all through the night.

And that was what we did during the awful spring of 1947 and so somehow we got ninety acres of oats into the ground, some of it in land which had been rough plowed through Bob's foresight the autumn before and was all ready for disking, fitting, and drilling, We got in our oats in one of those two-day breaks when, if the sun did not shine, the rain at least did not fall. Then the rains broke again and the cold persisted and in three or four days the oats were through the ground in a pale, misty shimmer of lettuce green across the wet, brown fields. And our hearts and stomachs felt better and our pride rose, because we had in the ground probably more oats than any farmer from the Appalachians to the Great Divide. On our loose, well-drained soil, oats did not mind the cold nor the rain. It was the kind of weather from which it benefited in the early stages. We were having March weather at least a month after March had passed.

There is in every good farmer a curious, overwhelming, almost malicious pride common to the human race but especially well-developed in the cultivator. It is born of satisfaction in being "smarter" than his neighbor, in having his acres look greener, in getting in his crops earlier, in having fields where the hay or the pasture is heavier. And conversely there is in every good farmer a kind of perverse satisfaction in the discovery that his neighbor's fields look poorly. The sight of a poor crop in someone else's field somehow warms the heart of the farmer whose own fields are lush and green.

Often when I have been driving across Ohio with Bob, he will grin, as we pass a miserable pasture or field of yellowish weedy hay and say, "I suppose that makes you feel awfully good." And I'm afraid that sometimes it does. The pride of a good farmer is often his worst sin, but it is also what makes a good farmer and what helped to feed this nation and the rest of the world in the difficult years when lack of machinery and labor made farming a back-breaking, long-houred job. It is that same pride which makes the good farmer resist subsidies and government payments and all the paraphernalia of a "kept" agriculture. In his heart a good farmer wants to show that he cannot be "licked," and that without help from anyone he can grown abundant crops despite every handicap.

That is why a good farmer grows short-tempered and desperate when the weather turns against him. With each day of drought or flooding rain, he becomes more frustrated and savage, because the weather alone he cannot lick altogether either by machines or muscles or long hours in the field.

And so farmers everywhere that spring of 1947 grew ill-tempered and angry. They did not wail. It is only the poor farmer who wails and looks for scapegoats or excuses for his own failures of energy or intelligence. But that, of course, may be true of the whole human race. It just stands out clearly in the case of the farmer who long ago discovered what many others rarely discover—that in life there are no "breaks" except as one makes them for himself.

Still it did not stop raining. Time for planting oats receded into the distant unchangeable past and time for corn plowing came along, and still it rained and stayed cold. It was the year when Al Jolson's old song, "April Showers"* had a great revival and every juke-box and every radio was blaring forth:

*Copyright 1921 by Harms, Inc.

"Though April showers may come your way
They bring the flowers that bloom in May
And when it's raining, have no regrets
Because it isn't raining rain you know
It's raining violets."

It was a song that sounded very sour to the farmer that spring. The violets, which grew on banks like weeds in our country, were small, shriveled and frost-bitten. There were no warm showers. There were only flooding downpours, day after day as May slipped past toward June and Ellen said, "They ought to change that song to April Showers that bring the flowers that bloom in July."

Slowly countless farmers abandoned all hope of planting oats. They talked of other crops and of putting all their land into corn. Corn planting time came along and still it rained. Here and there in our hill country one could see farmers dripping wet on their tractors, turning over sod ground for corn planting. Sod ground, especially in soil like that of our country, can be plowed fairly safely when it is still too wet, because the roots and vegetation help to keep the ground open, aerated and keep it from packing. We too plowed sod in the rain and turned under the acres of rank sweet clover on the loose, alluvial soil of the farm we rent from the Muskingum Conservancy. We dared not even put a tractor wheel on the small acreage of waterlogged clay.

But even after the ground was plowed it was too wet to fit for planting. Day after day went by, each rain bringing us nearer to the last date at which corn could be planted and have any chance of maturing before the average frost date of October fourth. Then the rain stopped for a couple of days and again we worked night and day until all but ten acres of corn were in the ground. By our own standards at Malabar, we were three weeks late but with luck that corn, changed at the last moment to a quick-ripening short-season hybrid, would mature if the frost held off.

We were thankful that we had all our corn in save for the ten acres of clay which we could not touch because it was as wet and sticky as glue. So we planned to put that into buckwheat, let it serve the bees and then plow it into the soil for the benefits it would give us the following year. "At any rate," said Bob, "it will look pretty, and it's better than leaving the ground bare or to grow up in weeds."

And again, smugly and pridefully, we settled back, aware that we had probably more corn in the ground than any of the farmers to the west of us all the way into the corn country where the fields were still more like the carp ponds of Austria and Czechoslovakia than the fertile fields of the mid-western bread-basket country. But still it rained and remained cold, and we began to worry over whether the seed would rot in the ground. Then for three days the rain suddenly stopped and capriciously the weather changed from cold to oppressively hot with a hot baking sun and a new peril developed—that even with all the organic material we had pumped into the soil for years and the fresh crop of sweet clover turned under, the soil was so wet that the hot sun might bake the surface and prevent the tender, germinating corn from piercing the surface. So on the third day I climbed aboard the tractor, attached the rotary hoe and drove it full speed back and forth across the surface of the cornfield because the faster you drive it, the more efficiently it works, breaking up the surface and throwing the tiny weed seedlings and bits of crumbling earth high into the air.

Driving at full tractor speed, I felt good. The sun was shining. The alluvial gravel loam was dry enough for the rotary hoe to work efficiently. The Conservancy farm lay alongside the big artificial lake formed by one of the dams of the Muskingum Flood Prevention Project. The lake beneath the clear skies and hot sun was a brilliant blue. The distant wooded hills were tropically green and lush from all the rain. The birds, mute during the weeks of downpour, chorused from every tree, bush and hedgerow and from the marshy land along the lake came the sound of splashing caused by the thrashing about of the big carp engaged in an orgy of reproduction. And in my heart was the gnawing old farmer's pride that we had outwitted even the weather. It was one of those fine days which is recompense for weeks of bad weather.

At sundown I drove happily home and ran the rotary hoe briskly over the plantations of beans, peas and sweet corn. And then at supper time as the shadows began to fall across the valley and the lush forest, there came a sinister note of warning.

Out of the symphony of birds singing and the music of the frogs in the ponds below the house, there emerged a note which fell on the ears and assaulted my senses as violently as a shrill fife playing loudly and discordantly in the midst of a great orchestra. It was the cry of the tree frogs calling for rain. It came from all sides, the same monotonous, trilled note which in time of drought can be the most lovely instrument in the whole symphony of Nature.

I said, "Listen to those damned tree frogs! Haven't they had enough? I'd like to go out and strangle every one of them!" And from across the big table I heard a loud chuckle from Anne.

When I asked, "What's so funny?" She said, "Just the picture of you going around the farm strangling every tree frog with your bare hands."

Tree frogs do not, as legend has it, "call for rain." On the contrary they call when the atmospheric conditions foretell rain. They are not suppliants; they are prophets. I looked out of the window and against the brilliant sunset, big, dark, unmistakably wet clouds were piling up at the end of the valley. I couldn't believe it could rain again. There couldn't be any more water in the skies.

That evening everybody on the farm was feeling good and on such evenings the men and the kids on the place are all likely to gravitate to the lower farm. It is a kind of public forum in the center of the thousand acres and when the rain is falling people gather in the machine shop where Kenneth is kept busy during the bad weather repairing machinery or ingeniously making machines which we can't buy because they are in short supply or don't exist. On fine evenings we seem to gather there spontaneously just to talk or enjoy the evening or sometimes to go fishing in the pond that lies below the shop.

We were feeling pretty good because our oats stood high and strong and green in the fields and because our corn was in the ground, the grains swelling and popping in the damp ground, warmed for the first time by a hot sun. While we talked, pridefully, the dark clouds at the head of the valley piled up higher and higher and the tree frogs sang more and more shrilly. When I pointed out the clouds, Bob said, "Well, we haven't got anything to worry about. Think of those poor guys in the flat country with their fields still under water. Even if it stopped raining it would take two weeks for the ground to dry out enough to get a plow into them."

Yes, we all felt pretty good.

We all went home at last, still feeling good. Two things were certain—that we were ahead of most farmers and that no matter how hard it rained we had lost and were losing none of our precious soil. It stayed where it was meant to stay, held in place by that thick pasture and hay sod or the protecting sodded strip which prevented it ever getting away from us.

Tired from the all-day jolting ride on the rotary hoe, I fell into that deep sleep that comes only after physical labor in the open air, the kind of sleep which you can *feel* yourself enjoying with an almost voluptuous pleasure. Even the dogs were tired from the long day in the field and forgot their snack in their eagerness to go to bed. They fell asleep in their chairs even before I found myself lying with eyes closed and the book I was reading fallen aside. I awakened long enough to turn out the lights and fell into that warm, pleasant oblivious sleep which must be like the reward of death to very old people who have led long, full and happy lives.

I slept "like a log" until about two in the morning when a prodigious clap of thunder which rocked the whole house awakened me. The thunder was bad enough but there was another sound even worse. It was the sound of rain on the roof, a sound which in the dry hot days of August comes like a celestial benediction. Now it sounded like a curse from Hell for not only was it the sound of unwanted rain but of ropes and buckets and torrents of it, the sound of Niagaras of unwanted water streaming from gutters and spouts which could not carry it off fast enough. And above and through the sound of the rain on the roof came another sound of water even more menacing—that of the spring brook which ran through the garden below the house.

It was a sound I had not heard in seven years, since first we controlled run-off water on the hills and pastures above. Now, after all these years, the clear little creek was roaring again. It meant not only that it was raining hard and that the water-soaked land could drink up not one more rain drop, but that this was flood and perhaps disaster. I rose and went to the door and

Prince, who sleeps on the foot of the bed, jumped up and went with me. There I heard another sound, even more ominous—the roar of Switzer's Creek a quarter of a mile away which had been clear and well-behaved, never going out of its banks since farmers upstream had begun taking proper care of their fields. Now it was roaring again. It could only mean flood.

With a feeling of helplessness I went back to bed, to lie there sleepless and worry over the fact that all the work I had done with the rotary hoe was useless since these torrents of water would pack the earth harder than ever, worrying over the cattle, the calves, the horses in the bottom fields. I knew from the roar of Switzer's Creek that this time it was not merely rain but a cloudburst of the proportions that sweep away bridges and houses and drown livestock in the fields. I slept a little more, fitfully, and each time I wakened I heard the unwanted hateful rains streaming down and the increasing roar of the streams.

At daylight I went to the door and looked out over the valley. Part of the lower pasture was flooded but the livestock was safe on high ground, drenched and grazing peacefully in the downpour. Through the middle of the flooded field ran the swift, muddy current carrying with it whole fences, trees, rubbish, bits of hog pens and even a brand new milk can bobbing along on its way from some spring house upstream to the reservoir lake below.

It rained thus until nine o'clock in the morning when suddenly the awful downpour ceased and everyone on the farm—men, women and children—streamed out of the houses toward the bridge over Switzer's Creek. There was the kind of excitement among us which comes perhaps as a recompense to people in the face of destruction and disaster, a kind of exhilaration which brings all people, whatever their temperaments or differences of character, together on a common level.

The first concern of the men was the new floodgate that Bob and Kenneth and Jesse had constructed only a day or two before to separate the two bottom pastures. It hung from a heavy piece of steel pipe between the two concrete buttresses of the township bridge, made thus so that when the water rose it would swing out and float. To build it had taken a great deal of time and hard work.

The gate was still there, swinging out almost flat on the

surface of the rushing water. Now and then a log or a whole tree swept swiftly beneath it without lodging or tearing it loose. It was a good piece of engineering. Everybody was proud of it.

Then, with all the dogs, the men crowded into the jeep to inspect the rest of the farm. The wheat fields, so green and lush even the day before, were beaten down in spots as if a giant had flung great pails of water against the wheat. In the wild swamp and woodland we call the Jungle, the water poured through the trees high above the banks. Here and there a log or a tree had become lodged, collected a bundle of flotsam and jetsam, and the diverted waters had cut out a whole new channel. We stood there on a high bank, silent, watching the flood, awed yet somehow exhilarated by the terrible, unpredictable, incalculable power of rushing water.

And last of all we set out for the Conservancy farm on the edge of Pleasant Hill lake built years ago to check just such floods as this. We went with forebodings for we knew that the dam would be kept closed to hold back the water and protect the helpless people in the towns downstream along the Muskingum River all the way to the Ohio and perhaps even down the Mississippi to the Gulf of Mexico. As we neared the Conservancy farm the forebodings grew for the rising waters of the lake had already covered the lower road. There had never been such a flood before in all our experience so we could not know what that high water meant to the fields of which we had been so proud because our oats were all above ground and flourishing and our corn planted even in the midst of the weeks-old rain.

Cautiously I felt my way with the jeep through the high water. We just made it and as we came out the other side on the high ground we found out what the water on the road meant. It meant that our pride, the oats field on the Conservancy farm, lay under four to six feet of muddy water. In the shallow water near the banks we could see the rippling wakes left by the big carp as they moved in to take advantage of the plowed muddy oats field which they found ideal for spawning. For a long time we stood there watching the water-traced movements of the big invisible carp.

Then Kenneth said, "I guess we might as well make something out of this mess. I think if you all make a drive we might corner some of these big carp." So the men and the boys, down to

George Cook who is nine, took off their pants and waded out in their shorts into the cold water making a chain to trap the carp in shallow water. Even the five Boxers joined in. As if they understood the game they moved forward in a line with the men and boys trying to drive the carp into the shallows. Only Bobby, who was four and might have found the water over his head, stood on the bank and shouted advice as one big carp after another turned swiftly and darted between us, sometimes even between one's legs.

It wasn't any good. Every carp escaped but somehow the game raised our spirits. We all decided that probably the water would be released quickly from the dam and the oats field would be left free of it again before the crop and the beautiful stand of sweet clover sowed in it would suffer any damage.

At last we made our way home to disperse to the monotony of regular tasks which could and did bring a kind of numb solace and resignation in such occasions.

That afternoon the air cooled and the bright sun came out and two days later the gravelly cornfield was dry enough to repeat the whole process with the rotary hoe, all the long hours of rough tractor riding at top speed, to break up the crust all over again and let the young seedlings through. While I worked back and forth across a big sixty acre field, the air turned muggy and hot once more and the wind shifted a little to the south, which is always a bad sign. I kept listening above the rumble of the tractor for the sound of train whistles. In our country when one hears the whistles of the Pennsylvania locomotives it means dry weather; when one hears the B & O [Baltimore and Ohio], it means rain. In midsummer one prays for the B & O. For once I wanted to hear a Pennsylvania whistle. Presently, as I was finishing the job with the rotary hoe, I heard a whistle. It came from a B & O freight train pulling up the long grade to Butler and never have I heard it more clearly!

At about the same time great black clouds began to appear again at the head of the valley and the accursed tree frogs began to sing. I knew that once again I had gone over that cornfield only to have all my work undone.

At twilight I rode the tractor the two miles back to the house. The setting sun disappeared beneath clouds and as I rode the drive up to the Big House, great solitary drops of rain began to fall. Before I got into the house the drops began to come down by the trillions, in torrents. I thought, trying to deceive myself, "Very likely it's only a big thunderstorm and will quickly be over." The water in the reservoir had already gone down about two feet in two days leaving part of our oats field bare in time to save it. If we had another heavy rain it would mean, with the lake level above flood stage, that instead of the young oats plants being released before they were drowned, the whole field would be flooded again and perhaps the cornfield that lay above it.

I was wrong. The rain was no thunderstorm. It was the same kind of flooding rain that had come down two nights earlier. Indeed it was worse, if possible. Eight o'clock came and nine and ten and still it poured. The little brook in the garden began to roar and then from the valley came the louder roar of Switzer's Creek.

I took a couple of good drinks and went to bed to read, thinking I could take my mind off what could only be disaster. But it wasn't any good. I tried reading novels, agricultural editorials, magazines, but through all the print and ideas, good and bad, came the devilish sound of torrents of water pouring off the roofs and the rising roar of the little brook. And at last when my eyes grew tired and I began to feel drowsy, I heard the ring of the telephone. I knew it was someone on the farm ringing because the sound is different when the ring is made by cranking the phone handle instead of pushing a button in the central office. I thought, "This is it. Something bad has happened on the farm!"

Bob's voice answered me. He was calling from his house below, not far from the creek. He said, "I think we've got a job. The horses in the bottom are scared. They're running up and down crying out. One of them tried to get across the creek and is marooned on the island. We've got to look after them and the cattle."

I asked, "Is it worse down by the bridge?" And his voice came back, "Brother, you ain't seen nothing."

I dressed, gloomily, worrying about the animals and especially the horses. Cows and steers are generally phlegmatic. They either take things calmly or go completely wild, but horses and especially saddle horses, get frightened, like people, and for me the horses, like dogs, are people. I took only one of the dogs with me. I chose Prince because Prince owns me—I don't own Prince—and he is the steadiest of them all save old Gina who has always been wise and calm. But Gina was too old and plump for wild adventure. Too many dogs might only make confusion. And besides they were likely to follow me into the water if I had to go there and be carried away in the flood. Prince was a good swimmer and he would obey me and not get panicky. So Prince, delighted and excited, jumped to the seat of the jeep.

Bob met me at the bridge, water streaming from his hat and jacket. He had an electric torch and with that and the lights of the jeep I saw quickly enough that I hadn't seen anything until now. The water was so high that it was seeping through the wooden floor of the bridge and sliding past beneath with a terrifying speed. A whole log struck the edge of the bridge and made it shudder and then slipped under the water out of sight in a second. In the earlier flood there had been backwaters and whirlpools beneath the bridge where rubbish gathered but now there was nothing but rushing water going past so fast that I felt a sudden dizziness and instinctively stepped back from the edge.

He told me about the panic of the horses. "I heard them all the way up at the house."

I said, "Get in. We'll take the jeep out in the field and use the lights." He didn't think we could make it with the jeep but I knew better then he did what it could do.

He said, "I'll get my car, leave it on the road and put all the lights on the field and join you."

While he got his car I opened the pasture gate and drove through. Even the high ground was running with water and wherever there was a depression the water stood in deep pools. I put the jeep into four-wheel drive in low gear and she did what she was supposed to do. She plowed through mud and water until the lights penetrated a little distance into the mist and driving rain, enough for me to see that only a rim of bluegrass remained above the flood. The lights picked up two things, both white—the white spots on the Holstein cows who had gone to the high ground and were either grazing or lying down and the white blaze on the forehead of Tex, my own mare, as she came toward me splashing through two feet of water.

Tex is a beautiful Kentucky mare, chestnut with a white blaze, and the proudest and most spirited of horses. She rules the others and it is impossible to catch any of the others in the field until you have first captured Tex. The other horses follow her with docility. But she is not too easy to catch and likes to play a game of enticing you near to her and then suddenly kicking her heels and rushing off. But in the flooded field she wasn't behaving that way and now ran straight toward the lights of the jeep followed by another horse. As I got down she came up close and whickered. There were no antics now. She was afraid and wanted to be taken care of. Then the lights of Bob's car were turned into the field and I saw that the other horse was Tony, Hope's horse, young and strong, who is by nature a clown. But tonight he wasn't clowning. He too whickered when I spoke to him.

I recognized Tony with a sinking heart because I knew then that the missing horse marooned on the island in the flood was Old Red. The others were strong and spirited and could have taken care of themselves even in the terrible current that was running, but Old Red was old and tired. He was a little deaf and nearly blind. He was the one you felt sorry for.

Old Red had brought up the little children until they had learned to ride well enough to handle the younger, more spirited horses. If they fell off he would stand still until they picked themselves up and climbed back on. He never got flustered or showed off and reared like Tex and never clowned as Tony did. He was twenty-one years old when we bought him because he was calm and docile. He was just a horse, never a high-spirited queen like the thoroughbred Tex nor a wild, impish polo pony like Tony. Sometime in his youth, when perhaps he had been a carriage horse on some farm, he had been abused, for on his shoulder he bore the scars of old galls from a collar. He wasn't a clever horse or a spirited horse or a beautiful one. He was always just a kind, patient, old slob. And now, at thirty years of age with his joints stiffened and his teeth mostly gone, he was marooned on an island in the midst of a roaring flood such as the county had not seen in half a century. I wished it had been one of the others.

As I took hold of Tex's halter, for the first time without her giving an indignant toss of the head, Bob came up out of the darkness and rain and mist with the light. He was carrying a long rope.

"I thought," he said, "we might need this to get over to the island to get the horse off."

I told him the missing horse was Old Red and that I'd better take the other two to the barn before they turned completely panicky and uncatchable.

Tex led easily enough. She wanted the dry safety of the barn and Tony followed as always at her heels. Prince, despite the fact that, like all Boxers, he hates getting wet, trudged along beside us, his ears down and his stub of a tail pressed low in an effort to get it between his legs. Bob went off through the water to check on the cattle on the high ground. On the way back the roar of the flood seemed to grow steadily louder. After the two horses were safely in the barn, I discovered on my return to the field that the water was still rising.

Far off through the rain I could see the faint glare of Bob's torch as he checked the cattle and in the light from the two cars I could see the stream of logs, trees and driftwood moving swiftly down on the surface of the current, but I couldn't see the island or Old Red.

I waded into the water and was joined presently by Bob but as the water rose deeper and deeper above our ankles and knees, it was clear that we were never going to make the island.

Then out of the mist the willows of the island emerged but there was no island. There was only swift flowing water covered with leaves, bits of sod and branches. And then, out of the mist, catching the light from the cars, appeared a ghostly Old Red. He was walking up and down, whickering loud enough to be heard above the sound of the water.

I called out to him and he stopped, looked toward me and then started in my direction but as soon as he reached deeper water he turned back to the island and the shallow water.

There wasn't any way to get to him. The water had risen so high that on the whole of the farm there wasn't a rope long enough to permit us to reach the island, and even with a rope tied about your waist, there wouldn't be much hope of getting through the torrent. Knowing horses, I knew that even if you made it, there was small chance of getting a horse in a panic to follow you.

I shouted to him again and again and each time the old horse started toward me and each time when he got into deep water he turned back to the island.

Meanwhile both Bob and I were drenched. The water ran inside our jackets and down our bodies. Prince, miserable in the dampness, crouched beside me. At last I gave up.

"There's nothing to do," I said, "but hope that he'll stay there and that the water won't get much higher."

And so we turned away with a sickening feeling through the rain and water, leaving the old horse where he was. The other horses were in the barn and the cattle all safe on high ground. There wasn't anything to do but go home. We had hot coffee at Bob's house and as I said good night to Bob, he said, "Maybe I opened my big mouth too soon—saying we hadn't anything to worry about." I laughed but I knew what he meant —that probably sunrise would find most of our corn and oats deep under the waters of the big lake.

By the time I got back to the bridge the planks were under water and before I drove across it I got down to make sure that the planks were still there and the bridge safe. You could not make sure but I got back into the jeep and took a chance. I speeded up the jeep and made a dash for it. The water flew high on both sides so that together with the pouring rain and the rushing water it seemed for a moment that all of us, Prince, myself and the jeep, were caught in a raging torrent of water. The planks were still there and we made it.

At home Prince and I dried ourselves off and joined Mary for hot soup and a snack with all the dogs, who treated the wet and miserable Prince with such resentment for having been the chosen one on the expedition that a fight developed between him and his brother, Baby. Then I went to bed after taking two sleeping pills so that I would not waken in the still early hours of the morning and hear the terrible rain and think of Old Red marooned alone on the island in the rising flood.

It was nearly eight when I wakened and the rain had stopped. The old orchard on the hill above my room was streaked with early morning sunlight and the red sandstone rock looked brighter and the trees lusher and more green than I had ever seen them. But in the back of my mind there was a sore spot which could not be healed until I went to the windows at the other side of the house which overlooked the bottom pasture. I had to know what had happened to Old Red.

It must have stopped raining some time during the night for the water had gone down and the surface of the island, littered with branches and trees and old boards, was now above the flood. But among the willows there was no sign of Old Red. I felt suddenly sick and in a last hope I thought, "Perhaps he is all right after all. Perhaps he's just around the corner below the slope." And I went back to the far end of the house and looked out, and there behind the slope, peacefully munching bluegrass with the few teeth he had left, was Old Red, behaving as if nothing had happened.

After breakfast Kenneth and I climbed into the jeep with the dogs and set out for the Conservancy farm. The jeep was the only car which had a chance of making it. We already knew the worst, for from the Bailey Hill we could see the lake—an enormously enlarged lake covering twice its usual area with clumps of trees here and there barely visible above the water. This time we couldn't get through the lower road at all. Not only was the road under ten feet of water but Charley Tom's pasture was under ten feet of water also. The bridge structure was out of sight.

So, turning round, we took the only other course of reaching the Conservancy farm; we took to a rutted abandoned old lane and the open, soggy fields and somehow we made it. As we came over the crest of a slope we saw the full extent of the disaster. All the oat fields and half the corn land was covered by water and here and there in low spots in the field there were great ponds of water as big as small lakes.

This was, in reality, a disaster. We sat for a time in silence looking at the wreckage. It wasn't only the money loss but the loss of the long hours of work and care we had all put into these fields.

Then Kenneth said, "There's a new milk can bobbing on the edge of the current. We might as well salvage something."

So together we set to work to get that solitary milk can out of the swirling torrent. It was not easy but by the use of long tree branches and poles we maneuvered the floating milk can to a point where, wading in up to his hips, Kenneth salvaged it. He fastened it to the back of the jeep and we climbed in and set out for home. There wouldn't be any recompense in cash for the damage done by the waters of the lake; we rented the whole farm from the state with the gamble that some day there might be just such a flood. And anyway, money is poor recompense to a good farmer; he wants his crops and the satisfaction that goes with raising them.

For three weeks most of the Conservancy farm remained under from five to twenty feet of impounded water, kept there to prevent its menace from being added to the already disastrous floods on the Mississippi. When the water went down at last not one living thing remained but only the desolation of logs and fence posts and driftwood scattered across the barren fields. Even the trees were killed along with the blackberries and elderberries that filled the hedgerows. We had not only lost our crops, but we had to clear the fields of their desolation. What little corn or oats remained on dry ground was growing but looked pale and yellowish in the water-soaked ground.

And elsewhere on the upper farm more rich wheat was beaten to the earth to mildew and smother the precious seedings. The bluegrass behaved in the water-soaked earth exactly as it did in time of drought. It grew tough and went to seed early and it was possible to clip it only on the high ground. Everywhere else in the fields, the power mower bogged down and had to be pulled out.

Good farmers are by nature optimistic; otherwise the uncontrollable vagaries of Nature—the floods, the droughts, the plagues of locusts—would long ago have discouraged them and the world would have been left starving. We were no different from other farmers—we hoped that the great flood had marked the end of the persistent intolerable rains.

We were wrong. June passed into July and still the rain continued, not simply showers or simple rains but cloudbursts coming sometimes twice a day. Even the fish ponds fed from tight sod-covered land and springs overflowed their barriers and big trout and bass escaped into the Clear Fork and the lake below. Came time to fill the silos with grass and silage and we began cutting and hauling but quickly found that every tractor had to carry a long chain so that we could pull each other out of the mud, a minor disaster which happened ten or fifteen times a day. Twice the big John Deere dug itself into the mud up to its belly and a string of four lighter tractors, chained together, could not drag it out. In the end with four-by-fours chained to its giant wheels it succeeded in lifting itself out of the mud.

Somehow the silos got filled with the lush, heavy alfalfa, brome grass and ladino, but even the grass was so filled with moisture that it had to be wilted a long time before it could be safely put away. Weeds grew in the corn and more wheat was beaten down in the fields of which we had been so proud. The oats which remained grew more and more lushly and all but the tough, stiff-stemmed new Clinton variety were beaten to the ground while weeds began to grow up through them.

Then the weather turned warm but the rains continued and at night when the air cooled the whole valley was blanketed in heavy white mists which appeared at sundown, rising in smokelike writhing veils above the trees. For days the valley seemed more like Sumatra or Java than midsummer Ohio country. Rust appeared for the first time in our experience on the ripening wheat and mildew on the leaves and fruit of the fruit trees. Some of the grapevines began to die back from the tops, a sign that their water-logged roots could no longer stand the lack of oxygen and the wetness of the earth. Three times the vegetable garden was replanted and three times drowned out, sometimes standing for days under three or four inches of water.

Then came a brief respite which in itself was very nearly a disaster. There was no rain but in its place there was a brilliant, burning sun accompanied by hot winds which burned the moisture out of the top soil but not out of the subsoil where the water still soaked the roots of all vegetation. It baked a crust over open ground and burned the over-lush leaves of the crops. At night the moisture still rose from the soaked ground in heavy blankets of fog. It was as if now it was the earth rather than the sky which was raining.

Somehow we managed to combine the wheat, although we lost from five to fifteen bushels per acre of wheat literally beaten into the earth by the torrents of water. Except for thirty acres of good oats on the highest ground, the crop was ruined. In the heads there were no grains at all but only chaff. And from over the rest of the Middle West then arose a cry that drought was ruining the crop just at the crucial moment of tasselling and pollenization. Because there had been so much rain the corn had set shallow roots on the surface of the soil and now suddenly that surface had been burned, baked and hardened.

But in our valley even the short, vicious heat was only a delusion. As it came time to make hay and clip and bale straw, the rains began again, not simply rains but the old cloudbursts. Ragweed grew higher and higher in the standing straw and the hay, partly dry and then soaked, rotted in the fields. Weeds everywhere grew like the fierce tropical growth that overwhelms settlements and plantations in a few weeks in the Tropics when the battle against them is relaxed for a season. The whole farm, usually so neatly and proudly kept, acquired a disheveled, unkempt, half-tropical appearance.

And so it went, on and on, through the end of July and then August and well into September. There was no hay-making season at all, even for the second cutting, and when there was a day or two of sunshine the hay, dried during the day, became drenched again each night from the moisture rising out of the water-soaked ground and from the heavy, damp fogs which settled each night in the valley. At last we took in hay which was still damp. Some of it moulded, some of it heated and turned brown and a little came through as the good green hay which we always made in a summer that was even vaguely reasonable.

Only the pastures and the new seedings gave us any pleasure or satisfaction, for they were lush and green but even this was small compensation for all the lost labor and seed and fertilizer and the depression which arose from the sight of wet hay and weed-choked cornfields. The buckwheat planted later on wet ground produced a bumper crop but few farmers take pride in lowly buckwheat and the season was so wet that the bees could not even work the blossoms.

And then presently in the beginning of September the rains stopped and miraculously two weeks of hot weather day and night set in, and suddenly the corn, after dawdling along all of the summer, began to show signs of ripening and making a crop. The soil began to dry out for wheat plowing and the miraculous resiliency which preserves farmers against utter and paralyzing despair began to assert itself.

Gradually the season began to recede into the past. It was

becoming the "old season". It was time now to plow and fit for wheat, to clip the bluegrass pastures and the weeds for the last time in the evil year of nineteen forty-seven. With the turning of the first furrow the pride which was humbled began to rise again. The fields were full of moisture and the plowing was easy. The earth turned over behind the plow, dark and crumbling, and you smelled already the wheat harvest of the coming season which you knew would be the greatest harvest we had ever known. The lime trucks began moving across the remaining wornout high pastures raising visions of deep, thick clover. In the desolated oat fields of the Conservancy farm and on the poor strips of the Bailey Place the sweet clover stood deep and rank. The new season had begun.

One more disaster in the "Bad Year" still lay ahead—a hard frost with a clear, full moon which burned the alfalfa and the grapes before they were ripe and covered all the landscape of Pleasant Valley with glittering white rime. For a moment our pride rose again, even in a bad year, for our corn was ripe and hard, while to the west of us in *real* corn country thousands of acres of corn had been frosted while still green and soft. And then came the warm, clear weather of October, brilliant with the deep green of the new springing rye and wheat and the burning colors of the forest. From brilliant blue skies the sun shone all day long while the work for the new season went on its way and all hearts sang.

What was past was past but 1947 would go down among the legends of our valley as the "Bad Year," the worst year that any of us, even old Mr. Tucker, who was over ninety-one and had lived all his life in the valley, could remember. We would be proud again of our fields and we would feel a certain wicked satisfaction when other fields looked worse than our own but after the bad year it would always be a pride that was not quite so confident.

Fifteen Years After

And so we come to the end, the end of Louis Bromfield's days at Malabar and almost the end of Malabar itself. It was 1955. Bromfield was to live but one year after this essay was published. His novels were no longer popular, and hard times had come upon Hollywood, drying up that lush source of income so necessary to support an establishment as complex as Malabar Farm, with its boxer dogs and pet animals, its streams of visitors, and its sizeable agriculture and domestic staff. Bromfield's wife, Mary, had died, as had George Hawkins. His daughters, Anne, Hope, and Ellen, had all moved away. He is not alone at Malabar; the farm is still a going concern. But the almost elegiac quality of this piece betrays the author's intuited sense that the last chapter has already been written.

Reading this essay, from the advantage provided by several decades of hindsight, it is poignant to see how Bromfield misunderstood his work as a writer, his role as an experimental farmer, and his effort to expand the Jeffersonian lessons of Malabar onto the larger canvas of American political life. He casts doubt on his literary career, but his words about Malabar were his finest achievement. He casts doubt on his "ludicrous" vision embodied in "the Plan," but it was romantic energy that made Malabar possible, even if the ideas did not work out in all particulars. He was as powerless to affect large political events here as he was in Europe before the war, when he wrote so passionately against appeasement; and yet his political work in support of soil and water conservation programs and other advances of the "New Agriculture," as he called it, may well have been decisive in the effort to rebuild the renewable natural resource base after the Dust Bowl and the hard-farming of wartime had taken their toll.

He should have known better, of course, but how many of us recognize our own false assumptions? The performance was not

weak; the objectives were falsely constructed, a difficulty experi-
enced by nearly all creative people—the touch of hubris. In the
end, the failures of self-understanding are unimportant, espe-
cially when compared to the one, big thing that Louis Bromfield
got right: that his work at Malabar gave him a sense of belonging
to something larger than himself, "to something vast, but infi-
nitely friendly."

That was the gift of Malabar Farm to him; and that is his
gift to us as well, not fifteen years after, but nearly fifty.

F ifteen years have passed since the snowy winter day when I turned the corner of the road into Pleasant Valley and said to myself, "This is the place." I had come back after twenty-five years of living in the world to my own country, to the valley I had known as a boy. I knew the country in the marrow of my bones; I knew it even in the recurring dreams which happened in strange countries here and there over half the world. I knew the marshes and the hills, the thick, hard-wood forests, the wide fields and the beautiful hills behind which lay one lovely small valley after another, each a new, a rich, mysterious, self-contained world on its own.

I was sick of the troubles, the follies and the squabbles of the Europe which I had known and loved for so long. I wanted peace and I wanted roots for the rest of my life.*

When I saw the valley again after twenty-five years it was under deep snow and the farms I bought were under deep snow. I have recounted the whole story in detail in *Pleasant Valley,* while the first impressions were still fresh in my mind, and I am glad that I did this for I can read it all and know now how little I understood the changes that occurred while I was away and how little I foresaw or understood what lay ahead and how nearly all the values of my life were to be changed and enriched.

---

*I cannot say that with regard to the troubles, the follies and the squabbles I found much change or relief. The record of my own country in these times, with its politics, its meddling in the affairs of other nations, its spasmodic Utopia-nism, its militarism, its saber rattling, its attempts to dominate the world and dictate the policies of other nations, has been no record in which to take pride or to justify a sense of superiority in any American.

What I saw then, I saw through a haze of nostalgia, with homesick eyes. What I was seeking in part at least was something that was already on its way out of American life.

On that first snowy evening when I knocked at the door of the farmhouse which stood where the Big House now stands, I was, like many a man on the verge of middle age, knocking at the door of my long-gone boyhood. Tired and a little sick in spirit, I wanted to go back and, like many a foolish person, perhaps like all of us, I thought or hoped that going back was possible. I was sick even of writing novels and stories, although they had brought me considerable fortune and fame in nearly every country in the world. All fiction, save perhaps such books as *War and Peace,* which is more history than fiction, seemed to me at last to be without consequence and even trivial in contrast to all that was going on in the world about me. I knew and partly understood—better than most, I think—what was going on and what was ahead, certainly far better than the great majority of Americans, because I had lived for nearly a generation at the very midst of the turmoil and the decay which ended finally with the humiliation of Munich and the Second World War.

Most of the fellow countrymen to whom I talked on my return seemed almost childish in their naïveté and their lack of understanding concerning the significance of what was happening in Europe and in the world—just as many of them today seem childish in their refusal to face a world which is utterly changed, a world in which Soviet Russia and Red China and the awakening of Asia and the decadence of Europe and the end of the colonial empires are all simple facts which cannot be wished nor laughed off nor evaded. Peace and decency can only come by and through recognition of such facts and a recognition above all that the old world which many of us perhaps found agreeable enough is not coming back.

Those of us who lived in Europe and Asia between the first two world wars knew and understood pretty well both Nazism and Fascism, and we knew too all about Communism in all its manifestations and knew that there was nothing to choose between the doctrines; one was merely a perversion of an unnatural political and economic philosophy and vice versa. They were both derived from the philosophy of a sick and psychopathic German named Marx. The forces behind them were actually the forces of a world revolution which manifested itself in countless ways not the least of which was the slow death of the already obsolete colonial empires. These doctrines were created not merely by a philosophy, wishful thinking or even fanaticism: they were created by immense economic and political stresses and strains which involved such things as overpopulation, shortages of foods and raw materials, abysmal living standards, restricted markets. In short Nazism and Communism were merely the political manifestations of profound economic ills. They did not in themselves cause war and revolution. They were basically the outward political manifestations of much more real and deep-rooted evils. The guilt for the war could not be fixed on any one nation or group of nations. Every nation in one degree or another shared responsibility. The responsibility still remains. We in this country have solved nothing nor made any great contribution toward creating and maintaining peace. The Utopians and the Militarists have indeed merely accomplished the contrary.

Fifteen years after I hoped bleakly to escape from all the evils I knew so well at first hand, I have discovered bleakly that there is nothing superior about my own people and that they do not have any special wisdom or vision. We have merely been more fortunate than other peoples. We are generous because we can afford to be generous. We are perhaps open-hearted because we are still a young people, but we still understand very little about the evils of the world or how they can be cured or at least modified. We lack almost entirely the capacity of putting ourselves in the place of other peoples, and the knowledge of the average citizen concerning the life and the circumstances of other nations and peoples is primitive, frequently enough even among those who occupy high places in our government.

When I came back to the valley on that snowy morning fifteen years ago, I was trying to escape the evils of the past and the weariness of Europe. Somehow in the misty recesses of my mind there existed a happy image of this valley in which I had spent a happy and complete boyhood—the image of a valley shut away, immaculate and inviolate, self-sustained and complete and peaceful. It was an image in which the sun was always shining. It was not of course an image born of the mind and the intellect but one born of the emotions. At that time I did not fully understand what it was that moved me so powerfully. I have only come to understand it through the gradual corrosion of disillusionment and pessimism and since I have found something which I did not then know existed, something which I did not even know I was seeking . . . something which it is difficult or impossible to describe save that it is a combination perhaps of reality and truth and of values which were unsuspected. All this is closely related to the earth, the sky, to animals and growing plants and trees and my fellow men. All this is of course of immense importance to me personally; it is important to others only as a bit, a fragment, of human experience, that element which perhaps more than any other sets men apart from animals who, so far as we know, are not capable of reflection or philosophy.

And so in the light of all this, the writing of fiction, unless it was merely a story to divert a tired world or provide relaxation for it, came presently to seem silly. It still does, no matter how pompous, how pretentious, how self-important, how cult-ridden the writer or the product. In this age fiction writing is simply a way of making a living and for my money not a very satisfactory or even self-respecting one. There are better and more satisfying things to do. One degree sillier are the writings of those who write importantly about novels. Once when a person said to me, "Oh, I never read novels!" I was inclined to regard him with snobbish condescension as a Philistine. Now I am not so sure.

So when the door opened in the Anson house more than fifteen years ago and the familiar childhood smell of a farm kitchen came to me, I was aware of a sudden delight as if in reality I had stepped from the recurrent weariness and disillusionment back into the realities of my boyhood. The smell was one in which there was blended the odors of woodsmoke, of apple butter, of roasting pork sausage, of pancakes, of spices. Mrs. Anson, workworn and no longer young, her arthritic hands wrapped in her apron, stood in the doorway with her back to the gaslight of the big kitchen walled with hand-cut stone from the low cliffs behind the house. With a puzzled smile lighted by some ancient memory and recognition, she invited me in, and brought me hot coffee and spiced cookies. When I told her my name she remembered me dimly as a small boy who used to camp on the adjoining Douglass Place, which belonged to her cousins, and who fished in Switzer's Run that flowed through the valley below the house.

When I asked her if the place was for sale, she answered that she believed not but that we might talk to her husband who was out in the barn milking. And so she put on a shawl and we walked in the blue winter twilight across the squeaking snow to the barn where old Mr. Anson sat on a three-legged stool drawing milk from a Guernsey cow. And again at the barn door the smell of the warm stable, the granary, the steaming manure came to me in the form of the perfumes of Araby. For the moment I again renounced all the world in which I had lived most of my life and escaped from it back into the past, into the world of horses-and-buggies, of muddy roads, of church suppers, of everything that was the America of my childhood. I who had been everywhere and known the world and "all the answers" wanted only to come back into this world.

The Ansons could not make up their minds whether they wanted to sell until they talked to their children, and so after another cup of coffee in the big stone kitchen I set off down the winding road past the cottage where Ceely Rose had poisoned her parents and brothers, across the little bridge and finally to the highway. It was a *blue* winter night with that peculiar quality of blue in the sky and in the air itself which one finds in our part of the world and only a few other places, places like Northern France and the Castilian plain about Madrid. The air seems to become luminous like the unreal blue of skies on the cyclorama of a theater. I was happy. I was hopeful that I had really escaped and had come home.

That night the whole valley was covered by snow and the little creek fringed with ice. What lay beneath the snow I could not see. I was only to discover it when the spring came with a rush of green and wild flowers.

When the snow was gone, I discovered that the valley of my childhood was no longer there. Something had happened to it. It had been ravaged by time and by the cruel and careless treatment of the land. As a small boy I had never noticed that these once small, lovely, rich valleys throughout our countryside had already begun to change, growing a little more gullied and bare with each year, or that the pastures grew thinner and more weedy and the ears of corn a little smaller each season. When the snow was gone, I began to understand what had happened to it, perhaps because for so long I had lived in the rich green country of Northern France where the land is loved and where it is respected and cherished almost with avarice, perhaps out of grim necessity, but nonetheless respected and even held precious. It was clear that no such thing had happened in the valley. Some of the farms which lay below and around the Anson Place no longer raised crops at all. They had been rented out to year-by-year tenants or to neighbors who took everything off them until they would no longer grow anything. The houses were occupied by industrial workers who spent their days in the city factories.

Except where starving sheep on wasted farms were turned loose in the woods to find meager living as best they could off the seedlings and the sun-starved vegetation, the forests and the marshes were still the same. Here and there a woodlot had been brutally murdered by some fly-by-night timber speculator, the trees sold perhaps to raise money for interest on the mortgage of some dying farm; but otherwise the growth of the wild grasses, the trees, the briars provided evidence of the original and fundamental richness of the whole countryside. Wherever there was desolation and sterility it had been created by man, by ignorance, by greed and by a strange belief inherent in early generations of American farmers that their land owed them a living.

When I look back now, the vague and visionary idea I had in returning home seems ludicrous and a little pathetic. Somehow the picture I saw of the future was one in which vaguely there were blended the carefree happiness of my boyhood and the life in a great house in the countryside of England in the great days. If in the dream there was any other element it was that of security; I wanted a place which, again vaguely, would be like the medieval fortress-manor of France where a whole community once found security and self-sufficiency. In a troubled world I wanted a place which, if necessary, could withstand a siege and where, if necessary, one could get out the rifle and shotgun for defense.

Today, fifteen years later, we at Malabar have not achieved these romantic dreams nor have I won the escape into the boyhood past which brought about the decision to return. A return to the past can never be accomplished and the sense of fortified isolation and security is no longer possible in the world of automobiles, of radios, of telephones and airplanes. One must live with one's times, and those who understand this and make the proper adjustments and concessions and compromises are the happy ones. In the end I did not find at all what I was seeking on that snowy night; I found something much better—a whole new life, and a useful life and one in which I have been able to make a contribution which may not be forgotten overnight and with the first funeral wreath, like most of the writing of our day, but one which will go on and on. And I managed to find and to create, not the unreal almost fictional life for which I hoped, but a tangible world of great and insistent reality, made up of such things as houses, and ponds, fertile soils, a beautiful and rich landscape and the friendship and perhaps the respect of my fellow men and fellow farmers. The people who come to the Big House are not the fashionable, the rich, the famous, the wits, the intellectuals (although there is a sprinkling of all these) but plain people and farmers and cattlemen from all parts of the world.

Perhaps it will turn out that I have left behind some contributions not only to the science of agriculture, which is the only profession in the world which encompasses *all* sciences and *all* the laws of the universe, but to the realm of human philosophy as well. None of this could I have done within the shallow world of a writer living as most writers live. Without implying in any way a comparison or any conceit, I am sure that Tolstoy understood all this on his estate at Yasna Polyana, Voltaire at Ferney, Virgil on his Tuscan farm, indeed most writers since the time of Hesiod who felt sooner or later the illusion and the futility of fancy words and sought some sturdier and earthier satisfaction. Flaubert was neither a happy man nor a complete one, nor was Turgeniev or Henry James. One has only to read their letters or their diaries and sometimes their stories and poems to discover a shadowy sense of impotence and inadequacy.

The *complete* man is a rarity. Leonardo was one and Michelangelo and Shakespeare and Balzac. They lived; they brawled; they had roots; they were immoral; they had vices as well as virtues; they were totally lacking in preciosity and the pale, moldy qualities of the poseur or the seeker after publicity and sensation. The *complete* man is a happy man, even in misery and tragedy, because he has always an inner awareness that he has lived a *complete* existence, in vice and virtue, in success and failure, in satisfaction and disappointment, in distinction and vulgarity. Not only is he complete; he is much more, he *is* a man.

The older I grow the more I become aware wistfully of that goal of completeness. It is not something that can be attained by wishing or even by plotting and determination. The man who sets out deliberately to be a complete man defeats himself, for from the beginning he is of necessity self-conscious, contriving and calculating. He becomes the fake, the poseur, the phony. Some attempt to turn their own inadequacies into a defense by affecting a sense of snobbery or superiority. In this sense a writer like Henry James is pathetic. So are many writers of our own times with their lacy preciosities, their affectations, their pomp and pretensions, their fundamental shallowness and decadence.

But enough of all that. If such thoughts have any importance, it is an importance which primarily touches only the individual and the individual only in relation to the satisfactions which he may win from a life which is all too short if one considers the glories, the complexities, the mysteries, the fascination, of the world and the universe in which we live. Certainly one of the happiest of men is the good farmer who lives close to the storm and the forest, the drought and the hail, who knows and understands well his kinfolk the beasts and the birds, whose whole life is determined by the realities, whose sense of beauty and poetry is born of the earth, whose satisfactions, whether in love or the production of a broad rich field, are direct and fundamental, vigorous, simple, profound and deeply satisfying. Even the act of begetting his offspring has about it a vigor, a force, a directness in which there is at once the violence of the storm and the gentleness of a young willow against the spring sky.

I was born of farming and land-owning people and have never been for long away from a base with roots in the earth, despite the fact that the fortune and circumstances of life have from time to time brought me into the most worldly and sophisticated and fashionable of circles in a score of countries and capitals and frequently among the great, the famous and those, in the world of politics, who have made the history of our times. Still I know of no intellectual satisfaction greater than that of talking to a good intelligent farmer or livestock breeder who, instinctively perhaps, knows what many less fortunate men endeavor most of their lives in vain to learn from books, or the satisfaction of seeing a whole landscape, a whole small world change from a half-desert into a rich ordered green valley inhabited by happy people, secure and prosperous, who each day create and add a little more to the world in which they live, who each season see their valley grow richer and more beautiful, who are aware alike of the beauty of the deer coming down to the ponds in the evening and the mystery and magnificence of a prize-winning potato or stalk of celery, who recognize alike the beauty of a field with a rich crop in which there are no "poor spots" and the beauty of a fine sow and her litter.

These are, it seems to me, among the people who belong, the fortunate ones who know and have always known whither they were bound, from the first hour of consciousness and memory to the peace of falling asleep for the last time never to waken again, to fall asleep in that tranquility born only of satisfaction and fullness and completion. In a sense they know the whole peace of the eternal creator who has built and left behind him achievements in stone, in thought, in good black earth, in a painting upon a wall or some discovery which has helped forward a little on the long and difficult path his fellow men and those who come after him. It is these individuals who belong and who need not trouble themselves about an afterlife, for at the end there is no terror of what is to follow and no reluctance to fall asleep forever, since it is the direct and the natural thing for them to do. They are at once and in essence humble and simple people, no matter what fame they achieve or what admiration they have won from their fellow men. Because they belong and so have found their place and their adjustment in the intricate and complex pattern of the universe, they find even the tragedies and the suffering of their own lives only a part of a general vast pattern. They are, perhaps, more sharply aware of the significance of tragedy and suffering than less limited and egotistical folk; that very awareness and significance blunt the sharp edge of suffering and presently the pain wears away, leav-

ing only peace and even perhaps a strange sense of beauty and richness.

The mysteries of the human mind are certainly fascinating but more limited and, for me at least, less important and less interesting than the cosmic mysteries which take place within a cubic foot of rich productive soil, for essentially these "mysteries" of the human mind are merely a part of an infinitely greater and more intricate and complex mystery which utterly baffles all of us, even the wisest and most learned. One of the great errors of our time, and one which has brought us in our time much misery, is the attribution of an overweening and disproportionate importance to man and his mind. Man himself, as a physical machine, as a mechanistic, functional and living organism, is indeed marvelous as is every part of the universe; but his ego and self-importance, in our time, are given a distorted, decadent and tragi-comic importance.

Man is merely a part of the universe, and not a very great part, which happens to be fortunate principally in having evolved such traits and powers as consciousness, reflection, logic and thought. The wise and happy man is the one who finds himself in adjustment to this truth, who never needs, in moments of disillusionment and despair, to cut himself down to size because it has never occurred to him, in the beginning or at any time, to inflate his own importance whether through ignorance, morbidity, egotism or undergoing psychoanalysis (which is merely another name of one of the age-old manifestations of brooding impotence and frustration of the incomplete man).

It is only later in life, in the midst of what is still a somewhat turbulent and certainly a varied existence, that any full understanding and satisfaction of this sense of *belonging,* of being a small and relatively unimportant part of something vast but infinitely friendly, has begun to come to me. It is only now that I have come to understand that from earliest childhood, this passion to *belong,* to lose one's self in the whole pattern of life, was the strong and overwhelming force that unconsciously has directed every thought, every act, every motive of my existence.

This urge is by no means an uncommon one and is perhaps shared in one degree or another by every man or woman of real intelligence, although many fail to recognize it for what it is or to understand it. Certainly it is the profoundly motivating pattern in the life of a man like Albert Schweitzer just as it is of many a humbler thinker and teacher. It is indeed the very force of every good and real teacher; it is that element which distinguishes the creator from the desiccated savant, that distinguished Christ from Socrates, that makes all formal education seem futile and useless unless it is *understood* and *used*. Mere *learnedness* becomes insignificant and even useless when the fire is absent. This rarity of understanding is the reason why throughout the ages there has always been a cry that there are not enough teachers and why all the knowledge and all the formal training in the world produced by all the universities and colleges since the beginning of time cannot produce one more real teacher. I am afraid it is true that teachers, like good cattlemen and good farmers and good engineers and good cooks, are born and not made. So essentially are most really good people.

The egotistical, the resentful, the psychologically maimed can never really belong. Perhaps in the end the great failure of the Communist doctrine will be registered in history as a failure to produce great teachers, or any teachers at all or indeed any complete men who really belonged. The typical leader has been, almost without exception, the psychologically deformed, the egotist, the man hungry for power but not for understanding, altogether the man confused and limited by the stupidities of materialism and the domination and tyranny and terrors that spring from and surround his own ego. Few men in human history have had such power as Stalin but what honest and intelligent man would ever wish to have changed places with him? It is probable that he was a most limited man who never knew even the shadow of that satisfaction which comes to the complete man.

And now, dear reader, if you have survived these philosophical ramblings we shall get on to the business at hand—the business of drying hay, of finding means for making more money for the farmer, of helping to feed hungry people, and in general the satisfactions of life in the country. But do not overlook the fact that all of these things real, finite and even perhaps materialistic, are all very much a part of the pattern in the life of at least one busy and happy man even though he is a long way from being a complete one, just as they have become in these times more and more a part of the pattern in the lives of countless middle-aged and elderly businessmen, industrial workers, engineers, clerks, retired mechanics, and have been part of the pattern in the lives of a number of Presidents from Washington and Jefferson to General Eisenhower—men who have discovered sooner or later that somehow farming, and especially good and intelligent farming, comes closer to providing a key to adjustment and understanding of the universe than all the algebraic formulas of Albert Einstein.

Considering the general insignificance and unimportance of man, the pleasures of agriculture are perhaps more real and gratifying than the pleasures and even the excesses of the purely mathematical mind (which are certainly not pleasures to be underestimated). If the pleasures of mathematical debauchery or orgies in physics are to be treated as limited, it is only because they are denied the great mass of humanity and because all too often they induce and create the deformities and limitations of the incomplete man. Rousseau was in many respects a fool and at times a humbug and a liar but he had something in his conception of the Natural Man, something in which even the great wise and cynical mind of Voltaire, an infinitely more intellectual and sophisticated man, found a perpetual source of envy.

The greatest creative and intellectual vice of our times, and a factor which causes increasing distress and even tragedy, is the overspecialization which man has partly chosen and which has been partly forced upon him by the shrinking of the world, by the incredible speeding up of daily life and the materialistic impact of technological development upon our daily existence. The superspecialist tends to become not only an incomplete man but a deformed one. What perhaps limits forever the superspecialist or the "pure" intellectual stewing in his own juice is the fact that in his intensity and in the sharp limitations of his narrow field, he loses frequently the power to understand or even to conceive the principle of the complete man, flesh, appetites, weakness, follies and all, and so he loses in time all understanding in the true sense of the universe or even of the small world which surrounds him.

Afterword: Malabar Lost, and Found

W e Americans must have been starved for some vision of the good life toward the end of the Second World War, when *Pleasant Valley,* the first of the Malabar books, was published. (My own wartime volume, printed on thin paper as part of the war effort, carries a patriotic message from Bromfield on the dust jacket: "Buy Bonds! Make guns! Raise food! All this is important to the men who are doing the tough fighting.") *Pleasant Valley* was a huge best-seller—my copy is the tenth printing—and it no doubt improved the productivity of victory gardens throughout the nation, including a quarter-acre of vegetables plus two chicken coops under the management of my father, who was the book's original owner.

When *Pleasant Valley* was published, I was only fourteen years old and, as chief wartime weeder and chickie-doo scraper, was uninterested in reading further in a subject I'd had too much of already. And so the book languished unread by me on my father's shelves, and then on mine, for more than thirty years. But, over those years, agriculture changed greatly, and so did my relationship to it. At length, during the 1970s, when I was middle-aged and had taken a job as a government policy specialist in natural resources, I became quite involved, and then alarmed, about agriculture. From a macroeconomic standpoint, agriculture was succeeding during the 1970s, but its natural and cultural "resource base" was being diminished rapidly. The signs of the farm crisis of the 1980s were even then evident.

My duties as a policy specialist included giving little talks about emerging issues in my field. Accordingly, I distilled my concerns about agriculture and rural life into what I called "the twelve bad news cards" which I used as the basis for informal presentations to those who wanted to listen to me. They covered problems of larger and fewer farms, the urbanization of prime farmland areas, the vagaries of climate, the reduction in expected crop-yield increases, the effect of air pollution (acid rain) on yields, the nightmare of energy prices, the erosion of the soil, and the increasing possibility of genetic disaster as scientists moved their hybrid varieties further and further away from stable seed stocks, and on and on into a dim future in which only suburban crabgrass would survive.

Finally, I fell prey to my own bad news. As if war-weary, I became needful of some sort of optimistic vision, a sense of possibility that would deliver agriculture from a headlong rush to disaster. It was then, in this gloomy mood, that something—who knows what—guided my hand to the old book that I had inherited, *Pleasant Valley*.

Reading Bromfield was a tonic. The troubling issues, it turned out, had changed only in their particulars, and this forgotten novelist of the 1930s was speaking to me with an entirely fresh voice, filled with constructive ideas. I hurried to the library (several libraries, in fact, for Bromfield is not that easy to come by these days) to read the rest of his "farm books." I also read about him—the literary biography by David Anderson, which I have greatly relied on in preparing this anthology, the charming memoir by Bromfield's daughter Ellen Bromfield Geld, and some shorter essays. But never in that time of library haunting did it occur to me that Malabar Farm, the object as well as the subject of most of Bromfield's literary output during the last years of his life, might still exist. I had read the passage in *Pleasant Valley* in which he talks about wanting the state of Ohio to take over the farm someday; but I also knew that farms close to cities, even small Ohio cities, were being swallowed up by the relentless march of urbanization. My own California valley was once "pleasant" too, but its vineyards and orange groves had long since been converted to rooftops. In the suburban Maryland county where I later lived, the condos had spread thirty miles into the countryside, three times farther than the ten miles that separated Malabar from Mansfield.

Moreover, I had read that Bromfield had run out of money at the very end. Hollywood had fallen into deep financial crisis, and Bromfield had developed bone cancer, for which he needed expensive care, including blood transfusions. In a last-ditch effort to keep the farm operating, he sold the timber from a valued woodlot. Only an eleventh-hour infusion of funds by his friend Doris Duke saved the old trees from the chainsaw. Then Bromfield died, in 1956, of hepatitis contracted as a result of a transfusion. He was fifty-nine.

The family could not have carried on the work of Malabar, I knew. I read something of an effort to keep the place going by the organization Bromfield helped to found, the Friends of the Land. But I also learned from other sources that the group had gone out of business sometime in the 1960s. The trail seemed to stop there. End of the story.

Then one day, while looking over a road map of Ohio, and the interstate route between Cleveland and Columbus, I chanced to see the words "Malabar Farm" written in tiny print southeast of Mansfield, exactly where it was supposed to be. Immediately, I called everyone I could think of, including state officials in Ohio, to learn more about the fate of Malabar. Having feared the worst, I was relieved to discover that the state of Ohio eventually *had* taken over the place, just as Bromfield had hoped they would, although not until 1972 when the Malabar Farm Foundation, an interim owner after Friends of the Land dissolved, transferred title. Glory be. The Ohio Department of Parks sent me a brochure and suggested that I come out for a visit.

It was early spring, and I drove to Ohio the hard way, on two-lane roads over the mountains of West Virginia and into the Amish country of eastern Ohio, where there are as many quaint horse-drawn carriages and be-hatted, black-garbed people driving them as in Pennsylvania. I came into Pleasant Valley with much the same spirit of adventure in rediscovering a landscape as had Bromfield himself in 1939. Sure enough, there it was, with the gently rolling fields, the woodlots on the steeper slopes, the ponds rimmed with willows, the silos and barns, and up a long curving drive, the "Big House," white and many-winged. In a sense, I had come home, too.

It is a marvellous thing that the state of Ohio has done, to protect what had for me become very nearly a hallowed place. Many school children, groups of retired people who had read Bromfield during the thirties, and outdoor recreationists, who in winter go cross-country skiing at the farm, are the visitors. It is true that Malabar is no longer a fully functioning experimental farm. Though some farming goes on, even a few experiments, Malabar is, essentially, a park, owned and operated largely for recreational purposes by the Ohio Department of Parks. So it was a bittersweet visit that I made. No longer were the "plain dirt farmers" arriving in dusty cars from adjoining states to get some agricultural tips from that famous writer fellow. The roadside market to end all roadside markets was still there, but empty of produce. Still, I encountered a middle-aged couple filling plastic containers with water from the spring that had once kept the Malabar produce field-fresh. They told me they always came here for good water; had for years. Bromfield would have been pleased. Eventually, I adjusted to present realities. Louis Bromfield was gone; but they are gentle, good-hearted, enthusiastic people who have saved Malabar and who now keep it for the rest of us. I admire them for it.

Nowadays, you can take a tour of the farm given by an expert guide. There is a gift shop, in one of the garages. And those who take you through the house and grounds tell funny stories about the desk with twenty-eight drawers that Bromfield designed but never used, preferring to write at a card table instead, and how Lauren Bacall and Humphrey Bogart were married at Malabar in 1948, and how Mount Jeez got its name. The children can pet the animals, and you can take a hayride as if "the Boss" himself were at the reins. How can you not be glad of that?

Yet, for some, there is a poignancy still evident at Malabar. David Anderson, Bromfield's biographer, who knew and admired his subject, had to admit that this big, hearty man, this marvellously American assemblage of complexity and simplicity, could and did fail in the two principal goals he set for himself: to create a body of literary work that would last, and to create an experimental farm that would give hope to all the "plain dirt farmers" devastated by drought and depression. Today, few (if any) of his novels remain on the shelves of branch libraries, at least those outside Ohio. And the agriculture that he celebrated as a possible way of life in a Jeffersonian democracy has been harder to achieve, rather than easier. Farms are becoming fewer and fewer, with greater and greater capital requirements, and there is less need for those such as he, who are "teched." It would now be better to know how to run a computer than to run your hands lovingly over a tall stalk of corn.

Despite all this, Bromfield did in fact leave a permanent legacy; it was different from, but perhaps more important than, any he imagined. In his works and days at Malabar he demonstrated what was needed then, and is even more urgently needed now—a transcendent sense of *possibility* in the land and in living a full and rich life on it. Bromfield was not a disciplined thinker; he was inconsistent and full of foolish notions, especially some off-putting political ones. And yet, in what he wrote about farms and farming and the land, there stands a text, a kind of gospel, that mediates between the hopeful rural ideals of Jefferson and Liberty Hyde Bailey, and the conditions of our modern times in late-twentieth-century America. Bromfield translated, for us, past idealism into future possibility. Sometimes it was a bit roundabout, but it was accurate and true. Though many others at mid-century wrote paeans on rural land and life, Bromfield, I believe, stands alone as its great explicator. He was quixotic, to be sure, but he knew the past, and he could see how it might be fitted into a future.

"Tradition," he wrote, "has much to do with the beautiful garden, landscape, or farm. There should be a *rightness* in relation to the whole landscape, to the climate, to the country, to the regional architecture, to the type of soils, even perhaps to the existence of the natural birds and wildlife. It should have a relation to the past of the region, to history itself."

He saw it whole, this idea called the American land, and, at Malabar, he taught us to see it, too.

Select Bibliography

The Malabar books, by Louis Bromfield

The Farm. New York: Harper and Brothers, 1933.

This is a fictionalized autobiography of Bromfield and his family in Ohio. Though it precedes the establishment of Malabar, *The Farm* provides an exact fix on the author's Jeffersonian philosophy and his compulsion, if that is not too strong a word, to return from France to establish Malabar Farm as the realization of his family's destiny. *The Farm* is thought to be one of Bromfield's best novels from a literary standpoint.

Pleasant Valley. New York: Harper and Brothers, 1945.

The first of the Malabar books and the most uniformly interesting for the general reader. It was a best seller that went through many printings.

Malabar Farm. New York: Harper and Brothers, 1948.

A sequel to *Pleasant Valley* and a best seller as well. It is a mix of rather technical material on farm practice, first-rate essays, and the appealing "Malabar Journal," detailing life on the farm.

Out of the Earth. New York: Harper and Brothers, 1950.

The most discursive of the Malabar books, with detailed information on how the farm was run and what the results were from the various experiments.

From My Experience. New York: Harper and Brothers, 1955.

The Malabar wrap-up book, containing much material from earlier works. A bit more technical than *Pleasant Valley,* it is nevertheless quite accessible and interesting.

Animals and Other People. New York: Harper and Brothers, 1955.

A collection of animal pieces drawn from earlier Malabar books.

Biographies

Anderson, David D. *Louis Bromfield.* New York: Twayne Publishers, 1964.

A literary biography organized more around Bromfield's works than his days. Nevertheless, Anderson does a first-rate job of revealing Bromfield as a man as well as an author, and he tries hard to put Bromfield's postwar political conservatism into perspective.

Geld, Ellen Bromfield. *The Heritage: A Daughter's Memories of Louis Bromfield*. New York: Harper and Brothers, 1962.

A warm and quite well-written memoir.

Lord, Russell. "Afterword," in Louis Bromfield, *The Farm*. New York: New American Library, 1961.

Russell Lord was an agricultural journalist and author who edited *The Land*, the magazine of Friends of the Land, an organization Bromfield helped to establish and served as an officer. In this biographical essay Lord emphasizes the years at Malabar. Russell Lord's wife, Kate Lord, prepared the drawings for *The Land* and illustrated two of Bromfield's books, *Pleasant Valley* and *Malabar Farm*.

Collateral Sources

Bailey, Liberty Hyde. *The Holy Earth*. New York: Scribner's, 1915.

The great "Dean Bailey" of Cornell Agricultural College became Bromfield's agricultural mentor. Bailey was a prolific writer, encyclopaedist *(Hortus)*, and chairman of President Theodore Roosevelt's Country Life Commission. This book, on the spiritual value of farming and rural life, was his most influential; it especially affected Bromfield.

Betts, Edwin Morris. *Thomas Jefferson's Farm Book*. Princeton: Princeton University Press, 1953.

A facsimile reprint of Jefferson's farm notebook, plus, more significantly, a sizeable selection of Jefferson's letters and other papers concerning agriculture and farm life. This volume reveals the source of Bromfield's interest in Jefferson.

Bowers, William L. *The Country Life Movement in America, 1900–1920*. Port Washington, N.Y.: Kennikat Press, 1974.

An account of the movement that did much to inform Bromfield's views of the values of rural life.

Faulkner, Edward H. *Plowman's Folly*. Norman: University of Oklahoma Press, 1947.

The book that started the conservation tillage revolution and that, without Bromfield, might never have been published. It has recently been reprinted, with *A Second Look,* by Island Press in its Conservation Classics Series.

Howard, Sir Albert. *An Agricultural Testament.* New York: Oxford University Press, 1943.

The seminal work on organic agriculture. Howard had an important influence on Bromfield.

Schlesinger, Arthur M., Jr. *The Coming of the New Deal.* Boston: Houghton Mifflin, 1958.

Contains an especially good account of the agricultural crisis of the 1930s and of the New Deal measures, which Bromfield at first supported and then rejected, to stabilize farming in America.

Sears, Paul. *Deserts on the March.* Norman: University of Oklahoma Press, 1935. (Fourth edition, 1980).

Sears was at Oberlin when Bromfield established Malabar, and he became a valued advisor and friend. This study of erosion and the abuse of farmland has become a classic.

Chapter Sources

The essay on pp. 1–4 is from *Out of the Earth* (New York: Harper and Brothers, 1950), in which it was the Epilogue.

The essays on pp. 5–21, 22–41, and 93–132 are from *Pleasant Valley* (New York: Harper and Brothers, 1945).

The essays on pp. 42–83, 84–92, 133–59, and 192–214 are from *Malabar Farm* (New York: Harper and Brothers, 1948).

The essays on pp. 160–77, 178–191, and 215–28 are from *From My Experience* (New York: Harper and Brothers, 1955).

All excerpts are reprinted by permission of Harper & Row, Publishers, Inc., and the Estate of Louis Bromfield.

Charles E. Little is the author of five books on conservation and rural issues, most recently *Green Fields Forever* (Island Press, 1987), on the implications of new agricultural technologies. Over a distinguished career in conservation, Little has served as executive director of the Open Space Institute, senior associate of the Conservation Foundation, and head of natural resources policy research at the Library of Congress. He was founder and first president of the American Land Forum (now the American Land Resource Association). Little is a columnist on conservation topics, contributes articles and essays to several magazines and journals, including *Smithsonian* and *Wilderness*, and publishes books and research monographs in his field. He lives and works in Kensington, Maryland.

Designed by Martha Farlow.

Composed by Brushwood Graphics, Inc., in Century Schoolbook
with display lines in Italia Bold.

Printed by R. R. Donnelley & Sons Company on 50-lb. Cream White Sebago
and bound in Joanna—Arrestox A on spine and Kennett on sides.